HYBRIDIZATION OF BLOCKCHAIN AND CLOUD COMPUTING

Overcoming Security Issues in IoT

HYBRIDIZATION OF BLOCKCHAIN AND CLOUD COMPUTING

Overcoming Security Issues in IoT

Edited by

M. Lawanya Shri, PhD

E. Gangadevi, MSc, MPhil

K. Santhi, PhD

Chiranji Lal Chowdhary, PhD

First edition published 2024

Apple Academic Press Inc.
1265 Goldenrod Circle, NE,
Palm Bay, FL 32905 USA

760 Laurentian Drive, Unit 19,
Burlington, ON L7N 0A4, CANADA

CRC Press
2385 NW Executive Center Drive,
Suite 320, Boca Raton FL 33431

4 Park Square, Milton Park,
Abingdon, Oxon, OX14 4RN UK

© 2024 by Apple Academic Press, Inc.

Apple Academic Press exclusively co-publishes with CRC Press, an imprint of Taylor & Francis Group, LLC

Library and Archives Canada Cataloguing in Publication

Title: Hybridization of blockchain and cloud computing : overcoming security issues in IoT / edited by
    M. Lawanya Shri, PhD, E. Gangadevi, MSc, MPhil, K. Santhi, PhD, Chiranji Lal Chowdhary, PhD
Names: Shri, M. Lawanya, editor. | Gangadevi, E., editor. | Santhi, K., editor. | Chowdhary, Chiranji Lal, 1975- editor.
Description: First edition. | Includes bibliographical references and index.
Identifiers: Canadiana (print) 20230441572 | Canadiana (ebook) 20230441637 | ISBN 9781774912164 (hardcover) |
    ISBN 9781774912171 (softcover) | ISBN 9781003336624 (ebook)
Subjects: LCSH: Blockchains (Databases) | LCSH: Blockchains (Databases)—Industrial applications. |
    LCSH: Cloud computing.
Classification: LCC QA76.9.B56 H93 2023 | DDC 005.74—dc23

Library of Congress Cataloging-in-Publication Data

....

CIP data on file with US Library of Congress

....

ISBN: 978-1-77491-216-4 (hbk)
ISBN: 978-1-77491-217-1 (pbk)
ISBN: 978-1-00333-662-4 (ebk)

About the Editors

M. Lawanya Shri, PhD
Associate Professor, School of Information Technology and Engineering,
VIT University Vellore, Tamil Nadu, India

M. Lawanya Shri, PhD, is working as an Associate Professor in the School of Information Technology and Engineering at VIT, Vellore, India. She has published more than 40 research papers in international journals and 15 conference proceedings. She has published several book chapters and co-authored one book, *Computer Architecture for Beginners*. She serves as an editorial board member of *Informatics in Medicine Unlocked* (Elsevier). Her research work focus on blockchain technology, artificial intelligence, cloud computing, web services, and the Internet of Things.

E. Gangadevi, MSc, MPhil
Assistant Professor,
Department of Computer Science,
Loyola College, Nungambakkam, Chennai,
Tamil Nadu, India

E. Gangadevi, MPhil, is working as an Assistant Professor in the Department of Computer Science at Loyola College, Chennai, India. She has published two patents and more than 15 research papers in international journals and many book chapters. She has published a book on database management system (or DBMS) and a higher secondary computer science book for the state government of Tamil Nadu. Her areas of research are machine learning, deep learning, IoT, and cloud computing.

K. Santhi, PhD
Assistant Professor (Sr.),
School of Information Technology and
Engineering, VIT University Vellore,
Tamil Nadu, India

K. Santhi, PhD, is working as an Assistant Professor (Sr.) in the School of Information Technology and Engineering in the VIT, Vellore, Tamil Nadu, India. She received her MTech (CSE) from the VIT, Vellore. She has more than 14 years of teaching experience at VIT. Her areas of research include wireless networks, cloud computing, and computer architecture. She has published several research papers in peer-reviewed international journals. She is a life member of the Computer Society of India.

Chiranji Lal Chowdhary, PhD
Associate Professor, School of Information
Technology and Engineering,
VIT University Vellore, Tamil Nadu, India

Chiranji Lal Chowdhary, PhD, is an Associate Professor in the School of Information Technology and Engineering at VIT University, where he has been since 2010. He received a BE (CSE) from MBM Engineering College at Jodhpur in 2001, and MTech (CSE) from the M.S. Ramaiah Institute of Technology in Bangalore in 2008. He received his PhD in Information Technology and Engineering from the VIT University Vellore in 2017. From 2006 to 2010, he worked at M.S. Ramaiah Institute of Technology in Bangalore, eventually as a Lecturer. His research interests span both computer vision and image processing. Much of his work has been on images, mainly through the application of image processing, computer vision, pattern recognition, machine learning, biometric systems, deep learning, soft computing, and computational intelligence. He has given a few invited talks on medical image processing. Professor Chowdhary is the editor/co-editor of more than seven books and is the author of over 50 research articles on computer science. He filed two patents deriving from his research. Google Scholar Link: https://scholar.google.com/citations?user=PpJt13oAAAAJ&hl=en.

Contents

Contributors

V. Ananya
Student, Computer Science and Engineering, VIT, Vellore, Tamil Nadu, India

P. Anbalagan
Department of Computer Science and Engineering, Annamalai University, Annamalai Nagar, Tamil Nadu, India

G. Anuradha
System Engineer, TCS, Chennai, Tamil Nadu, India

R. Anusha
School of Computer Science and Engineering, VIT, Tamil Nadu, India

M. Balasubramaniyan
School of Information Technology and Engineering, Vellore Institute of Technology Vellore, Tamil Nadu, India

Korhan Cengiz
Department of Electrical–Electronics Engineering, Trakya University, Turkey

J. Deepa
Faculty of Information Technology, VelTech Rangarajan Dr. Sagunthala R&D Institute of Science and Technology, Avadi, Tamil Nadu, India

E. Gangadevi
Department of Computer Science, Loyola College, Chennai, Tamil Nadu, India

J. Geetha
Department of Computer Science and Engineering, Ramaiah Institute of Technology, Bangalore, Karnataka, India

K. Govinda
DSCOPE, VIT University, Vellore, Tamil Nadu, India

G. Hariharan
Student, Department of ECE, SVCE, Sriperumbudur, Tamil Nadu India

P. Kishore
Student, Computer Science and Engineering, VIT, Vellore, Tamil Nadu, India

K. Ajith Kumar
School of Information Technology and Engineering, Vellore Institute of Technology, Vellore, Tamil Nadu, India

Kishore Kumar
Student of University College of Engineering, Ariyalur, Tamil Nadu, India

P. Sathish Kumar
School of Information Technology and Engineering, Vellore Institute of Technology, Vellore, Tamil Nadu, India

Shivam Kumar
Student, MCA Department, Vellore Institute of Technology, Vellore, Tamil Nadu, India

Vikas Kumar
Student, MCA Department, Vellore Institute of Technology, Vellore, Tamil Nadu, India

Gargi Lohia
Student, Computer Science and Engineering, VIT, Vellore, Tamil Nadu, India

S. Meenatchi
School of Information Technology and Engineering, Vellore Institute of Technology Vellore,
Tamil Nadu, India

A. Murugan
Associate Professor and Head, PG and Research Department of Computer Science,
Dr. Ambedkar Government Arts College (Autonomous), Affiliated to University of Madras, Chennai,
Tamil Nadu, India

Pallavi D. Naik
Department of Computer Science and Engineering, Ramaiah Institute of Technology, Bangalore,
Karnataka, India

C. Navaneethan
School of Information Technology and Engineering, Vellore Institute of Technology Vellore,
Tamil Nadu, India

Charit Gupta Paluri
Student, Computer Science and Engineering, VIT, Vellore, Tamil Nadu, India

Saurya Raj Pandey
Student, Computer Science and Engineering, VIT, Vellore, Tamil Nadu, India

S. Kamal Prasat
Student, Computer Science and Engineering, VIT, Vellore, Tamil Nadu, India

Ritu Pravakar
Department of Computer Science and Engineering, Ramaiah Institute of Technology, Bangalore,
Karnataka, India

N. Rajeev Reddy
PhD Scholar, Department of Electronics and Communication Engineering,
Dr. M.G.R. Educational and Research Institute, Chennai, Tamil Nadu, India

S. Sirisha Reddy
Department of Computer Science and Engineering, Ramaiah Institute of Technology, Bangalore,
Karnataka, India

R. Saminathan
Department of Computer Science and Engineering, Annamalai University, Annamalai Nagar,
Tamil Nadu, India

S. Sanjay
Student, Computer Science and Engineering, VIT, Vellore, Tamil Nadu, India

K. Santhi
School of Information Technology and Engineering, VIT, Vellore, Tamil Nadu, India

R. Saravanan
Faculty of Information Technology, VelTech Rangarajan Dr. Sagunthala R&D Institute of Science and Technology, Avadi, Tamil Nadu, India

S. Saravanan
Department of Computer Science and Engineering, Annamalai University, Annamalai Nagar, Tamil Nadu, India

Priyanshi Sharma
Student, MCA Department, Vellore Institute of Technology, Vellore, Tamil Nadu, India

R. Shobarani
Associate Professor, Department of Computer Science Engineering,
Dr. M.G.R. Educational and Research Institute, Chennai–95, Tamil Nadu, India

M. Lawanya Shri
SITE, VIT, Vellore, Tamil Nadu, India

R. Swathi
School of Information Technology and Engineering, Vellore Institute of Technology, Vellore, Tamil Nadu, India

S. Thangaprasath
School of Information Technology and Engineering, Vellore Institute of Technology Vellore, Tamil Nadu, India

Savithri V.
Assistant Professor & Research Supervisor, Department of Computer Science, Women's Christian College, Chennai.

J. Vijayalakshmi
Research Scholar, PG and Research Department of Computer Science,
Dr. Ambedkar Government Arts College (Autonomous), Affiliated to University of Madras, Chennai, Tamil Nadu, India

T. Vimala
Associate Professor, Department of Electronics and Communication Engineering,
Dr. M.G.R. Educational and Research Institute, Chennai, Tamil Nadu, India

Abbreviations

2PC	two-phase commit protocol
AAL	ambient assisted living
ABE	attribute-based encryption
ADC	autonomous device coordination
AES	advanced encryption standard
AML	anti-money laundering
ANN	artificial neural network
API	application programming interface
BaaS	back-end as a service
BR	block reward
BSO	business-based smart operations
CA	certification authority
CDN	content delivery network
CNT	carbon nanotubes
CoAP	constrained application protocol
CoT	chain of things
CPS	cyber-physical system
CPU	central processing unit
DAO	decentralized autonomous organization
DAP schemes	decentralized anonymous payment schemes
dAPP	distributed application
dApps	decentralized apps
DDoS	distributed denial of service
DFS	distributed file sharing
DLT	distributed ledger technology
DoS	denial of service
DSCSA	Drug Supply Chain Security Act
ECC	elliptic curves cryptography
ECDSA	elliptic curve distributed signature algorithm
ECG	electrocardiogram
ECoG	electrocorticography
EEG	electroencephalogram
Elf Store	edge-local federated store

ERP	enterprise resource planning
ESB	enterprise service bus
EVM	ethereum virtual machine
F-AHP	fuzzy analytic hierarchy process
GIS	geographic information systems
HTLCs	hashed time lock contract
IaaS	infrastructure as a service
ICS	industrial control system
ICT	information and communications technology
IoHT	internet of healthy things
IoT	internet of things
IPFS	interplanetary file system
IRS	internal revenue services
IT	information technology
kNN	k-nearest neighbor
KYC	know your customer
LoRaWAN	long-range wide area network
MB	megabyte
ML	machine learning
MPC	most popular content
MQTT	message queuing telemetry transport
MSO	management strategy and organization
NB-IoT	narrowband internet of things
NFC	near-field communication
NIST	National Institute of Standards and Technology
NLP	natural language processing
NPA	non-performing assets
NPK	potassium, phosphorus, and nitrogen
OTC	over-the-counter
OTP	one-time password
PA	precision agriculture
PaaS	platform as a service
PDoS	permanent denial of service
PGP	pretty good privacy
PKI	public key infrastructure
POM	production and operations management
PoS	proof-of-stake
PoSP	proof of benefit power

PoW	proof of work
PPN	peer-to-peer networking
PQB	post-quantum blockchain
PSO	particle swarm optimization
PwC	PricewaterhouseCoopers
RCS	resilience control system
RFID	radio frequency identification
RHCS	remote healthcare system
RPG	regulators of pest growth
SaaS	software as a service
SD	sustainable development
SOA	service-oriented-architecture
SOC	service-oriented computing
SPHCS	smartphone-based healthcare system
SS2PL	serializability, strict two-phase locking
SVM	support vector machine
TF	transaction fees
TF-IDF	term frequency-inverse document frequency
Triple DES	triple data encryption standard
TSP	technology-based smart products
VAM	virtual automation metrology
WAN	wide area network
WHCS	wearable healthcare system
WHO	World Health Organization
WSN	wireless sensor network

Preface

Blockchain technology is a thriving technology trend that has gained precise attention from IT industries and business organizations across the globe. It is poised to envisage significant challenges to unleash economic benefits with advancements in the IT industry. The holistic delineation of blockchain technology revolutionizes existing technologies and diverse domains by enabling secure and fast transactions. The recent advancement of blockchain technology facilitates decentralized networks that are used in various fields for reliable business transactions. The distributed and decentralized technology arms users across the globe with proactive resistors over their data. Blockchain technology and its applications depict how the thriving technology trend sustains with various host platforms and blends with other technologies like cloud computing, IoT, intelligent systems, and big data analytics. This pioneering technology is utilized by various companies and business organizations to improve secure transactions by building smart contracts and decentralized applications.

The emergent blockchain technology has an intense impact on various business sectors, including financial services, the healthcare industry, the transportation industy, supply chain management, and so on, to materialize the decentralized global infrastructure with dedicated transactions on the network. The blockchain holistic depiction can be leveraged for secure transactions due to its consensus-driven, distributed, and decentralized distributed ledger. It has blossomed to assuage many challenging issues across various domains. The recent explosion of blockchain technology has shaped a dazzling impact on stakeholders, business experts, industrialists, and researchers.

This book explores all the aspects of blockchain technologies and facilitates an overview of the latest developments. It proffers the advancements of blockchain with various cutting-edge technologies and its diversified business applications. This book addresses various challenges, emerging issues, and problems in classical centralized architecture and how blockchain platform provides magical solutions and novel services with recent advancements for improving business processes.

This book focuses on blockchain technology-based distributed transactions for industrial applications. The aim of this book is to provide the big picture of blockchain technology with the integration of various cutting-edge technologies and its solution. It also addresses the challenges of diversified applications, deployment, feasibility study, and the services offered by blockchain technology.

## CHAPTER 1

A New Innovation of Blockchain in Industrial IoT 4.0 (IIoT)

R. ANUSHA[1], R. SARAVANAN[1], J. DEEPA[2], and KISHORE KUMAR[3]

[1]*School of Computer Science and Engineering, VIT, Tamil Nadu, India*

[2]*Faculty of Information Technology, VelTech Rangarajan Dr. Sagunthala R&D Institute of Science and Technology, Avadi, Tamil Nadu, India*

[3]*Student of University College of Engineering, Ariyalur, Tamil Nadu, India*

ABSTRACT

It's the beginning of machines taking over the world. It seems like everyone is talking about it; what exactly is it? Many people have different ideas about what exactly it is, what it does, and what it means to everyone. Yes, assuredly, it is IoT. IoT has unified connected devices that can talk to each other (machines) without requiring human-to-human and human-to-computer interactions. Many enterprises, like Fitbit, Apple Watch, etc., are extensively coming forward to deploy IoT for their particular industry. It also connects the internet with things. Open-source computing devices like Raspberry Pi, BeagleBones, Arduino, NodeMCU, etc., enable machine–machine communication in an industrial environment like automobile collision in avoidance/detection. Since one of the key features of IoT is "heterogeneity," it leads to privacy and security risk on consumer data (connected to IoT). Thus, here the 'Blockchain (BC)' exists. This

Hybridization of Blockchain and Cloud Computing: Overcoming Security Issues in IoT.
M. Lawanya Shri, E. Gangadevi, K. Santhi, & Chiranji Lal Chowdhary (Eds.)
© 2024 Apple Academic Press, Inc. Co-published with CRC Press (Taylor & Francis)

chapter brings you the application of BC in the smart community created by IoT, especially for IIoT. It describes the security breaches of IoT, the architecture of CPS, and some BC-IIoT uses.

1.1 INTRODUCTION

Industry 4.0 takes the previous industry into intelligent enterprises by adding a variety of technologies [1]. The drastic technology of IoT and Blockchain together bestow towards Industry 4.0 [1].

In IIoT, we are talking about thousands of millions of sensors all connected to the internet, and security is enormous. Industry 4.0 was in the 20th century, exactly the production automation made possible by electronics and computer processing. Still, an industrial network is centralized and has a third-party access operation. It suffers for flexibility, security, privacy, transparency, efficiency, data integrity, resilience, the trustworthiness of data, etc.

In the 21st century, Industry 4.0 evolved with the "SMART" self-processing of machines, i.e., interconnecting intelligent industrial devices. Industry 4.0 has introduced the manufacturing industries to new paradigms of IoT, large data analytics, cloud manufacturing, fog computing, etc. With this advanced technology, we are enabling the two important factors in Industry 4.0:

- "SMART" [enable to work]; and
- "SELF" [enable to work by].

The potential opportunities have been created such as:

- self-automation;
- self-awareness;
- self-prediction;
- self-comparison;
- self-reconfiguration; and
- self-maintenance.

Industry 4.0 was based on information and communication technologies (ICT) that enabled the fourth revolution to work as smart industries as well as smart manufacturing, production, etc., i.e., the virtual world was connected to the physical world with the help of CPS, CC, and IoT embedded system. These technologies play a vital role in the industry integration with other technologies that enable the 4th generation of the industry (Figure 1.1).

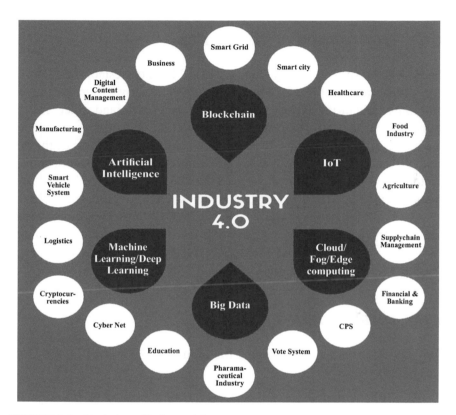

FIGURE 1.1   Evolution of Industry 4.0.

Let us learn about the general evolution of industry by stages and the main application of Blockchain, i.e., IoT. IoT devices have many implications for the industry and have enhanced the new technology integration of IIoT with Blockchain. The architecture of BC in the industry and the IIoT with Blockchain use have been discussed here.

1.1.1   FOUNDATION OF INDUSTRY 4.0

The enabling technologies of Industry 4.0 are the foundation of this fourth intelligence generation. This underlying technology defines the smart technology in Industry 4.0, e.g., the virtual automation metrology (VAM) achieves zero defects in the automation of the wheel.

1.1.2 EVOLUTIONARY OF INDUSTRY 4.0

The evolution of the industry from 1.0 to 4.0 has been established. The 1st generation started at the end of the 18th century and early 19th century, based on the manufacturing system which takes steam power and water. The 2nd generation in the late 19th century was based on electrical power, which led to mass production. The 3rd generation started in the middle of the 20th century; automatic and micro-things were introduced in the manufacturing sector based on ICT. The 4th generation deals with "smart" and "self-working" based on the enabling technologies (CPS, IoT, CC, and BPM).

The evolution revolves around the various enabling technologies which led Industry 4.0 to IIoT. Amalgamating the most significant technology called BC was a viral topic among the researchers to do the analysis of merits and demerits of BC-IIoT in Industry 4.0.

1.1.3 ENABLING TECHNOLOGIES

The key information technologies for Industrial 4.0 were BD, CC, IoT, and BC [4]:

1. **CPS:** The nucleus of Industry 4.0 is CPS. It is an autonomous system that integrates electronics, sensors, and actuators (hardware parts) and has communication compatibility [5]. The extension of ICT and virtual integration of physical and informative communication to enhance scalability, adaptability, resiliency, safety, compatibility, etc.
2. **IoT:** The internet of things has software and hardware integration with the help of sensors and the underlying pillars of IoT, i.e., RFID, WSN, M2M, and SCADA.
3. **Cloud Computing:** It is based on IaaS, SaaS, and PaaS, together with increased performance and low cost.
4. **Big Data:** The 5 V's were the key factors in categorizing the characteristics and structures of data since the volume of data is increasing because of the deployment of various technologies like AI, IoT, social networking, etc.

5. **BPM:** This is based on production and operations management (POM) which enables to examine, computation, replica, brutalization, reform, and enhance the manufacturing process. BPM enables the enterprise or organization to set its goals and collaboration between inter- and intra-collaboration of enterprises.

1.1.4 FIVE STAGES OF IoT IN MANUFACTURING AND DESIGN

➢ **Stage 1:** The computer-aided design model was used to design/redesign. Designed information was scanned by RFID; those data were transmitted over the internet on the cloud securely with the help of GUI [CAD model] [6].
➢ **Stage 2:** With the help of ML techniques, the CAD model data surfaces were continuously analyzed and refined for the creation of refined shapes [6].
➢ **Stage 3:** Based on the collected data and manufactured design, the categories of tools and machines have been listed using the internet from a DB [6].
➢ **Stage 4:** In order to retrieve the design information, this stage produces the planning information, which has been stored standardly [6].
➢ **Stage 5:** The entire plan has been defined and generated also, validated with the agents, and finally transferred to the machine for production [6].

1.2 ENACTMENT OF BLOCKCHAIN IN IIOT

Modern technology enables the participants to work globally, but the thing is to analyze how secure it is. Here to give solution Blockchain comes. It provides a secure stream for collaborating. Exactly traditional industry development differs from mutual benefit, i.e., Industry 4.0 generation enables the collaboration of all businesses and data models, etc. Blockchain has a superpower character called "Smart Contracts."

Here, the question came, what is Smart Contract?: According to the terms of the contract or agreement, which is intended to program execution automatically, it controls or documents legally relevant actions. This enables the "SMART" and "SELF" processing characteristics of the industry. The main attribute of Industry 4.0 is 'self-automation 'that can be enabled by Blockchain's Smart contract. The traditional contract system takes time to execute, but this SC makes less time and increases the transparency environment of industrial 4.0 growth.

The fourth revolution of Industry 4.0 enables smart factories, smart manufacturing, smart control, and monitoring process. It is the need of an hour to adopt this by Industry 4.0 by integrating with new emerging technologies like Blockchain, IoT, AI, Machine Learning (ML), etc.

Communication among all the machines in the secure channel by the Industry 4.0 will be developed based on IoT, i.e., IoT makes things connect and communicate with each other, but the thing here is, with the help of IoT and BC, we have to design and plan to collaborate each other with security. With IoT, things start collaborating and have a centralized Blockchain core, SC. This enables things to collaborate without worrying about trusted or trustless can transact with each other. This also makes the fully automated system, e.g., cyber-physical system (CPS), supply chain management, food industry, etc.

Thus, in the evolution of industry 4.0, out of many approaches, the efficient adoption in this series was Blockchain and IoT, elaborating the distribution to the trustless environment. Initially, the Blockchain was used in the financial and banking sector, i.e., currencies [Bitcoin] or cryptocurrencies. Now everybody understands that this will not work for that alone, and now it steps into all fields like healthcare, AI, IoT, agriculture, smart city, etc.

In Industry 4.0, CPS has vast space, and the fatigue of security and transparency of transactions through decentralized network technology evolved. The architecture of CPS will be discussed in Section 1.3.

Some of the benefits of BC in Industry 4.0:

- sustainability;
- traceability;
- employability; and
- privacy.

1.3   ARCHITECTURE OF CPS

In the evolution of Industry 4.0, there is in need to understand the proper definition of CPS. But still, there is no proper definition, as well as architecture. This section presents the guideline for the architecture of implementing CPS in Industry 4.0. Before implementing CPS, the following two main functional components must be analyzed:

- advanced connectivity; and
- smart data management and analytics.

The 5C's of CPS are as follows:

1. **Smart Connection:** This is the first step in developing a CPS application. It owned two steps: (i) reliable and accurate data and its components are collected from ERP, SCM, MES, and CMM; (ii) selecting the type of sensors to handle those data.

2. **Data-to-Information Conversion:** The relevant information has to be extracted from the data. The conversion of data to information was done by many tools and methodologies. This is said to be Smart-Analytics. This second level enhances the ability of 'self-awareness' for machines.

3. **Cyber:** At this level, the information converted has been pushed into it to form a machine network. The gathered huge data has to be specifically analyzed for their performance, and it enhances the 'Self-Compare' of machines, i.e., the machine performance was compared with every other machine, and it got the rate on the fleet as well as the individual machine performance was analyzed. With this rate, the future behavior of machines can be predicted. Hence it is called a "central Information Hub."

4. **Cognition Level:** Comparative information, as well as individual machine performance, was available. This level provides the acquired knowledge for monitoring the system. With this, the user can make a prior decision for maintaining the system. Thus, this level needs 'proper infographics,' i.e., that transfer the acquired information to the users.

5. **Configuration Level:** The entire information from the previous levels was given to physical space for monitoring the system. This level provides the proper solution to apply the corrective decision given by the cognitive level for physical space to monitor the system. Thus, it acts as a 'Resilience Control System '(RCS). This enhances the property of machines to be 'self-adaptive," self-configure.'

1.3.1 BC-IIOT USE-CASES

The modern world abides by much new technology, but because of the immense characteristics like decentralization, immutability, anonymity, distribution, transparency, and authenticity, this all leads this Blockchain to step into all the sectors. The own certification of products or machines is done by the use case of industrial IoT. The main use of BC in Industry 4.0 has been discussed below:

1. **Manufacturing Sector:** Let us consider the coffee machine. The manufacturer collaborates with this BC-IIoT to produce this type of machine because that has self-adaptive, aware, etc. Here, the machine implemented with this technology must predict three features: (i) temperature of the coffee, (ii) quality and quantity of water used, and (iii) amount of coffee powder used. This machine sends those data to the SC in BC. Thus, the quality or value of the product information was passed to the user. Thus, "self-automation" was achieved.

2. **Election System Sector:** As everybody knows, many forgeries have been done in the voting system at the time of the election. Since BC has beautiful consensus mechanisms and POA, i.e., proof of authority and GO-Ethereum concept can be helpful in this sector. The immutability destroys fraud in voting. It does not accept changes and multiple entries, which makes this system work securely [10].

3. **Music Industry/Production Sector:** Royalty in the music industry was quite a common problem. The smart contract can be used to protect IP rights for music for different users, movies, ringtones, etc. [8]. Around 40% of music consumption is streamed from platforms like Spotify or Soundcloud, Pandora, Tidal, Apple, etc. [11].

    • **Ujo:** Royalties in the music industry seek to solve the problem, i.e., the smaller artists still struggle for compensation, so the idea behind this Ujo is to provide both compensation and transparency for their work [11]. It is applicable to all the artists like painters, singers, etc.

4. **Education Sector:** In this sector, the smart contract has two processes: (i) identity management; and (ii) certification manage-ment, i.e., it is about document management systems. The trans-action was based on the certifier whose fingerprint register in the

Blockchain can give a hash value (SHA-256) and drag and drop digital certificates for verification. The transaction can validate the certificates, and they may know the start and the end date of the certificates. It also deals with the issuing organization. The main advantage was counterfeit protection and easy verification.

5. **Sustainable Supply Chain Network:** The central part of the SSCN was the digital cyber network. It has five parts: (i) technology-based smart products (TSP); (ii) business-based smart operations (BSO); (iii) sustainable development (SD); (iv) management strategy and organization (MSO); and (v) collaboration (C) [2].

1.3.2 HOW BC-IoT-INDUSTRY 4.0 SUSTAIN?

The combo of BC-IoT in Industry 4.0 has a wide range of intelligence introduced to it. Of course, this incorporating technology sustains in all ways because of its characteristics like decentralization, immutability, scalability, trustworthiness, anonymity, etc. The problem of interoperability, scalability, and so on has a solution based on this combo.

1.3.3 PERCEPTION OF INDUSTRY 4.0

The final perception of this revolution is adaptability, scalability, interoperability, etc., which means the drastic change from traditional to smart industry development, i.e., modifying everything to a digital format like digital business promotion, digital business model, digitalizing, and integrating the smart to industry.

1.4 INTELLIGENCE MANUFACTURING IN THE CONTEXT OF INDUSTRY 4.0 [1]

Intelligent manufacturing or smart manufacturing leads to "real, optimistic management between the enterprise and customers or partners, broker or business involved people." It involves intelligence manufacturing supported by various enabling technology in this generation. It also uses data models and SOA methods to be very smart.

The new emerging BC-IIoT tights the security and trust in smart industries, i.e., in Industry 4.0. This makes the new essence in intelligent industries. The main aspect of Industry 4.0 is to keep 3P's strong enough:

- Production;
- Productivity; and
- Product quality.

This is all done in a smart way by using these technologies in Industry 4.0. The entire enterprise resource planning (ERP) can be done by these enabling technologies, which abide by (OPM, SCM, SRM, CRM, PQM, POM, etc.

1.5   CONCLUSION

This chapter defines the involvement of IoT, BC, CC, SOA, BPM, CPS, BD, etc., in Industry 4.0. This chapter also defines the smart industries working based on which principles and enactment of BC-IoT in Industry 4.0. The significant impact of Industry 4.0 with BC tights the privacy of industries which improves the industries to act smart. IoT and other technologies make this generation produce products with zero defects.

KEYWORDS

- **cyber-physical system**
- **enterprise resource planning**
- **information and communication technologies**
- **management strategy and organization**
- **production and operations management**
- **virtual automation metrology**

REFERENCES

1. Lampropoulos, G., Siakas, K., & Anastasiadis, T., (2019). Internet of things in the context of Industry 4.0: An overview. *Int. J. Entrep. Knowl., 7*(1), 4–19. doi: 10.2478/ijek-2019-0001.

2. Manavalan, E., & Jayakrishna, K., (2019). A review of internet of things (IoT) embedded sustainable supply chain for Industry 4.0 requirements. *Comput. Ind. Eng., 127*, 925–953. doi: 10.1016/j.cie.2018.11.030.

3. Da, L., Xu, E. L., & Li, L., (2020). *Industry 4.0: State of the Art and Future Trends, 56*(8), 2941–2962.

4. Stupar, S., Kurtovic, E., & Bico, C. M., (2020). Key information technologies of Industry 4.0. *Proc. Fac. Econ. East Sarajev.*, (20), 59–75. doi: 10.7251/ZREFIS2020059S.

5. Elmamy, S. B., Mrabet, H., Gharbi, H., Jemai, A., & Trentesaux, D., (2020). A survey on the usage of blockchain technology for cyber-threats in the context of Industry 4.0. *Sustain., 12*(21), 1–19. doi: 10.3390/su12219179.

6. Anbalagan, A., & Moreno-García, C. F., (2020). An IoT based Industry 4.0 architecture for integration of design and manufacturing systems. *Mater. Today Proc.*, (xxxx). doi: 10.1016/j.matpr.2020.11.196.

7. Bodkhe, U., et al., (2020). Blockchain for Industry 4.0: A comprehensive review. *IEEE Access, 8*, 79764–79800. doi: 10.1109/ACCESS.2020.2988579.

8. Teame, K., Debie, A., & Tullu, M. (2022). Healthcare leadership effectiveness among managers in Public Health institutions of Addis Ababa, Central Ethiopia: a mixed methods study. *BMC Health Services Research, 22*(1), 1–11.

9. Lee, J., Bagheri, B., & Kao, H. A., (2015). A cyber-physical systems architecture for Industry 4.0-based manufacturing systems. *Manuf. Lett., 3*, 18–23. doi: 10.1016/j.mfglet.2014.12.001.

10. Post, B., (2020). *Smart Industries* (pp. 756–763). No. ICCMC. [Online]. Available: https://www.bangkokpost.com/business/1914104/smart-electronics (accessed on 11 August 2022).

11. "Coursera. https://www.coursera.org/learn/iot-cyber-security/home/welcome (accessed on 11 August 2022).

12. Wang, Q., Zhu, X., Ni, Y., Gu, L., & Zhu, H., (2020). Blockchain for the IoT and industrial IoT: A review. *Internet of Things, 10*(66), 100081. doi: 10.1016/j.iot.2019.100081.

13. Topics, T., (2013). *Industry 4.0: Are We There Yet?*. doi: 10.34190/EKM.20.112.

CHAPTER 2

Blockchain Technology in Estimating Crow Intelligence Using Artificial Intelligence

SAVITHRI V.[1], G. HARIHARAN[2], and G. ANURADHA[3]

[1]*Assistant Professor & Research Supervisor, Department of Computer Science, Women's Christian College, Chennai.*

[2]*Student, Department of ECE, SVCE, Sriperumbudur, Tamil Nadu India*

[3]*System Engineer, TCS, Chennai, Tamil Nadu, India*

ABSTRACT

The study about the human–crow relationship is the purest form of affection and love. In India, the crow population is estimated at around 19 million. Penetrating into the minds of the birds is still challenging, and research has to be scaled more for human–crow conversation. Block technology technique in an intelligence system that helps to read the mind of the crow and makes improvising by extracting the features of the crow's eyeballs movement, mouth movement, face value, left eye movement, right eye movement, mouth expansion, and mouth shrink. Extraction of the pixel value is considered as input, and we have trained the system using multilayer perception, radial basis function, and support vector model. The desired output is verified for accuracy by comparing the values with the standard statistical values as defined by the veterinary doctors. The proposed system implements a voice blockchain technique

Hybridization of Blockchain and Cloud Computing: Overcoming Security Issues in IoT.
M. Lawanya Shri, E. Gangadevi, K. Santhi, & Chiranji Lal Chowdhary (Eds.)
© 2024 Apple Academic Press, Inc. Co-published with CRC Press (Taylor & Francis)

and sensor technology with radio frequency identification (RFID) to detect signal variations. The multilayer perception and radial basis function were implemented in two different tools; SPSS and JustNN tool. The output of both algorithms is based on statistical measures compared and encrypted using blockchain technique. The concluded output is again converted into speech to humans for better understanding.

2.1 INTRODUCTION

Blockchain technology is a recent hot topic that is widespread in the cloud for securing distributed data in cloud computing. The study about the human-bird interaction is very less, and it's an effort to insight into the depth study of human-crow interaction in a private secured manner by applying AI to read the feelings of the crow. Crow is the most inimitable bird, which has the unique quality of better interaction with a human when compared to other birds. The percentile growth of crows is decreasing due to a drastic increase in hunting and lack of guardianship. Artificial intelligence is the machine sense from an environment and produces an action of the output. The term is applied in intellectual approaches such as acting humanly, acting rationally, thinking humanly, and thinking rationally. Learning, perception, reasoning, and problem-solving are the major research components in AI. Acting humanly is one kind of learning concept in AI. The study of human-level intelligence is another field of AI. The study of intelligence is nothing but learning, reasoning, knowledge representation, knowledge awakening, and many more of the human senses. The human work is done by the computer, and it transmits the communication to humans. There is no physical sense like humans; instead, computers precepts from the environment. The psychological experiment is in reality and combined together with a computer model. The experimental investigation is fed into the computer from human activities, and it is done through a psychological way. Humans may think right or wrong in day-to-day activities, but computer rectifies their own mistake and learn from the mistake. Thinking rationally is the expert who knows the laws of logic. Syllogism is a logic that provides a pattern for the correct conclusion. Logic is classified as formal and informal logic. Formal logic is the historical development of logical notation in the program. Informal logic is a logical notation in the sense of a computer embedded with memory that contains a description of thorough reading in the way of human logical thinking. This way is called logicism. The rational agent is something that perceives the middleman and acts according to it. The laws of thought are sometimes assumed from the rational agent to represent rational knowledge and rational reason. The study of the AI approach design rational hidden causal agent for the act of rationally and give a solution for the given problem.

A hidden causal agent is the special feature of a crow that perceives an environment and reacts to the sense. A rational agent uses the performance measure for the criteria of what the world is like now and what action should take now. An agent learns from the mistake and recognizes the problem. Focusing on human–crow interaction is a must in order to avoid hackers of crows and to increase the growth rate of crows. The proposed system helps to know much about crows to help them and feed them in order to increase the growth rate of crow generation and understanding through ML. Hash is the core component, but every block of the bitcoin blockchain is categorized into the following components:

- Read the crow features;
- Hash function; and
- Blockchain validation.

2.2 LITERATURE REVIEW

Blockchain technology is the recent cloud computing topic implemented in AI. This new approach helps to read the intelligence of the crow in AI in a privately secured manner. The crows like veggies, i.e., cakes, savory, proffered food, etc. Normally, it comes in groups [1]. The author discusses the crow's features, population, food, and qualities [2]. The author explains that the birds offer nonprofessionals unparalleled opportunities to contribute to scientific knowledge [3]. The study referred to the Fraser Darling effect to note the density of breeding birds, the spread of laying, and the median date of egg-laying for social stimulation of reproduction [5]. The study proposes the pigeon interaction compared with ML neurons using signal processing [6]. The author proposes an intelligent system to study the behavior of birds. In this proposed system, the scope extended further to read the mind of a crow using intellectual learning [7]. The author's view about blockchain technology is applied to biometric analysis and reviewed with various existing studies [8]. The study reveals the blockchain technology implemented in the agricultural sector for food production [9]. The study reviewed how blockchain is implemented successfully in economists and technology [10]. The study reveals how climatic changes affect blockchain technology financially [11]. The study reveals the security protocol for public and private stakeholders in blockchain technique [12]. The proposed system gives insight into blockchain technology in wildlife.

2.3   DATA COLLECTION

Datasets are extracted through life sciences links. Much research is not implemented in human crow interaction. In order to have depth knowledge about the study, data extracted and six features' values are extracted and implemented in JustNN and SPSS tools to compare and check the accuracy of this study.

2.3.1   DATASET SAMPLES IMPLEMENTED IN JUSTNN AND SPSS TOOLS

Face Value	Mouth Expand	Left Eye	Expand Eye	Right Eye	Eye Expansion
150	239	86	64	32	40
66	124	44	32	18	22
161	267	76	68	41	45
163	270	55	69	50	49
149	239	88	68	37	41
67	126	44	37	19	25
159	268	78	69	41	45
162	271	58	69	53	52
151	233	87	64	36	40
68	126	49	35	19	24
164	269	78	68	41	46
165	271	58	67	50	51
151	234	86	64	38	41
68	126	47	32	19	32
163	268	78	68	41	45

Face Value	Mouth Expand	Left Eye	Expand Eye	Right Eye	Eye Expansion
165	272	58	65	52	49
156	240	86	64	21	40
69	126	47	36	18	29
169	269	78	69	41	48
166	270	58	69	57	50
154	239	86	65	39	42
73	125	47	36	17	45
168	269	77	68	47	45
169	273	56	64	52	49
153	239	89	71	34	40

2.3.2 HASH FUNCTION IMPLEMENTED FOR BLOCKCHAIN TECHNIQUE

Blockchain is a technology that records information, so it is very hard to change or hack the system. A hash function is the most important function used in the blockchain technique. It is mainly used in business analysis, but this study takes it to another dimension where block techniques can also be implemented in human crow interaction.

Features	Face Value	Mouth Expand	Left Eye	Expand Eye	Right Eye	Eye Expansion
Hash values	101	201	301	401	501	601

In the above table, the hash function is implemented separately for each feature from the dataset, and the resultant value is displayed.

2.3.3 DATASET SAMPLES IMPLEMENTED IN JUSTNN

JustNN is a Neural Networks tool that helps to learn, train, and test the features for effective results. The six features from the dataset are extracted and implemented in the JustNN tool to compare the performance and efficiency of the study in an effective manner.

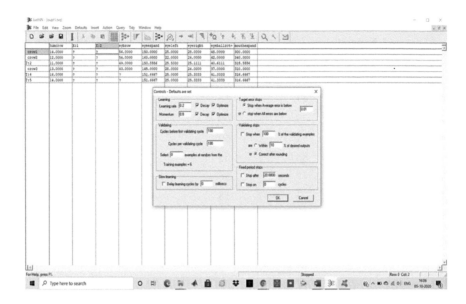

2.3.4   DATASET SAMPLES IMPLEMENTED IN SPSS

SPSS is a statistical tool for social sciences which normally used to analyze data statistically and manipulate data using ANOVA and MANOVA. To check the efficiency of this study and to analyze the prediction in a statistical method, the dataset is implemented in this tool.

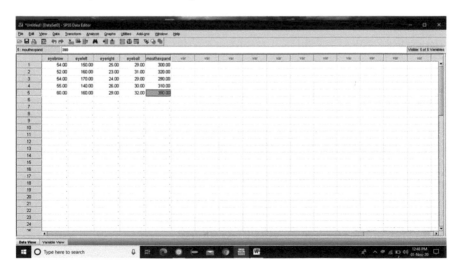

2.4 RESULTS AND DISCUSSIONS

Blockchain technology with hashing method is used to improvise the human-crow interaction. The pixel values that have six attributes of crow images are determined and it is converted to their hash function and further implemented in a neural network. Multilayer perception employs a hyperplane to separate data points. ANN's alternative versions are SVM and SVR, which are considered substitute ML algorithms.

2.4.1 RADIAL BASIS

Radial Basis is used here to map the maximum movement of the mouth widening and gestures with that of the variation from the original values as determined by the veteran doctors. This maps the values, and a hyperplane can then be plotted based on the feature-extracted values.

2.4.2 BLOCKCHAIN TECHNIQUE

Blockchain Technique makes virtual reality applicable to the natural environment. It brings advanced technology into real-world objects. Blockchain Technique is used with sensors to detect the mindset of the crow. The same is converted as a signal. MyoWare sensor is used here to read the voice signal.

2.4.3 MACHINE LEARNING

Multilayer Perception is the single or multilayer of Artificial Neurons. The input should have one node with a weighted bias and an output layer. Deep learning models can be developed effectively.

2.4.4 SUPPORT VECTOR MACHINE

SVM is the best classifier in neural networks for statistical calculation. Better predictions can be made using datasets in SVM (Table 2.1).

TABLE 2.1   Multilayer Perception and SVM Predicted Value

MLP Predicted Value 1	MLP Predicted Value 2
150.1236	241.4128
66.40299	123.1027
161.4318	263.9883
163.9415	271.9729
150.1236	241.4128
66.40299	123.1027
161.4318	263.9883
163.9415	271.9729
150.1236	241.4128
66.40299	123.1027
161.4318	263.9883
163.9415	271.9729
150.1236	241.4128
66.40299	123.1027
161.4318	263.9883
163.9415	271.9729
150.1236	241.4128
66.40299	123.1027
161.4318	263.9883
163.9415	271.9729
150.1236	241.4128
66.40299	123.1027
161.4318	263.9883
163.9415	271.9729
150.1236	241.4128

2.4.5 TRAINING, TESTING, AND VALIDATION

By training and testing the features, the basic characteristics of the ROC curve are generated for validation and prediction. To validate the efficiency of the resultant data, the training and the testing data are implemented in the confusion matrix, which accurately predicts the false resultant as false and the true resultant as true.

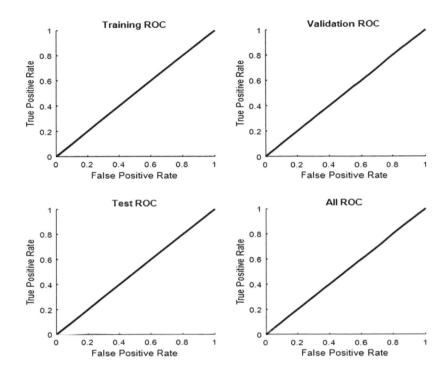

2.4.6 STATISTICAL PREDICTED SUMMARY OF SPSS

Statistical prediction is made in the SPSS tool by analyzing the dataset in a multilayer perceptron model.

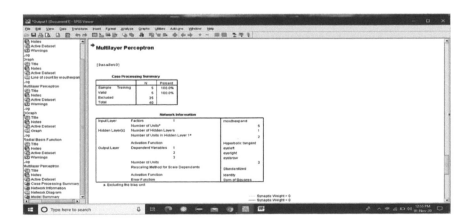

Case Processing Summary						
	Cases					
	Included		Excluded		Total	
	N	Percent	N	Percent	N	Percent
faceheight * mouthexpand * mouthshrink	4	100.0%	0	0%	4	100.0%
facewidth * mouthexpand * mouthshrink	4	100.0%	0	0%	4	100.0%
eyewidth * mouthexpand * mouthshrink	4	100.0%	0	0%	4	100.0%
eyeexpand * mouthexpand * mouthshrink	4	100.0%	0	0%	4	100.0%

2.4.7 STATISTICAL PREDICTED SUMMARY OF JustNN

The statistical prediction was implemented using the JustNN tool, where the training and testing data were done and validated. The below diagram shows the learning time of neural networks, minimum errors, testing time, validation, and results.

2.4.8 NN WITH VARIATION IN TESTING TIME AND LEARNING TIME

The diagram represents the changes in the testing time, which made a change in accuracy.

2.4.9 STATISTICAL PREDICTED SUMMARY OF SPSS WITH SVM

The diagram explains the efficiency of MLP-SVM in the SPSS tool for deep learning proves better compared to MLP in the JustNN tool.

The proposed system predicts 100% accuracy by training and testing the dataset in multilayer perception, radial basis function, and support vector model in the SPSS tool.

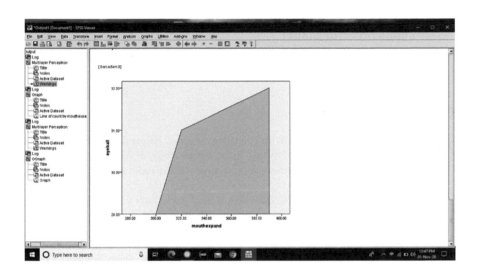

2.5 CONCLUSION AND FUTURE WORK

Blockchain technique implemented to human–bird interactions is the special initiation of ML in Blockchain technique to read the mind of the birds. The proposed system helps to detect the mind of a crow using SVM and MLP with a voice recognition sensor. This system helps to understand more about the crow and helps to increase its growth of the crow. The new attempt made in this study helps the society of ornithology in a privately secured manner. Further, the proposed system can be extended for implementation in other creatures. The proposed system predicts 100% accuracy by training and testing the dataset in multilayer perception and radial Basi and SVM in the SPSS tool.

KEYWORDS

- artificial intelligence
- blockchain technology
- multilayer perception
- neural networks
- radio frequency identification
- support vector model

REFERENCES

1. Dhanya, R., & Azeez, P. A. (2010). The House Sparrow Passer domesticus population of Arakku township, Andhra Pradesh, India. *Indian Birds, 5*(6), 180–181.
2. Gadgil, M., (1972). The function of communal roosts: Relevance of mixed roosts. *IBIS, 114*, 531–533.
3. Lan, C. T. N., & Lord, M., (1972). Dispersion, population ecology and migration of eastern great reed warblers *Acrocephalus orientalis* wintering in Malaysia. *International Journal of Avian Science, 114*(4), 451–494.
4. Barbara R., (1972). MacRoberts, social stimulation of reproduction in herring and lesser black-backed gulls. *International Journal of Avian Science, 114*(4), 495–506.
5. Letzner, S., Gunturkun, O., & Beste, C. (2020). How birds outperform humans in multi-component behavior (Retraction of Vol 27, Pg R 996, 2017).
6. Veit, L., & Nieder, A., (2013). Abstract rule neurons in the endbrain support intelligent behavior in corvid songbirds. *Nat. Commun., 4*, 2878.
7. Ante, L., (2020). Smart contracts on the blockchain-A bibliometric analysis and review. *Telematics and Informatics, 57*, 101519.
8. Antonucci, F., Figorilli, S., Costa, C., Pallottino, F., Raso, L., & Menesatti, P., (2019). A review on blockchain applications in the agri-food sector. *J. Sci. Food Agric., 99*(14), 6129–6138.
9. Böhme, R., Christin, N., Edelman, B., & Moore, T., (2015). Bitcoin: Economics, technology, and governance. *J. Econ. Perspect., 29*(2), 213–238.
10. Bolt, J., (2019). *Financial Resilience of Kenyan Smallholders Affected by Climate Change, and the Potential for Blockchain Technology. CCAFS.*
11. Buterin, V., (2015). On public and private blockchains. In: Buterin, V., (ed.), *Ethereum BLog, Vitalik Buterin.*
12. Cachin, C., & Vukolić, M., (2017). *Blockchain Consensus Protocols in the Wild. arXiv preprint arXiv:1707.01873.*

CHAPTER 3

Toxic Comment Classifier

K. GOVINDA[1] and KORHAN CENGIZ[2]

[1]SCOPE, VIT University, Vellore, Tamil Nadu, India

[2]Department of Electrical–Electronics Engineering, Trakya University, Turkey

ABSTRACT

A gigantic measure of data is created consistently through web use emerging from intelligent online interchanges among clients [20–25]. Even though the present circumstance contributes fundamentally to improving the nature of human existence, unfortunately, it additionally includes incredible perils since online compositions with high harmfulness can root individual assaults, online provocation, and tormenting exercises [26–30]. In this century, web-based media has formed many occupation possibilities, and simultaneously, it has become a selective spot for individuals to openly provoke their sentiments expressly. Among a portion of these clients, a few gatherings are exploiting these stages and abusing their opportunity to create their poisonous mentality (for instance, annoying, verbal provocation, unsafe dangers, foul remarks, and so on). The 2017 Youth-Risk-Behavior-Surveillance-System (Center for Any Disease Control and Prevention) evaluated that about 14.9% of secondary school understudies were harassed by electronic methods in the previous year beforehand as the review was finished. With the sudden expansion in harmfulness levels in online discussions via web-based media stages, the requirement for the utilization of profound learning calculations for

Hybridization of Blockchain and Cloud Computing: Overcoming Security Issues in IoT.
M. Lawanya Shri, E. Gangadevi, K. Santhi, & Chiranji Lal Chowdhary (Eds.)
© 2024 Apple Academic Press, Inc. Co-published with CRC Press (Taylor & Francis)

poisonous remark order and location has become a major centralization of numerous online stages. In the previous few years, there were a few endeavors to perceive an effective model for online poisonous remark characterization forecasts.

Nonetheless, these means are as yet in their beginning phases, and new techniques and structures are required. The conversation AI group, an activity financed by Jigsaw and Google (both are a piece of Alphabet endeavor), is reliably chipping away at the apparatuses that can help improve online discussions. One territory of the center is the investigation of hurtful online exercises, such as harmful remarking (for example, remarks that are arranged as impolite, rude, or most likely make an individual leave a conversation). Till now, they've made an assortment of openly accessible models that are supported through the Perspective API, including the poisonousness level. Yet, the current models are as yet making blunders, and they don't permit the clients to pick among the sorts of harmfulness they may be keen on finding.

Parallelly, the massive volume of statistics that have constantly been appearing for a while makes the creation of new machine learning (ML) algorithms and computational tools for handling this information an overbearing need. Gratefully, the developments in hardware, cloud computing, and big data have allowed great advancement of Deep Learning approaches which have shown a very promising performance so far. Toxic comment classification is a newly developing research field with numerous studies that have addressed various methods in the detection of undesirable messages on communication platforms. This chapter focuses on the comparison of deep learning algorithms applied to the classification of the toxicity of the online comments that had been made.

3.1　INTRODUCTION

The web has become the biggest stage to speak to our aptitudes. Different websites permit individuals to utilize their stage to grandstand their aptitudes through recordings, articles, and other data in a few designs. Most of the websites give an office for commenting on any transferred data. In any case, there's a chance that people can utilize accursed dialect in their comments. This chapter proposes to classify toxic comments constructed on the types of toxicity. Examples of toxicity categories can be insult, hate, severely toxic, obscene, threat, etc. This chapter uses different ML algorithms like support vector machines (SVMs), KNN, Naïve Bayes, etc., to determine the six types of toxic comments and their performances.

The online interactions among people generate a huge amount of data, giving rise to what we call "Big Data." If we are not using specific tools and strategies such as Machine Learning (ML) and Natural Language Processing (NLP), extracting valuable information in real-time is difficult. Some common examples of such data sources include the interactions linked to social networks, blog articles, etc. An infinity of information that many companies make use of to offer free or paid services to many users [3]. In this situation, the downside is characterized by the number of risks connected with toxic comments since the compensations related to the said kind of information (social comments, online reviews, political opinions, etc.) are drastically reduced by those who often interfere with verbal attacks, bullying, harassment, threats to the person. And in general, actions lead some members to abandon the discussion.

The foundation for the issue emerges from a wreck of online discussions, where individuals take an interest effectively and offer remarks. Since the remarks now and again are likewise injurious, annoying, or maybe scorn based, it turns into the duty of the facilitating associations to affirm that these discussions don't appear to be of the negative sort [4]. The mission was, therefore, to construct a model that would make necessary predictions to categorize the comments into various categories. The goal is to create a model ready to be able to distinguish the toxicity level with the most accuracy and to deliver a relative study between the various algorithms used for the advancement.

An immense measure of studies has been finished on remark grouping inside the news, account, and other undifferentiated areas. One such examination of group remarks from the broadcast space was made with the help of a collection of highlights like the range of remarks, capitalized and accentuation events, and verbal highlights like spelling, obscenity, and lucidness utilizing the straight and tree-based classifier [8].

Many studies recently examined scorn discourse utilizing neural organization frameworks; Badjatiya et al. utilized general analyses with various profound learning plans to survey semantic word inserting to switch harmful remarks to recognizable proof [13]. In another investigation, a notion examination model of YouTube remarks, utilizing a profound neural organization, was arranged that drove around 70–80% precision [14]. Additionally, the general utilization of different styles of neural organization techniques for input characterization has been widely utilized in late-distributed writing [6, 15–17].

Nonetheless, these methodologies just tended to some of the undertaking's difficulties while others stayed unsolved [18].

Some revealed that broad quantities of writing have demonstrated that directed learning procedures are the premier, often utilized techniques for digital tormenting discovery. All things considered, other non-regulated procedures and techniques are perceived to be employable on digital harassing acknowledgment. Likewise, Karlekar and Bansal [19] detailed an expanded number of non-public attacks and misuse that are shared and posted on the web. During this investigation, creators introduced the assignment of consequently ordering and examining different kinds of badgering, upheld stories shared on the net discussion Safe City and utilized marking levels of grabbing, staring, and remarking; their outcomes demonstrated that solitary name CNN-RNN. This model recommended accomplishes a precision of 86.5. Perhaps the most unfamiliar issues are an approach to distinguish calculations that may execute high affectability inside the recognition of harmful remarks. Obviously, distinguishing remarks that aren't poisonous as harmful is baffling for the clients, and there ought to be a lot of exertion to make a calculation with the absolute best level of sensitivities.

Poisonous remark arrangement could be a moderately new field, and lately, various investigations have been administered to naturally characterize harmful remarks. The paper [13] by Nobata et al. proposed a regulated grouping calculation technique with the use of n-grams and manual improvement of RE examples to distinguish the oppressive language [13]. Stood et al. utilized the generally characterized boycotted words and altered the distance measurements of the calculation to distinguish the profanity, which allowed them to use maxims like sh*!+ (or) @ss as ill-bred [13]. Hirschberg and Warner recognized the disdain discourse text by deciphering a corpus of web locales and client remarks equipped towards identifying anti-Jewish scorn [14]. Nobata et al. utilized truly arranged online client remarks from Yahoo Finance and some news pages for recognition of the online scorn discourse [13]. Chen et al. likewise did the component designing method for additional arranging of remarks into damaging, non-oppressive, and uncertain [15]. Georgeakopoulos and Plagianakos thought about the exhibition of five distinct classifiers, to be specific; calculated regression, BoW approach

SVM, NB, k-nearest neighbor (kNN), and random trees, and found that multinomial NB outshone all additional methodologies in arranging the harmful remarks [16].

A couple of dedicated papers that address the effect of merging unmistakable substance changes on the show precision for assessment arrangement. Uysal and Gunal have indicated the impact of progress on substance characterization by taking into thought four changes and their all-possible blend on news and e-mail space to notice the classification accuracy. Their test examinations created the impression that picking reasonable mixes may end in basic improvement in arrangement accuracy [17]. Nobata et al. used standardization of numbers, replacing incredibly long dark words and repeated emphases with a vague token [6]. Haddi et al. explained the piece of change in suspicion examination and delineated with the assistance of SVM on movie review information bases that the accuracy's advancement basically with the fitting change and have a decision. They utilized change techniques, for example, eliminating the blank area, extending shortened forms, expelling stop words, and nullifying them [18].

Different papers fixate more on the displaying when contrasted with change. For the outline, Wang watches out for channeling out anything from the corpus that is not the letter set. Regardless, this would channel out all the numbers, pictures, Moment Messages (IM) codes, and abbreviations, for example, $#!+, *tingle, absolutely particular significance to the words, or pass up a great opportunity for a piece of information. In another assessment, Bao et al. used five changes to be explicit URLs feature reservation, nullification change, repeated letters standardization, stemming, and lemmatization on Twitter data and associated a straight classifier open in a WEKA AI mechanical assembly. They found the precision of the characterization increases when URLs feature reservation, invalidation change, and repeated letter standardization are used while lessening when stemming and lemmatization are associated [19].

3.2 PROPOSED METHOD

The multi-label classification of comments needs to be achieved. The development methodology entails the following steps: dataset description, text pre-processing, solving the multi-label classification problem, feature extraction, and model training.

3.2.1 DATASET DESCRIPTION

The dataset utilized is accessible on Kaggle. The dataset comprises 10,734,904 words, out of which the number of special words is 5,32,299. The 10 most common words are "the," "to," "of," "and," "a," "I," "is," "you," "that," and "in." The English Oxford lexicon comprises 1,71,476 words. The issue with the over insights is that we are tallying a word capitalized or lowercase as diverse words inside and out. This would not include any significance to the assist preparing our information.

3.2.2 TEXT PRE-PROCESSING

The efficiency depends upon the pre-proccssing of data, as pre-processing reduces ambiguity in feature extraction. Hence, data pre-processing is an important step in text classification. The pre-processing includes converting all text to lowercase and removing special characters, numbers, punctuation marks, URLs, usernames, and stop words.

3.2.2.1 DATA CLEANING

The information utilized comprises numerous Wikipedia comments, which have been labeled by people concurring with their relative harmfulness. The information incorporates the following:

- **train.csv:** The preparing set contains comments with their twofold labels.
- **test.csv:** The test set foresees harmfulness probabilities for these comments.

On analyzing the prepared dataset, it was noted that the harmful levels within the comments are classified as appeared below.

The dataset comprises 10,734,904 words, out of which the number of one-of-a-kind words is 5,32,299. To channel and clean our data, we perform the taking-after process:

- Remove unrelated characters (!"#$%&() *+,-./:;<=>?@[\\]^_`{|}~\t\n).
- Alter all letters to lowercase (HeLlO → hello).
- Tokenization of our words (hi how are you → [23, 1, 5, 13]).

- Normalize our input length with padding (hi how are you → [23, 1, 5, 13, 0, 0, 0]).

Misspelled words, slang, or different word modulations are not shared into a single base word. However, the advantage of using a Neural Network is that they excel with raw inputs; hence, we would not pre-process the data further for better accuracy.

Some statistics on the pre-processed data:

- **Vocab Size:** 2,10,337;
- **The Longest Comment Size:** 1,403;
- **Average Comment Size:** 68.22156908210138;
- **Max Comment Size:** 37.

After pre-processing the data, our word size drops down to a controllable 2,10,337.

3.2.2.2 EMBEDDING

The information representation regularly utilized in our lexicon is the one-hot encoding, where each word is changed into a vector with a one compared to its area. For illustration, in case our word vector is [hi, how, are, you], and the word we are trying to find is "hello," the input vector would be [1,0,0,0]. This tends to work fine unless our lexicon is tremendous, which is 2,10,000 in this case. This implies that we would like conclusion up with word vectors that comprise primarily a bunch of 0s. We have subsequently taken the approach of employing a Word2Vec procedure to discover embeddings for our words. The benefits of this nonstop inserting are that words with a prescient comparative control will appear closer together on our word vector. Although, the disadvantage to this is that it produces more of a black box where the words with the most analytical power get mislaid in the numbers.

3.2.3 FEATURE EXTRACTION

The Bentonite was activated by adding concentrated H_2SO_4 (1:1 w/v) with constant stirring. The material was kept in a hot air oven at 110°C for 12 hours. This material was washed with distilled water and soaked in a 2%

NaHCO$_3$ solution overnight to remove the residual acid. Then the material was washed with distilled water, until the pH of the adsorbent reached slightly above 7.

3.2.3.1　TF-IDF VECTORIZER

It is simple for people to order pictures or text, yet it is hard for PCs, which manage numbers, and to be more exact, they measure numbers as electrical motivations. Hence, any information should be changed over into that structure so PCs can handle it and give us back the outcome. Along these lines, highlight extraction assumes a significant part in handling text. So, prior to preparing the model, we should vectorize the info information. Highlight extraction should be possible by applying the term frequency-inverse document frequency (TF-IDF) utilizing n-gram features-unigram (1-word) and bigram (2-words) to discover the heaviness of a specific element in a book. Subsequently, highlights are sifted dependent on the greatest weight.

*TFIDF score for term i in document j = TF(i, j) * IDF (i)*

where

IDF = Inverse Document Frequency

TF = Term Frequency

$$TF(i, j) = \frac{\text{Term i frequency in document j}}{\text{Total words in document j}}$$

$$IDF(i) = \log_2 \left(\frac{\text{Total documents}}{\text{documents with term i}} \right)$$

and

t = Term

j = Document

$$\textbf{Tf.Idf}(c, d, w) \;=\; \textbf{Tf}(d, w) \log \left(\frac{N}{\textbf{Df}(c, w)} \right)$$

where; N is the number of documents in collection.

3.2.3.2 N-GRAM FEATURES

When n-gram highlights are connected, more than one word is considered at a time. This can be beneficial as numerous times a few words pass on assumptions more successfully when utilized together. An n-gram of estimate 1 is referred to as a unigram; measure 2 could be a bigram. N-grams captures more setting around each word. N-grams nearly continuously boosts exactness. The N-gram recurrence strategy gives a cheap and profoundly compelling way of classifying records.

3.3 EXPERIMENTAL METHODS AND MATERIALS

3.3.1 SUPPORT VECTOR MACHINE

Given a piece of labeled training, the algorithm yields the ideal hyper-plane which categorizes modern input information. It works effectively on huge datasets without as well much computation. To maximize the edge between the information focuses and the hyperplane, the hinge loss function is utilized. The SVM algorithm executed in practice employing a kernel. The hyperplane is learned in linear SVM by changing the issue utilizing a few linear algebras.

$$\text{A separating hyperplane: } w^T x + b = 0$$

$$(w^T x_i) + b > 0 \quad \text{if } y_i = 1$$

$$(w^T x_i) + b < 0 \quad \text{if } y_i = -1$$

3.3.2 LOGISTIC REGRESSION

It could be a simple technique. We try and predict the probability of variables belongs to a "0" class or "1" class. It uses a logistic function that always returns a worth between 0 and 1 to model a binary variable quantity. The logistic function is given by If the worth is above the edge, the category is predicted as "1" class, else it's predicted as "0" class.

$$P = \frac{1}{1 + e^{-(-.5596 + 1.2528X)}}$$

3.3.3   K-NEAREST-NEIGHBOR

The KNN algorithm won't learn within the training phase, it only saves all the training examples. At the time of prediction, for the test instance at the algorithm finds the training example x_i, y_i which is closest to x_t. Euclidean distance is employed to calculate the space between the test data and every row of coaching data. The formula to calculate the Euclidean distance between two data points v and u is given by:

$$D(a,b) = \sqrt{\sum_{i=1}^{n}(b_i - a_i)^2}$$

K neighbors are selected with the shortest distance from the test data, and voting is disbursed to decide the output.

3.3.4   DECISION TREE

It is a stream diagram tree-like structure, where every one of the inside hubs means a test on an element, every one of its branches indicates a result of a test, and each leaf hub holds a class name. The highest hub of a tree is the root hub. A way is followed from the establishment to a leaf hub, which holds the classification forecast for that tuple. The instructive and order steps of choice tree enlistment are basic and quick. Choice trees are valuable in light of the fact that the improvement of choice tree classifiers doesn't need any space information. Their portrayal of obtained information in the tree structure is direct to acclimatize clients. Choice tree classifiers have great exactness. The matter of constructing a call tree is expressed recursively. First, it's necessary to pick out an attribute to position at the basis node and make one branch for every possible value. The attribute with the very best information gain is chosen because of the root node. When the complexity of a tree increases, overfitting may occur, which successively reduces the accuracy of test data. To avoid over-fitting, pre-pruning, and post-pruning methods are used. In pre-pruning, we stop early (while growing the tree) if the gain isn't statistically significant. While in post-pruning, we grow full trees and take away the nodes supported cross-validation.

The Gini index and entropy calculation equation are as follows:

$$I_G(p) = \sum_{i=1}^{J}\left(p_i \sum_{k \neq i} p_k\right) = \sum_{i=1}^{J} p_i(1-p_i) = \sum_{i=1}^{J}(p_i - p_i^2)$$

$$= \sum_{i=1}^{J} p_i - \sum_{i=1}^{J} p_i^2 = 1 - \sum_{i=1}^{J} p_i^2$$

$$\mathrm{H}(T) = I_E(p_1, p_2, \ldots, p_J) = -\sum_{i=1}^{J} p_i \log_2 p_i$$

3.3.5 RANDOM FOREST

An arbitrary woodland is a group of numerous choice trees. Arbitrary backwoods are assembled utilizing a strategy considered sacking in which every choice tree is utilized as equal assessors. Whenever utilized for a grouping issue, the outcome depends on the lion's share vote of the outcomes got from every choice tree. For relapse, the forecast of a leaf hub is the mean estimation of the objective qualities in that leaf. Arbitrary woodland relapse takes the mean estimation of the outcomes from choice trees. Irregular woods lessen the danger of over-fitting, and precision is a lot higher than in a solitary choice tree. Besides, choice trees in an arbitrary woodland run in equal, so the time doesn't turn into a bottleneck.

The achievement of an arbitrary timberland profoundly relies upon utilizing uncorrelated choice trees. On the off chance that we utilize the equivalent or fundamentally the same as trees, the general outcome won't be vastly different from the consequence of a solitary choice tree. Arbitrary backwoods accomplish uncorrelated choice trees by bootstrapping and highlighting arbitrariness. Subsequently, after the training, estimates for unobserved models x' can be completed by an average of the estimates from all the distinct regression trees on the x':

$$\hat{f} = \frac{1}{B}\sum_{b=1}^{B} f_b(x')$$

where; B is the no of times bagging is performed on the set. Moreover, an approximation of the indecision of the estimate can be completed as the standard deviation of the calculations from all the distinct regression trees on the $x.'$

$$\sigma = \sqrt{\frac{\sum_{b=1}^{B}(f_b(x') - \hat{f})^2}{B-1}}.$$

3.3.6 *NAÏVE BAYES*

Credulous Bayesian order could be a probabilistic way to deal with AI. It's based on the Bayes theorem; for example, the probability of an event realizing that B has happened likely could be determined. Occasion B speaks to the proof and, like this, the speculation to be affirmed. The hypothesis runs on the conviction that everybody's indicators/ highlights are free; accordingly, the presence of 1 wouldn't influence the inverse. This can be the Bayes approach to gullible rearrangements. The likelihood of 1 occasion, B, is autonomous of another B occasion happening. The information acquired inside the underlying evaluation of client information determined the likelihood of whether that new remark is harmful or non-poisonous. The way to deal with grouping an online remark as hostile or harmful would start by contemplating our assortment of training information named poisonous and non-harmful.

The likelihood that a message is poisonous, P(Toxic), was then determined to uphold the extent of harmful messages happening inside the informational preparation collection. There's no necessity to compute the likelihood of the message content, P (message content). The likelihood that the new message's substance is found during a poisonous word pool is required to uphold the gullible rearrangements of the Bayes theorem. The gullible suspicion determines the probability of the new message being poisonous in light of the result of the word showing up or not showing up inside the harmful word pool. In like manner, the probability of the new message being non-harmful is determined, and furthermore, the characterization of the new message would depend on the probability proportion.

1. **Multinomial NB:** These chips away at the Naïve Bayes calculation for the polynomial circled information and is one in all the two exemplary guileless Bayes variations used in content characterization (where the data are typically signified as the word vector checks utilized; however, TF-IDF vectors likewise are known to figure well by and by). The appropriation is parametrized by vectors $\theta_y = (\theta_{y1}, \ldots, \theta_{yn})$ for each class y, where n is the quantity of highlights (in content characterization, the components of the jargon) and θ_{yi} is the likelihood P(xi|y) of this element 'i' showing up during an example having a place with class 'y.'

    The parameters θ_y are assessed by a leveled form of determined probability, i.e., ratio counting:

$$\hat{\theta}_{yi} = \frac{N_{yi} + \alpha}{N_y + \alpha n}$$

where; $N_{yi} = \sum x \in Txi$ is the number of times that feature i appears during a sample of sophistication y within the training set T, and $N_y = \sum i = 1 n N_{yi}$ is the total count of all features for sophistication y.

2. **Bernoulli NB:** This requires tests chosen to be denoted as binary-valued feature vectors; just in case, given the other data, a Bernoulli NB occurrence might binarize. The conclusion rule for Bernoulli Naïve Bayes is established on:

$$P(x_i \mid y) = P(i \mid y) x_i + (1 - P(i \mid y)) (1 - x_i)$$

which contrasts from multinomial NB's broadcast that it unequivocally punishes the non-event of a feature i that is a pointer for innovation y, where the multinomial variety would fundamentally disregard a non-happening highlight. On account of substance arrangement, word occasion vectors (rather than word check vectors) are also accustomed to prepare and use this classifier. Bernoulli NB may perform route better on a couple datasets, especially those with more limited reports. It's judicious to pass judgment on the two models if time licenses.

3.4   RESULTS AND DISCUSSION

The dataset is of 95,981 examples of remarks alongside their names. It had been noticed each 1 out of 10 examples was poisonous, and each 1 out of 50 examples was indecent and annoying, yet the events of test being serious harmful, danger, and personality scorn was very uncommon. The initial five segments don't contain any harmful words henceforth they are delegated non-poisonous as shown in Figure 3.1.

The next step is to check the percentage of toxic comments in the dataset. It seems that 90% of the comments fall in the toxic category as shown in Figure 3.2.

```
In [34]: ▶ data = pd.read_csv('train.csv')
            data.head()
```

Out[34]:

	id	comment_text	toxic	severe_toxic	obscene	threat	insult	identity_hate
0	0000997932d777bf	Explanation\nWhy the edits made under my usern...	0	0	0	0	0	0
1	000103f0d9cfb60f	D'aww! He matches this background colour I'm s...	0	0	0	0	0	0
2	000113f07ec002fd	Hey man, I'm really not trying to edit war. It...	0	0	0	0	0	0
3	0001b41b1c6bb37e	"\nMore\nI can't make any real suggestions on ...	0	0	0	0	0	0
4	0001d958c54c6e35	You, sir, are my hero. Any chance you remember...	0	0	0	0	0	0

Entries with all 0 under the 6 categories are neutral and considered as non-toxic.

FIGURE 3.1   The training dataset used for classification.

```
data.toxic.value_counts(normalize=True)

0    0.904156
1    0.095844
Name: toxic, dtype: float64
```

FIGURE 3.2   Percentage of toxic comments present in the dataset.

In the first visualization, we can observe that comments were of varying occurrences from less than 2,000 to 15,000. The majority of comments occurred up to 15,000, as shown in Figure 3.3.

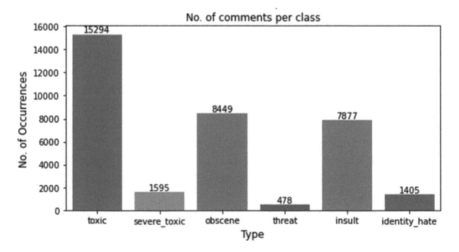

FIGURE 3.3   The total comments are present in every category of comments.

The second visualization plots the % of comments belonging to various categories. Toxic comments were uppermost in quantity, after that obscene, insult, severe-toxic, identity-hate, and threat in declining order as shown in Figure 3.4.

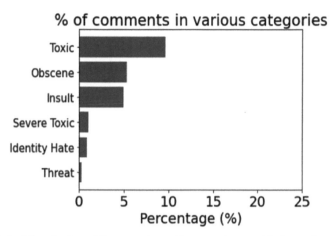

FIGURE 3.4   Visualization of the percentage of comments present in the various categories.

The following step removes the punctuations, capital letters, spaces, etc. So as to make the data more suitable for further classification as shown in Figure 3.5.

```
# Text preprocessing steps - remove numbers, capital letters, punctuation, '\n'
import re
import string

# remove all numbers with letters attached to them
alphanumeric = lambda x: re.sub('\w*\d\w*', ' ', x)

# '[%s]' % re.escape(string.punctuation),' ' - replace punctuation with white space
# .lower() - convert all strings to lowercase
punc_lower = lambda x: re.sub('[%s]' % re.escape(string.punctuation), ' ', x.lower())

# Remove all '\n' in the string and replace it with a space
remove_n = lambda x: re.sub("\n", " ", x)

# Remove all non-ascii characters
remove_non_ascii = lambda x: re.sub(r'[^\x00-\x7f]',r' ', x)

# Apply all the lambda functions wrote previously through .map on the comments column
data['comment_text'] = data['comment_text'].map(alphanumeric).map(punc_lower).map(remove_n).map(remove_non_ascii)

data['comment_text'][0]
```

```
6]: 'explanation why the edits made under my username hardcore metallica fan were reverted  they weren t vandalisms  just closur
    e on some gas after i voted at new york dolls fac  and please don t remove the template from the talk page since i m retired
    now        '
```

Separate our dataset into 6 sections. Each section is comment + 1 category.

FIGURE 3.5   Removal of all numbers, capital letters, and punctuations.

By creating the word cloud, I will be analyzing the type of toxic words present in the dataset. More visible the word, the greater the frequency it has in the dataset. I have implemented the WordCloud in two categories: identify hate and insult.

Earlier, we saw that comments that are toxic (and other forms of toxicity) make up less than 10% of the comments in the data. This leads to the issue of class imbalance.

We can deal with class imbalance by taking a subset of the data where the proportion of the toxic comments are at least 20% (ideally 50%) in relation to non-toxic comments.

For a start, we can take 5,000 rows of comments that are toxic and concatenate them row-wise with those that are not toxic so that we have a balanced dataset.

Now we need to create a simple function that takes in a dataset and allows user to choose dataset, toxicity label, vectorizer, and number of n-grams as shown in Figure 3.6.

```python
def cv_tf_train_test(df_done,label,vectorizer,ngram):

    ''' Train/Test split'''
    # Split the data into X and y data sets
    X = df_done.comment_text
    y = df_done[label]

    # Split our data into training and test data
    X_train, X_test, y_train, y_test = train_test_split(X, y, test_size=0.3, random_state=42)

    ''' Count Vectorizer/TF-IDF '''

    # Create a Vectorizer object and remove stopwords from the table
    cv1 = vectorizer(ngram_range=(ngram), stop_words='english')

    X_train_cv1 = cv1.fit_transform(X_train) # Learn the vocabulary dictionary and return term-document matrix
    X_test_cv1  = cv1.transform(X_test)      # Learn a vocabulary dictionary of all tokens in the raw documents.

    # Output a Dataframe of the CountVectorizer with unique words as the labels
    # test = pd.DataFrame(X_train_cv1.toarray(), columns=cv1.get_feature_names())
```

FIGURE 3.6   Vectorization and removal of stopwords.

Now I have created a TF-IDF vectorizer object for each category and calculated the F1-scores across all models as shown in Figure 3.7.

The table given in Figure 3.7 shows the F1-score of all the models on the basis of the categorization of toxicity. Figure 3.8 is the graphical representation of the table given in Figure 3.7.

	F1 Score(toxic)	F1 Score(severe_toxic)	F1 Score(obscene)	F1 Score(insult)	F1 Score(threat)	F1 Score(identity_hate)
Log Regression	0.861234	0.927879	0.908655	0.896599	0.628821	0.699029
KNN	0.185120	0.857416	0.519056	0.257992	0.720000	0.230159
BernoulliNB	0.776521	0.803707	0.787830	0.783762	0.311828	0.549206
MultinomialNB	0.874958	0.936170	0.901463	0.897411	0.504762	0.485857
SVM	0.876133	0.926004	0.921378	0.902619	0.786765	0.797516
Random Forest	0.838055	0.934874	0.909091	0.883993	0.795539	0.768448

FIGURE 3.7 F1-scores of all the models.

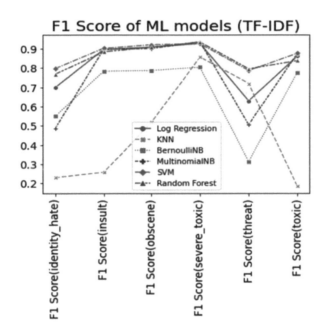

FIGURE 3.8 Graphical representation of all the models.

We can see that SVM outperforms all the other models in terms of accuracy in the classification of toxic comments as the graph line of SVM is observed to be the highest. Now we need to test if our model is actually working or not.

Random forest has assigned a probability of 1 that comment 1 is toxic. Comment 2 has only a low toxicity probability of 0.16 (Figure 3.9).

```
# Sample Prediction
comment1 = ['You piece of shit']
comment2 = ['What is up garden apple doing']

comment1_vect = tfv.transform(comment1)
randomforest.predict_proba(comment1_vect)[:,1]
```

```
array([1.])
```

```
comment2_vect = tfv.transform(comment2)
randomforest.predict_proba(comment2_vect)[:,1]
```

```
array([0.16036935])
```

FIGURE 3.9   Prediction of comments using random forest.

3.5   CONCLUSION

This chapter focuses on pernicious comment classification, where online comments are classified into various predefined categories. There are ceaseless trials experimenting and computing the presence of toxicity of assorted kinds on the web platforms, including the micro and macro blogging sites by the industries further because the research communities for an efficient model that detects and predicts the web pernicious comments. This is important within the research field because of the tremendously growing online interactive communication among users. This work is devoted to finding the most effective possible optimum solutions for the classification of online pernicious comments, which further classifies the toxic comments into six labels provided by the datasets on the Kaggle platform. The analysis shows that a SVM is preferable than other algorithms as the graph line of the SVM is the highest among all. Therefore, we can say that the SVM can be considered the perfect model for the toxic comment classification.

KEYWORDS

- **machine learning**
- **Naïve-Bayes**
- **natural language processing**

- **random forest**
- **support vector machine**
- **term frequency-inverse document frequency**

REFERENCES

1. CrowdFlower, (2016). *CrowdFlower Data Science Report*, 8, 9.
2. https://www.statista.com/statistics/272014/global-social-networksranked-by-number-of-users (accessed on 11 August 2022).
3. Lenhart, A., Ybarra, M., Zickuhr, K., & Price-Feeney, M., (2016). *Online Harassment, Digital Abuse, and Cyberstalking in America.* Report 11.21.16, 1–59.
4. Nobata, C., & Tetreault, J., (2016). *Abusive Language Detection in Online User Content*, 145–153.
5. Joulin, A., Grave, E., Bojanowski, P., Douze, M., Jégou, H., & Mikolov, T., (2016). *FastText.zip: Compressing Text Classification Models*, 1–13.
6. Zhang, X., Zhao, J., & Lecun, Y., (2015). *Character-Level Convolutional Networks for Text,* 1–9.
7. Prathyusha, D. J., & Govinda, K. (2019). Securing virtual machines from DDoS attacks using hash-based detection techniques. *Multiagent and Grid Systems, 15*(2), 121–135. doi: 10.3233/MGS-190305.
8. Sood, S. O., Antin, J., & Churchill, E. F., (2009). *Using Crowdsourcing to Improve Profanity Detection, 69–74.*
9. Warner, W., & Hirschberg, J., (2012). *Detecting Hate Speech on the World Wide Web* (pp. 19–26). no. Lsm.
10. Chen, H., Mckeever, S., & Delany, S. J., (2017). Presenting a labeled dataset for real-time detection of abusive user posts. *Proceedings of the International Conference on Web Intelligence – WI, 17, 884–890.*
11. Dhanya, A. S., & Govinda, K. (2019). Sentiment analysis on goods and services tax bill. *Journal of Computational and Theoretical Nanoscience, 16*(43621), 2237–2240. doi: 10.1166/jctn.2019.7879.
12. Maas, A. L., Daly, R. E., Pham, P. T., Huang, D., Ng, A. Y., & Potts, C., (2011). Learning word vectors for sentiment analysis. *Proceedings of the 49th Annual Meeting of the Association for Computational Linguistics: Human Language Technologies*, 142–150.
13. Rajasekaran, R., Govinda, K., Reddy, A., Reddy, U. S., & Reddy, Y. (2019). Visual analysis of temperature time series and rainfall using big data. *Journal of Research on the Lepidoptera, 50*(3), 39–52. doi: 10.36872/lepi/v50i3/201023.
14. Rajasekaran, R., Masih, J., & Govinda, K. (2019). An analysis of mobile passcodes in case of criminal investigations through social network data. *International Journal of Computers and Applications*. doi: 10.1080/1206212X.2019.1662169.
15. Bao, Y., Quan, C., Wang, L., & Ren, F., (2014*). The Role of Pre-processing in Twitter Sentiment Analysis,* 615–624.

16. Somasekhara, R. M. C., Sivaramakrishna, L., & VaradaReddy, A., (2012). The use of an agricultural waste material, jujuba seeds for the removal of anionic dye (Congo red) from aqueous medium. *J. Hazard Mater., 203*, 118–127.

17. Ramasubbareddy, S., Govinda, K. & Swetha, E. (2020). Facial expression recognition system using convolutional neural networks. *International Journal of Recent Technology and Engineering, 8*, 603–607. doi: 10.35940/ijrte.B1119.0782S419.

18. Kumari, B. V. S., Prasad, G., Ramasubbareddy, S., Govinda, K. (2020). Optimized task scheduling for cloud computing using PSO and GA. *International Journal of Recent Technology and Engineering, 8*, 608–611. doi: 10.35940/ijrte.B1120.0782S419.

19. Maas, A. L., Daly, R. E., Pham, P. T., Huang, D., Ng, A. Y., & Potts, C., (2011). Learning word vectors for sentiment analysis. *Proceedings of the 49th Annual Meeting of the Association for Computational Linguistics: Human Language Technologies*, 142–150.

20. Chowdhary, C. L., Sai, G. V. K., & Acharjya, D. P., (2016). Decreasing false assumption for improved breast cancer detection. *J. Sci. Arts Year, 16*(2), 157–176.

21. Chowdhary, C. L., (2018). Application of object recognition with shape-index identification and 2D scale-invariant feature transform for key-point detection. In: *Feature Dimension Reduction for Content-Based Image Identification* (pp. 218–231) IGI Global.

22. Govinda, K., Nair, A. S., & Ramasubbareddy, S. (2020). Map reduce, pig and hive on climatic condition. *International Journal of Innovative Technology and Exploring Engineering, 8*, 1144–1148. doi: 10.35940/ijitee.K1231.09811S19.

23. Wang, S., & Manning, C., (2012). Baselines and bigrams: Simple, good sentiment and topic classification. *Proceedings of the 50th Annual Meeting of the Association for Computational Linguistics*, 90–94.

24. Govinda, K., Singh, A., & Ramasubbareddy, S. (2019). Privacy protection in smart grid using blind signature method. *International Journal of Innovative Technology and Exploring Engineering, 8*, 1162–1165. doi: 10.35940/ijitee.K1234.09811S 19.

25. Chowdhary, C. L., Muatjitjeja, K., & Jat, D. S., (2015). Three-dimensional object recognition based intelligence system for identification. In: *2015 International Conference on Emerging Trends in Networks and Computer Communications (ETNCC)* (pp. 162–166) IEEE.

26. Chowdhary, C. L., & Acharjya, D. P., (2018). Singular value decomposition–principal component analysis-based object recognition approach. *Bio-Inspired Computing for Image and Video Processing*, 323.

27. Subbaiah, C. V., & Govinda, K. (2019). Survey of QoS routing applying soft computing techniques in MANET. *Journal of Advanced Research in Dynamical and Control Systems, 11*, 1480–1486.

28. Schuster, M., & Paliwal, K. K., (1997). *Bidirectional Recurrent Neural Networks, 45*(11), 2673–2681.

29. Chowdhary, C. L., (2019). 3D object recognition system based on local shape descriptors and depth data analysis. *Recent Patents on Computer Science, 12*(1), 18–24.

30. Chawla, N. V., Bowyer, K. W., Hall, L. O., & Kegelmeyer, W. P., (2002). SMOTE: Synthetic minority over-sampling technique. *Journal of Artificial Intelligence Research, 16*, 321–357.

CHAPTER 4

Blockchain in Healthcare: A New Dimension to Healthcare Data Security

R. SAMINATHAN, S. SARAVANAN, and P. ANBALAGAN

Department of Computer Science and Engineering,
Annamalai University, Annamalai Nagar, Tamil Nadu, India

ABSTRACT

Present-day healthcare shifts its paradigm towards a patient-centered healthcare system with a higher order of security. The law of compliance concerning healthcare data is strictly enforced, and policies are effectively utilized as per compliance. The trend of smart healthcare is growing with the rapid use of modern technologies such as cloud, blockchain, 3D printing, wearable devices, etc. Preserving the healthcare data in offline storage is not a feasible part due to its large collective nature from the connected wearables devices. Hence, modern healthcare systems leverage the use of online storage with cloud computing. These advancements in data storage and processing lead to an increase in several potential risks and vulnerabilities. It includes large data breaches in the cloud storage. To address the issue of healthcare data security, this chapter presents the possible solutions for utilizing Blockchain technology. This chapter also gives a complete overview of the present healthcare system and analyzes the drawback of each approach.

Hybridization of Blockchain and Cloud Computing: Overcoming Security Issues in IoT.
M. Lawanya Shri, E. Gangadevi, K. Santhi, & Chiranji Lal Chowdhary (Eds.)
© 2024 Apple Academic Press, Inc. Co-published with CRC Press (Taylor & Francis)

4.1 INTRODUCTION

Nowadays, the healthcare industry plays a vital role in the era of the development of nations and states. As the world's population has been increasing rapidly, there is a huge demand for better healthcare facilities. Some of the diseases are unpredictable, which requires extra attention in monitoring. In the healthcare industry, diagnosis and health monitoring are important parameters. Most people are not visiting hospitals for their health issues due to their busy schedules, which may cause many health issues. Primarily the maximal numbers of healthcare systems are innovated to predict and analyze the healthcare of the people who do not have time to visit the hospital due to their work schedule. It can also keep track of their health status at regular intervals. As per the proverb "prevention is better than cure," earlier detection is the better way to take care of health issues because earlier recognition is the foremost way which helps the patients with their health status [1–3].

In a most populated nation like India, healthcare is the major issue where the people from rural areas don't get proper healthcare facilities which in turn increases the issues. With the help of development in technology, there is a need for smart healthcare systems which regularly monitors and diagnoses the patient's health status and alerts them. At present, due to the increased population of aged people, they may suffer from chronic illness and health-related issues. These people require special attention and may require a large number of hospital beds, which impacts the medical structures [4]. These people require special care and attention in real-time and periodic monitoring of their health status. With the development of technology, smart healthcare systems have been introduced. Smart healthcare is the health-related services and care system that uses the technologies such as wearable devices like smartwatches, fitness trackers, personal digital assistants, mobile devices, etc. The major technology used in the smart healthcare system is IoT, mobile internet, cloud computing, big data, blockchain, microelectronics, and artificial intelligence. The technology used in this system collects and accesses information from the particular individual and responds in an intelligent manner. This chapter discusses the major aspect of the present-day healthcare system, such as smart healthcare systems, IoT-based smart healthcare systems, components of smart healthcare systems, remote healthcare systems (RHCS), and smartphone-based healthcare systems (SPHCS). This chapter also gives insight into the usage of blockchain in the healthcare industry. Further, this chapter comprehends the existing security issues and their enhancement with the present healthcare industries.

4.2 SMART HEALTHCARE SYSTEM

Smart healthcare is introduced from the concept of smart planet proposed by IBM. As the name suggests, smart planet means sharp infrastructure that uses tiny sensors to collect and transfer information by means of the Internet of Things (IoT) using internet technologies. It can coordinate and integrate all data and can provide accurate data. The collected information is shared between the patients and the medical services like hospitals, health centers, etc., and with the concerned doctor. These smart devices are wearable and portable. IoT-based smart healthcare system monitors the parameters like temperature, blood pressure, pulse rate, etc., in real-time. A smart healthcare system consists of participants like doctors, patients, hospitals, scientific, and research institutions [1–7]. It involves in multiple dimensions like monitoring, diagnosing, research, decision-making, and management. From the viewpoint of patients, the devices can be wearable, which are used to monitor the health status of the patient. The patient can look for medical assistance through healthcare virtual assistants such as Google Assistant, Microsoft Cortana, Apple Siri, etc. A virtual assistant is used to treat diseases and used to improve the mental health of humans, and it also helps the psychotherapist in order to bring the spiritual health of the patients. From a doctor's viewpoint, the doctor can suggest and diagnose health issues through an intelligent clinical decision support system. Doctors can manage medical reports through laboratory information management systems, picture archiving, communication systems, etc. [8].

4.3 IoT-BASED SMART HEALTHCARE SYSTEM

In the present world, IoT makes remarkable achievements in the development of wireless technology. IoT takes us to the next level in technology. IoT makes use of internet technologies to collect data, process the data and transfer the data to desired destination. Data collection can be made through a large number of sensors that records the changes and store the data in the server. Basically, communication in IoT can be done in three ways: (i) machine-to-machine communication, (ii) human-to-machine communication, and (iii) human-to-human communication. Generally, IoT is defined as the connection between a large number of physical devices, such as sensors, computing devices, and software through the network. IoT uses smart devices attached to the internet, which can be operated anytime and anywhere [9–11].

In health monitoring systems, IoT plays an important role. IoT can be used to keep track and controls mechanical, electrical, and electronic devices through the internet. Punit et al. [6] presented a system that provides better and more efficient health services to patients by implementing cloud-based network information. This proposed system monitors the health parameters such as patients heart rate, blood pressure, etc., and sends an emergency alert to the doctor through the mobile application [6]. Krishna & Nalini [7] presented the system, which is mainly designed for real-time monitoring of the important parameters of the patients. The collected data is transferred from mobile phones or laptops to the authorized person using a cloud server. The collected data is stored and processed for further processing and decision making. It uses an Arduino board, Raspberry Pi board, and cloud computing for monitoring body temperature, blood pressure, oxygen saturation percentage, and heart rate [7]. Malti & Bani [3] presented a system that uses carbon nanotube (CNT) electrodes for continuous ECG monitoring. The proposed system uses sensors for signal acquisition from the patients. The acquired data is transferred to a smart device, and from the smart device, the data is transferred to the doctor, hospital, or ambulance. The alert message is received by the family member or doctor through the smart device [3].

Durga & Ram [9] presented the architectural view of smart healthcare system using IoT. The system architecture monitors the body parameters in real-time. The sensor collects the data and processes the information using a microcontroller. From microcontroller, the data is transferred to the MySQL database server. The database server keeps the data and provides better accessibility. The data can be viewed with the help of the Android app on mobile phones. By using decision-making algorithms the decisions can be made, and the alert message is sent to the concerned person [9]. Srilakshmi et al. [5] presented about security-related issues in the software-defined network. Due to wireless connection, the network is more prone to vulnerable attacks or threats. Sensors are used to collect the information from the network, and the stored data is captured in the cloud. The stored data is present at the top of the layer known as software-defined network. The health reports are maintained very confidential. Based on the sensed information, an immediate alert is sent to the patients and proper medicine or drug can be given to the patient in the absence of the healthcare provider [5].

By using IoT in the healthcare system, the burden due to medical infrastructure and rise in medical expenses are reduced. By real-time and accurate method, the health status is monitored in a regular interval, and an alert message is sent to the concerned person. IoT gives a wide variety of healthcare applications in health monitoring from remote areas, health monitoring of patient, health monitoring through wearable devices, health monitoring through smartphones, etc. To promote the value and support for human life, smart devices with IoT is used. In health tracking, IoT-based Smart devices are attached to the patient body to track important parameters such as blood pressure, body temperature, rate of respiration, pulse rate, and also blood glucose levels. These parameters are kept as medical databases in the hospital server for future reference, and these parameters are used for prognostication and treatment [12].

The collected databases are stored in the hospital depository. When a patient reaches the hospital due to health issues, doctors can easily get the data related to that person. By checking past health records, it leads to proper treatment for the health issue. IoT promotes a bridge between the patients and the healthcare experts for better diagnosis and consultation. It supports the system in getting the information precisely and accurately. IoT-based healthcare services are easy and affordable to everyone. It keeps the tracking of day-to-day physical activities at one end to control the symptoms and helps in tracking the health goal of the individual on the other end. It elevates the healthcare infrastructure towards user-friendly, adaptability, wearable, and flexible automation. In IoT, the sensors collect a huge amount of data from the patient, and the collected data is stored in the server or in the cloud. Once the data is stored in the cloud or server, it can be accessed from anywhere using internet technologies. The data stored in the server should be protected from external hackers and malware. The data collected from the sensor occupies a lot of space. To maintain the data in an efficient manner, IoT analytics is implemented [13].

The unprocessed data is converted into reliable data by means of extraction of data. In a smart healthcare system, the important features are classified as: (i) personalized, (ii) persuasive, (iii) predictive, (iv) participatory, (v) perpetual, (vi) programmable, and (vii) preventive. In IoT, the collection of raw data is very easy and reliable. Those are taken from the sensors in real-time from an infinite number of patients for a tremendous amount of time. The sensors accurately measure and keep track of health status parameters. By using IoT in healthcare systems, the costs for medical expenses are reduced. It enhances communication between the patients and the healthcare provider. Databases are maintained confidentially, which gives the update of patient health records and enriches the patient's healthcare [14–17].

4.4 CLOUD PLATFORM

In the medical field, telecommunication plays an important role in transferring patient's information during emergency situations. The advancement of IoT employs self-reliant, self-controlled, and self-organized devices which can smartly cooperate with other devices. In the medical care industry, the major requirement is to keep monitor the patient's health periodically to ensure quality and safety. Whenever there is a critical condition, the patient's data should be available on the data access center. For continuous health monitoring of patient and for data communication, the ThingSpeak cloud platform is implemented. ThingSpeak cloud platform is implemented using Arduino Uno, ESP8266, SEN1174, and LM35. The major advantage of this platform is to provide high-quality monitoring, high-security level through Wi-Fi modules and secure communication by cloud database. It is a low-cost and low-complexity prototype [18, 19].

The hardware setup is an interfaced circuit made up of temperature sensor, heart pulse sensor, keypad, microcontroller, Wi-Fi module, LCD display, and ThingSpeak cloud platform. Arduino board is the heart of the system. It is used to collect the data inputs from the sensors and transfer the information to the destination. From the microcontroller, the data are transferred to the Wi-Fi module (ESP8266). The Wi-Fi module is to communicate the information to the ThingSpeak module. Heart pulse rate is measured from the interfacing device SEN1174. It operates with direct current of 5 V and draws 4 mA current from the power supply. To measure the body temperature with high accuracy LM35 temperature sensor is used [20]. To enter the password, a 4×4 keypad is used. The resulting

output of heart pulse rate and body temperature is displayed on the 16×
2 LCD display. When the device is switched ON, the sensor will read the
temperature and pulse rate of the patient. The collected data is communi-
cated to ThingSpeak cloud platform through Wi-Fi which can be accessed
by doctors and family members [20].

4.5   COMPONENTS OF A SMART HEALTHCARE SYSTEM

The different attributes of smart healthcare systems include sensors,
medical equipment, communication devices, applications, which are used
by doctors, patients and healthcare providers, and end users/patients.

4.5.1   SENSING

The first and initial stage of the proposed infrastructure is sensing. In
this stage, the sensors in the architecture are used to sense the different
anatomical movements and specifications by a well-equipped electrophys-
iological sensor such as wearable sensors, blood pressure sensor, blood
temperature sensors, electrocardiogram (ECG), oxygen concentration,
biosensors, electroencephalogram (EEG), respiration rate sensor, electro-
corticography (ECoG), etc. The sensor is the main and key component in
the development of the healthcare system. These different types of sensors
are used to measure the parameters like blood pressure, glucose level,
heart pumping rate, respiration rate, etc. [20].

4.5.2   CONTROLLER UNIT

For the first stage in processing microcontroller/controller unit is used. The
data collected from the sensor unit is processed at this stage. Generally,
microcontroller is a small self-controlled computer on single integrated
chip, which is more or less similar to system on chip. It consists of a
memory unit and different peripheral input-output devices. It can perform
various arithmetic and logical functions. Examples of Microcontroller
are Intel processors, Arduino microcontrollers, PIC, ARM processors,
Raspberry Pi, etc.

4.5.3   COMMUNICATION MEDIUM

The collected data should be transferred by the devices through the network at any time, anywhere. It enables the incorporation between the network and the applications. Communication can be carried out in two ways: (i) short-range communication, and (ii) long-range communication. Short-range communication includes Bluetooth, Radio Frequency Identification (RFID), Wi-Fi, and Near Field Communication (NFC). Long-range communication includes Wide Area Network (WAN), Long Range Wide Area Network (LoRaWAN), IoT, and Narrow Band Internet of Things (NB-IoT). Wireless communication in IoT enables RHCS efficiently and smarter. In short-range communication, communication is carried between the devices and nearby places. In long-range communication, the communication is carried out between the main controller and remote controller, which are located at the base station, such as healthcare centers [22].

4.5.4   MEMORY AND COMPUTING DEVICES

The most important component in a smart healthcare system is the memory unit and the computing unit. The raw data is taken from the sensors and stored in the database. In the storage unit, the patient's record is maintained in the database. Whenever the patient visits the hospital or health service provider, the doctor can update the information about the health issues. For storing large amount of data, cloud computing technology is used. Cloud computing is useful in sharing resources in a reliable manner. In IoT-based healthcare system, cloud computing or fog computing is used. The technologies chosen depend on the location and amount of the data. Most of the IoT application uses cloud computing because of its huge advantages. The advantages of cloud computing are data storage, security, heterogeneity, better resolution, privacy, and confidentiality. The sensors data can be stored in the cloud, and later, the stored data can be used to monitor through cloud computing.

4.5.5   DATA AND DECISION-MAKING SYSTEM

The data precision can be made from the large amount of data collected from the patients based on intelligent and knowledge algorithms. The informa-tion can be collected from the patients through sensors like body sensors, temperature sensors, pressure sensors, etc. The stored data can be utilized for future processing. By knowing the patient's health history, it is easier for the doctors to give the proper and better treatment. The data analysis can be done through ML approach and big data analysis. Big data has various advantages in different industries which are generating large amount of data.

4.6   CLASSIFICATION OF SMART HEALTHCARE SYSTEM

Healthcare systems can be classified into two types: (i) conventional healthcare systems, and (ii) smart healthcare systems. The motivation behind smart healthcare system is to assist and enlarge the traditional healthcare system. Conventional healthcare systems can be classified into Ambient Assisted Living (AAL), and Wearable Health Care Systems (WHCS). Smart healthcare systems can be classified into RHCS and SPHCS. When smart healthcare system is connected to IoT, the system becomes smarter and more intelligent [11]. In smart healthcare system architecture, the devices are attached to each other while the sensors are collecting data from the patient. The sensor data is transferred to the cloud, from the cloud server, and the data can be accessed anytime, anywhere by cloud computing. By using a smart healthcare system, the doctor or the healthcare provider can track and monitor the medical assets of the patients. The healthcare system includes ECG, EEG, body temperature monitoring, body pressure monitoring, glucose level monitoring, oxygen level monitoring, etc., for aided healthcare services. In remote health monitoring, the data is collected in a real-time basis and transferred from the remote location to the healthcare provider using NFC devices. In SPHCS, smartphones and smart applications are used to monitor the parameters like pressure, temperature, etc. AAL is an example for personal healthcare system. It is used to enhance and monitor the elderly persons, specially challenged people, etc., from their living space in a secure and convenient form as a personal assistant. Wearable smart healthcare system uses wearable devices such as smartwatches, fitness trackers, and smart belts to monitor the patient health [12].

4.7   SECURITY-RELATED ISSUES IN SMART HEALTHCARE SYSTEM

In a smart healthcare system, the data collected from the sensors are transferred to the base station through wireless connection. The data transferring through wireless technology may be subject to vulnerable threats or security attacks. The security threats include Denial of Service (DoS), fingerprint, and timing-based snooping, router attacks, select, and forwarding attack, sensor attack, and replay attack. To prevent the threat, it is necessary to maintain and examine the security measures, vulnerabilities, and counter-measures. The attackers in IoT are classified into two types, such as internal attackers and external attackers. Internal attackers exist in the system, and they perform malicious activities inside the system. These attacks can be easily found. External attackers found outside the system and they perform malicious activities. In this attack, it is difficult to find the attacker existence because they exist outside the system [14–17]. They silently monitor the operation of the system and perform the attacks or malicious activities like modifying health records, etc.

4.8   SECURITY ATTACKS ON THE HEALTHCARE DEVICES

Based on the eHealth environment, security attacks can be classified into two types: routing attacks and location-based attacks. The routing attack types are router track, select, forwarding, and replay attacks. The location-based attack includes DoS, finger, and timing-based snooping and sensor attacks. In a routing-based attack, the attack happens in the data transmission routes where intruders attack the route of data to send or drop data packets. In a location-based attack, the attack happens at the end node, where the intruders attack the service of the system at the destination node [10].

4.8.1   DENIAL OF SERVICE ATTACK

In a DoS attack, the attack makes services inaccessible to the users by making the computer or network to shut down at any point of time. By making the system shut down, the other nodes at the system can't share the data by sensing the channel busy. In DoS, the patient health record can be controlled by attacker without proper authentication and permission to access data. The denial of attack makes the transmission node busy so that the other nodes in the network can't share the data. DoS attack happens at the data transmission node. This attack makes the data transmission between the nodes to be misplaced or inaccessible. In this attack, the attacker can modify the data; the modified false data is transferred to the receiver, which leads to false information of the patient. The DoS attack leads to false statements such as false health records and false emergency calls. This false data may lead to patient death. DoS attacks happen on each layer of the network [10].

4.8.2 FINGERPRINT AND TIMING-BASED SNOOPING

In a wireless network, the network is impotent to find the malicious threats that happen in data transmission from the sensor to sensor, then from the sensor to destination in an encrypted form. In this threat, the physical layer requires broadcast time and fingerprint for each message where the fingerprint is defined as the impression created by friction in fingers. This type of attack is called fingerprint and timing-based snooping. In this attack, the intruder silently listens to data transmission happens from sensor to sensor with time interval and fingerprint stamps. After detecting all the data, the attacker can modify the records of the patient [10].

4.8.3 ROUTER ATTACK

The most important factor of the healthcare system is data transmission. The data can be modified on the data transmission path where the receiver receives the false health record [10]. The routing of data happens through the wireless network, which is more prone to attack.

4.8.4 SELECTIVE FORWARDING ATTACK

It is the type of black hole attack where the attacker gets outburst to a single or multiple sensors to attenuate this attack. The attacker acquires the data from any sensor and then drops the data packets and sends the dropped packets to other sensor nodes. This attack creates more problems in the system if the sensor node is near to the remote station. It is very hard to detect the reason for the data packets dropping. This attack is more harmful because it transfers incomplete data which reaches the receiver end [10].

4.8.5   SENSOR ATTACK

In a sensor network, the sensor node may fail or leave the network due to accidental failure or malicious activities that happen in the network. Due to lack of power at the network, the sensor node may leave. Using this chance, the attacker can enter the network by replacing the failed sensor node and perform malicious activities. The unauthorized person in the network can make false data by modifying, can insert the false data in the network due to lack of authentication [10].

4.8.6   REPLAY ATTACK

A replay attack happens when an unauthorized person enters the network. The primary idea of the attacker is to build trust in the network. The attacker monitors all the activities in the system and sends a message to the receiver when the transmitter stops the data sharing. A replay attack is also known as a playback attack [10].

4.9   BLOCKCHAIN TECHNOLOGY IN HEALTHCARE

Blockchain technology is a system that has a larger database secured by cryptography form so that the system can prove the time, integrity, and identification for the people and machines without the traditional. Typically, blockchain technology stores the larger databases in the form of blocks [21, 22]. The connection of blocks results in chain formation. The storage database is called data ledger. The transaction in the ledger is authorized by the digital signature at each time. Digital signature refers to the mathematical representation which is used to authenticate the integrity of the software, message, or document [23]. The digital signature in the blockchain verifies each time of transaction and prevents stealing the data. So, the data in the data ledger is highly secured.

Blockchain works by using three important factors. They are cryptographic keys, peer-to-peer communication in shared network and computing, which is used to keep the transaction and record of the network. Cryptographic keys are classified into two types (i) public key (ii) private key. In blockchain technology, the transaction records are encrypted into blocks to provide high security. The input data in the blockchain is encrypted into hash value. In blockchain, for controlling the database there is no central authority. Each block in the blockchain consists of data, hash, and nonce. Each block consists of data. Once the block is created, a 32-bit whole number is generated randomly called nonce which then generates a hash block header. Hash defines a 256-bit number combined with nonce which consists of a huge number of zeros. The value of hash is extremely zero. When the first block is created, a hash function with nonce is created with encrypted form. Hash function is used to convert one form of data into encrypted forms like human fingerprints and a mathematical operation. When the transaction starts, the hash value is created by a hash function, which in turn returns a digital signature that allows the third party to verify the transaction details like time, identity, integrity of data, etc. The main component of blockchain is the nodes. The nodes in the network can be connected together to form blocks. In blockchain technology, once the data is entered into the chain, it cannot be altered or changed, and it is visible to all the participants in the network [23, 24].

The nodes participating in the blockchain are called miners. In public blockchain, anyone can engage in reading, adding, and validating the blocks. In this process, the transactions are public and can be authenticated by public key cryptography. In private blockchain, only a single entity is allowed and it's not public. In this process, the transactions are not public and cannot be viewed by anyone, so it is not distributive. The transaction is in encrypted form and unavailable to the public. Consortium blockchain are often called public blockchain which can be accessed by a group that controls read, modify, and validate transactions on the blockchain. In this blockchain, the user authentication may guarantee or not and the blockchain may open or not.

The combination of IoT, blockchain, and ML are used for the detection of malicious activities in the healthcare system. IoT uses Internet technologies to block and get data generated from the wearable devices like smartwatches, etc., worn by the patient. The databases are collected and stored in the form of multiple transactions, and it also support control access. Blockchain supports the medical research by providing pseudo-anonymity of the patient identification and provide authenticated and authorized data for research. The ML approach is used to find the anomalies and forecast the analyzed data that are passed to the doctors for basic identification. The IoT module is used to access and sense the data that are collected from the wearable devices that are worn by the patient or the biosensors that are kept at the surrounding of the patient who is under monitoring [24].

The wearable devices monitor the basic parameters like heart rate, body temperature rate, blood pressure, oxygen saturation level and sleep stage monitoring. If the patient is bedridden, the biosensors or IoT sensors are placed on the body of the patient to monitor the vital parameters in real-time. The next module is blockchain technology. Blockchain stores large amount of data and the data is maintained as secured and encrypted form. Two types of blockchain architecture are used. The personal healthcare blockchain uses personal wearable devices to monitor and capture the data. The stored data can be further accessed by the doctor to proceed with proper medication. The data from the wearable devices is stored in the cloud-by-cloud computing which is maintained by the blockchain technology. The external record management blockchain is used for the purpose of maintaining the data that is being generated when the patient visits the doctor. The blockchain stores the data being generated by the health centers, medical test reports, pharmacy bills, prescriptions, and image data. The machine-learning modules are based on the data created by the patient for the detection of any abnormalities in the data. Whenever an abnormality is sensed, a notification or alert message is forwarded to the doctor. Based on the alertness, a suitable action is taken immediately [22–24].

4.10 CONCLUSION

This chapter is concluded by leveraging the advantages of the present-day healthcare system. Here, a deep insight about the healthcare systems, their components, and their services were discussed. Further, this chapter also exhibits the usage of blockchain technology in healthcare industries. It also gives a research overview of the current challenges and its pathway. This will help the researcher to explore all the possibilities of research in the domain of healthcare with blockchain. From the study, it is clear that blockchain technology will create many breaks in order to reduce complexity in the current healthcare data security and enables the option for trustless collaboration with highly secured immutable information.

KEYWORDS

- **blockchain**
- **carbon nanotubes**
- **electrocardiogram**
- **Internet of things**
- **remote healthcare system**
- **smartphone-based healthcare system**

REFERENCES

1. Manjulata, S., Mithilesh, A., & Mitul, K. A., (2020). Comprehensive investigation on IoT based smart healthcare system. *First International Conference on Power, Control and Computing Technologies (ICPC2T 2020).*

2. Shariq, A. B., & Arshad, A., (2019). IoT smart health security threats. *19th International Conference on Computational Science and Its Applications (ICCSA 2019).*

3. Malti, B., & Bani, G., (2017). IoT based smart health care system using CNT electrodes (for continuous ECG monitoring). *International Conference on Computing, Communication and Automation (ICCCA 2017).*

4. Sabyasachi, C., Satyabrata, A., & Hee-Cheol, K., (2019). A secure healthcare system design framework using blockchain technology. *International Conference on Advanced Communications Technology (ICACT 2019).*

5. Srilakshmi, A., Mohanapriya, P., Harini, D., & Geetha, K., (2019). IoT based smart health care system to prevent security attacks in SDN. *Fifth International Conference on Electrical Energy Systems (ICEES 2019).*

6. Punit, G., Deepika, A., Jasmeet, C., & Pulkit, K. D., (2016). IoT based smart healthcare kit. *International Conference on Computational Techniques in Information and Communication Technologies (ICCTICT 2016).*

7. Krishna, C. S., & Nalini, S., (2017). Healthcare monitoring system based on IoT. *2nd IEEE International Conference on Computational Systems and Information Technology for Sustainable Solutions.*

8. Tran Le, N., (2018). Blockchain in healthcare: A new technology benefit for both patients and doctors. *Proceedings of PICMET 18: Technology Management for Interconnected World.*

9. Durga, A. M. B., & Ram, S. M., (2017). Design and implementation of smart healthcare system using IoT. *International Conference on Innovations in Information, Embedded and Communication Systems (ICIIECS 2017).*

10. Sibi, C. S., Vaidehi, V., & Steven, W., (2019). Cyber attacks on healthcare devices using unmanned aerial vehicles. *Journal of Medical Systems, 44*(29), 1–10. Springer.

11. Islam, S. M. R., Kwak, D., Kabir, M. H., Hossain, M., & Kwak, K., (2015). The internet of things for health care: a comprehensive survey. In: *IEEE Access* (Vol. 3, pp. 678–708).

12. Zhou, Z., Yu, H., & Shi, H., (2020). Human activity recognition based on improved Bayesian convolution network to analyze health care data using wearable IoT device. In: *IEEE Access* (Vol. 8, pp. 86411–86418).

13. Meenalosini, V. C., Anupama, N., Suresh, C. S., Matthew, P., & Sibi, S. C., (2020). Skin cancer classification using convolutional capsule network (CapsNet). *Journal of Scientific and Industrial Research, NISCAIR-CSIR, 79*, 994–1001.

14. Pathinarupothi, R. K., Durga, P., & Rangan, E. S., (2019). IoT-based smart edge for global health: remote monitoring with severity detection and alerts transmission. In: *IEEE Internet of Things Journal* (Vol. 6, No. 2, pp. 2449–2462).

15. Ray, P. P., Thapa, N., & Dash, D., (2019). Implementation and performance analysis of interoperable and heterogeneous IoT-edge gateway for pervasive wellness care. In: *IEEE Transactions on Consumer Electronics* (Vol. 65, No. 4, pp. 464–473).

16. Mezghani, E., Exposito, E., & Drira, K., (2017). A model-driven methodology for the design of autonomic and cognitive IoT-based systems: Application to healthcare. In: *IEEE Transactions on Emerging Topics in Computational Intelligence* (Vol. 1, No. 3, pp. 224–234).

17. Akshay, T., Sibi, C. S., Sangeetha, D., VenkataRathnam, M., & Vaidehi, V., (2019). Role-based policy to maintain privacy of patient health records in cloud. *Journal of Super Computing, 75*(9), 5866–5881. Springer.

18. Liu, L., Xu, J., Huan, Y., Zou, Z., Yeh, S., & Zheng, L., (2020). A smart dental health-IoT platform based on intelligent hardware, deep learning, and mobile terminal. In: *IEEE Journal of Biomedical and Health Informatics* (Vol. 24, No. 3, pp. 898–906).

19. Seneviratne, S., et al., (2017). A survey of wearable devices and challenges. In: *IEEE Communications Surveys & Tutorials* (Vol. 19, No. 4, pp. 2573–2620).

20. Pacchierotti, C., Sinclair, S., Solazzi, M., Frisoli, A., Hayward, V., & Prattichizzo, D., (2017). Wearable haptic systems for the fingertip and the hand: Taxonomy, review, and perspectives. In: *IEEE Transactions on Haptics* (Vol. 10, No. 4, pp. 580–600).

21. Wang, S., et al., (2018). Blockchain-powered parallel healthcare systems based on the ACP approach. In: *IEEE Transactions on Computational Social Systems* (Vol. 5, No. 4, pp. 942–950).

22. Kumar, A., Krishnamurthi, R., Nayyar, A., Sharma, K., Grover, V., & Hossain, E., (2020). A Novel smart healthcare design, simulation, and implementation using healthcare 4.0 processes. In: *IEEE Access* (Vol. 8, pp. 118433–118471).

23. Zarour, M., et al., (2020). Evaluating the impact of blockchain models for secure and trustworthy electronic healthcare records. In: *IEEE Access* (Vol. 8, pp. 157959–157973).

24. Ismail, L., Materwala, H., & Zeadally, S., (2019). Lightweight blockchain for healthcare. In: *IEEE Access* (Vol. 7, pp. 149935–149951).

CHAPTER 5

Blockchain Technology-Based Industrial Internet of Things: Research Challenges

M. LAWANYA SHRI[1] and E. GANGADEVI[2]

¹SITE, VIT, Vellore, Tamil Nadu, India

²Department of Computer Science, Loyola College, Chennai, Tamil Nadu, India

ABSTRACT

Industrial Internet of Things (IIoT) technology is growing popular among industries over the world. The IIoT employs and raises demand for sensor technology. The widespread development of industrial applications using wireless networks and cloud computing with the Internet of technology has expedited IIoT technology. The integration of cloud computing with the Internet of Things is majorly used to monitor enormous among of generated data. In order to reduce cost, IIoT faces many challenges in finding solutions to the changes in process control, automation process, and resource constraints. Blockchain technology is an emerging technical term trend set that grasps the attention of researchers. Blockchain technology is shaping the industrial sectors to carry out secure transactions in a trustless and decentralized environment. This chapter discusses how blockchain technology solves the above issues in the IIoT.

Hybridization of Blockchain and Cloud Computing: Overcoming Security Issues in IoT.
M. Lawanya Shri, E. Gangadevi, K. Santhi, & Chiranji Lal Chowdhary (Eds.)
© 2024 Apple Academic Press, Inc. Co-published with CRC Press (Taylor & Francis)

5.1 INTRODUCTION

The development of industries and online shopping is a trend set, and the growth of industries depends on lifestyle changes and society's demand. Various industrial sectors need proper maintenance and incorporate advancement based on the technologies used. The rapid growth in turn triggers many challenges and issues in the industry. The rapid use of the internet in industries requires proper use of technology that sense and generates data for monitoring and maintenance purposes. Thus, there is a need for emergent sensor technology called IoT to come into the picture in most of the developing and developed industries. The integration of cloud computing with the Internet of Things (IoT) solves many research issues where industries do not require all computing resources on their own. Instead, they are using cloud computing to store data, deploy the applications developed on their own, and make use of readymade software based on pay as you go model.

IoT is a cutting-edge technology trend that enriches and transmutes human life and affords massive economic benefits. It is a most trending and vibrant topic in IT industries and distended its margin into the fields such as Smart Homes, Agriculture, Retail, Health Care, and so on. IoT technology affords many benefits in several fields and provides various solutions to problems in various domains. Despite the existence of such benefits, certain hindrances make restrictions to IoT. The foremost challenge faced in IoT technology is the security issue, which is a significant pillar of internet. As the number of connected devices is increases, there is a chance for connectivity issues and developing security vulnerabilities.

The compatibility issue is the major flaw in IoT technology, where there is no specific international standard for monitoring and tagging devices. Some devices prompt error messages when it is connected to mobile phones or other devices. It is virtually incredible to build up a global ecosystem that communicates devices with one another; there are no exclusive application protocols used in IoT technology for communication between many networked devices. The need of unique universal protocol is required for the application devices to communicate with each other.

Privacy of data is the most important issue when the data is collected from a heterogeneous environment through IoT sensors. The data stored has social boundaries, and proper implementation of IoT with privacy and confidentially is a widespread challenge. The lack of standards has the greatest impact on implementing the IoT devices, and the developers are liable to develop the model with a lack of standards.

IoT encompasses many associated sensors and devices that are placed in different locations to sense the environment with the use of various protocols, standards, and supported applications for communication. Testing and validating the standards with connected devices through the internet is the most challenging factor. The limitation depends upon increasing the data transfer and stored size with a highly efficient security mechanism.

The reshaping technology trend Industrial Internet of Things (IIoT) is beneficial for product manufacturing, identifying and correcting the defects in the product, solving logistic issues, product transportation, energy saving, and utility control. The smart sensor objects are scattered for collecting massive amounts of homogenous data that can further be used to identify the bottlenecks and faults and discover the vulnerabilities, consequently affecting the performance of industries worldwide. However, there are many issues that need to be resolved in IIoT. One among those is security and privacy-preserving of data. Blockchain technology is an emerging technology that mainly solves security problems. This chapter depicts the use of blockchain in the industrial sectors to carry out secure transactions.

Blockchain technology is a dedicated chain of structured blocks for storing data in a comprehensible and robust way. Blockchain is a collection of blocks that stores data securely with the help of hash code. It is a validating data ledger that is distributed in nature. Cloud computing is a collection of remote servers that helps consumers store the data, manage, and process the data based on pay as you go model. Cloud computing is a collection of data centers where each data center runs many servers. Cloud computing helps the consumer make use of resources through the internet efficiently by reducing maintenance costs or by investing in needed computing resources. The resources offered by the cloud computing environments are software resources, hardware, and runtime environments to deploy the user-created applications in pay as you use model. Virtual machines run and execute the tasks submitted by the users. If there are many tasks loaded to the virtual machine in the data center, this leads to downtime and outages in which it reduces the system performance.

5.2   RELATED WORK

The IIoT is a ground-breaking technology that interconnects a set of smart sensors and storage devices that stores the generated data for monitoring and sharing the data. The most important objectives in IIoT security are to monitor and maintain the software failures that arise due to integrity problems that, in turn, damage the physical resources, reduce productivity, and harm to humans. In order to address the above issues, the software in industries should be monitored to ensure reliability and integrity. Shruthi et al. [1] discuss the IoT and its architecture. The various elements of IoT for identification and sensing the devices using sensors and the storage used for the sensed data are discussed. Zang et al. [2] presented a study on IoT with clustering of networks that shows widespread advantages with respect to flexibility, robustness, extendibility, and centralized environment. Zang et al. [3] proposed a group-centric IoT recommender system using machine learning (ML) and big data analytics, which integrates mainly the social communities with mobile computing.

Chen et al. [4] presented a model that consists of context-aware security techniques and for collecting sensed data from vehicular ad-hoc networks. This security technique mainly focuses on how to protect the sensed data using authentication, access control policies, and encryption and decryption mechanisms. Huang et al. [5] proposed a novel technique software monitoring with controllable overhead for IIoT security. There are many limitations to using the software, like lack of monitoring of the status of running software, software deployment in IIoT, and snapshot for identifying the integrity and vulnerability. Arora et al. [6] presented a hardware monitoring technique of the processor model in which it observes the random execution of program traces in order to check the software failures in IIoT.

Gao et al. [7] provided the process of implementing a blockchain system model and depicted how blockchain functions in IoT in a detailed manner. Peter et al. [8] outlined a smart contract mechanism in blockchain technology for secure transactions in bank ledgers. The author discussed about "Internet of money" and the migration process to blockchain. Wahab et al. presented a survey on blockchain technology and possible key for privacy control. The deep and thorough analysis of cryptographic technique and digital signature technique based on blockchain are presented. Feng et al. provided a detailed review based on privacy problems and how blockchain can help to solve the issues are presented. The defense method and its technical aspects based on blockchain in IoT systems are discussed.

5.3 APPLICATIONS OF BLOCKCHAIN TECHNOLOGY IN IOT

5.3.1 BLOCKCHAIN-BASED IIOT

Blockchain technology is a buzz word for the researchers to solve many issues in current recent years. It provides a suitable solution for many problems using a decentralized and distributed ledger. The distributed ledger is the main key for blockchain by sharing with many consumers who are not known. The authorization and authentication mechanism in blockchain is embedded, so with these two, no consumer can access the data stored in the ledger. Hacking becomes very difficult and could not find any vulnerability during transaction processing. The blockchain technology has a very high brunt on diverse industries, and most of the industries are adopting it. Blockchain can minimize the data theft and fraud by removing all the vulnerability [9].

5.3.2 TRADING ACTIVITIES

Blockchain technology continues to rule headlines over the world. The constant list of projects and pilots has been competing for our attention because the digital revolution is gathering speed. But people are now speculating what benefits and probabilities that these technological updates can wake up the world of trade finance.

Technology-based solutions serve the simplest once they tend to solve several real-world issues, making the work easier and relieving from onerous things. As the current digital age is aware of swipe-to-buy and one-click checkout processes for trading, people would like to own a modification that creates a chance to do their business easier than before. The maintenance and expansion of the world's $8 trillion open account trade finance market are greatly captivated with the straightforward accessibility and strength of funding mechanisms. Taking trade finance because the fuel for world commerce into consideration, it is simple to watch why blockchain has such influence over the trade finance world [10].

Financial markets offer commercialism of monetary securities like equities, derivatives, bonds, and currencies. There are widely three sorts of markets:

1. **Money Markets:** These are short-run markets where the money is lent to corporations or alternative banks to do internal bank disposition. The foreign exchange comes underneath this class within which currencies are listed.
2. **Credit Markets:** This largely consists of retail banks where they borrow cash from central banks and loan it to alternative companies or households within the style of mortgages and typically loans.
3. **Capital Markets:** These offer the facility of buying and selling of financial instruments mostly like stocks and bonds. These may be divided into two types:
    i.   **Primary Markets:** These markets bring problems with stocks directly to the investors through the companies.
    ii. **Secondary Markets:** These markets offer the investors to resell their securities to alternative investors via stock exchanges.

Multiple electronic commercialism systems are used for exchanges today to provide the ability of trading of financial instruments.

A market could be where parties are involved in exchange physically, electronically, or virtually. Numerous financial instruments like stocks, equities, foreign exchange, commodities, and different types of derivatives are down for commerce in these marketplaces. Recently, several financial establishments have opted for software platforms to trade numerous types of instruments. Trading is outlined as an activity provided for consumers and sellers of several financial instruments to get profit and to protect from risk. There are a few types of traders, like investors, borrowers, hedgers, asset exchangers, gamblers, etc. Traders are aforementioned to be having a brief position after they sell a contract and an extended position when they buy a contract. The multiple ways in which trades are transacted are through brokers or directly on an exchange or Over-the-Counter (OTC), where consumers and sellers trade directly with one another. Brokers are the agents who settle trades for their clients and act on their client's behalf to deal at their very best worth [11].

5.3.3 *TRADE LIFE CYCLE*

The common trade life cycle includes many stages from the order placing to execution through a gradual process:

1. **Pre-Execution:** An order is being placed at this stage.
2. **Execution and Booking:** The order that is placed would be matched and executed, it is transformed into a trade. At this stage, the contract between counterparties is matured.
3. **Confirmation:** Here, both counterparties confirm the particulars of the trade.
4. **Post Booking:** This stage is provided with numerous verification processes that are required to establish the correctness of the trade.
5. **Settlement:** This can be the final stage of trade and very crucial in the trade life cycle
6. **Overnight:** This is the end-of-day process that involves report generation, profit and loss calculations, and numerous risk calculations.

5.4 REASONS FOR USING BLOCKCHAIN IN THE TRADE INDUSTRY

Blockchain ensures transparency, trust, and security whereas reducing time interval, eliminating the usage of paper and saving cash. This forces everybody to play honest in business along with removing the dangerous actors. This improves transparency so the business can automatically eliminate the risk of manipulation by participants within the chain.

The facility of trade finance directly between parties associated and increasing their potential within the market like Marco Polo is provided by introducing an end-to-end trade finance network for banks and their company clients. The exchange of trade-related information and delivering finance to the full ecosystem is made easier that proves that the trade finance network has the potential to be a game-changer rather than being another initiative.

This potential makes the bankers see the advantages of trade finance would get adopting blockchain technology. As blockchain is a decentralized system, it permits the involved parties to determine any agreement while not involving any kind of middlemen like lawyers, public accountants, civil servants, notaries or any other parties that are required to attest the information's integrity. Blockchain solely would like a Smart Contract which is a set of codes which will facilitate concerned parties to exchange money or other valuables in a transparent, trustable, and a secure method. As the involvement of the third parties or middlemen is reduced, the value associated with them is also reduced or vanished completely. Because, blockchain provides the ability to regulate self-executing, self-verifying of transactions that permits parties to eliminate the involvement of intermediaries such as clearinghouses. This technology has been very useful in the financial industry, particularly in trading activity.

5.5 BLOCKCHAIN IN INSURANCE SECTORS

5.5.1 BENEFITS OF BLOCKCHAIN IN THE INSURANCE SECTOR

Blockchain will change innovative and troubling changes within the insurance business just like it enabled the recording of cryptocurrency (like bitcoin). Some influences that blockchain is created in the insurance industry are:

- Alleviating the paperwork;
- It develops a system within which some claims are verified and handled very quickly;
- Minimizes the fraud;
- Improves the standard of information used throughout the under-writing; and
- It improves the efficiency across the insurance value chain like processes where claims are paid automatically.

Even though technology is dynamically changing the insurance industry, there is one technology that is more crucial than others. As the number of blockchain applications in insurance is growing daily, we tend to say that within a few years, each player within the area will be using that application. This brings several opportunities of embracing the modification by Fintech and smaller insurance firms.

5.5.2 BLOCKCHAIN INSURANCE APPLICATIONS

The main quality of blockchain that created the insurance industry to adopt this technology is cutting the middlemen. Currently, in the insurance industry, so much of personal information is at stake because of the bogging of several checks and rechecks. If all that information is within the blockchain, all those checks are often simply distributed and therefore the information which is trusted will directly flow between parties. This saves both time and money, and this is what that transforms the industry.

5.5.3 BLOCKCHAIN IN LIFE INSURANCE INDUSTRY

Blockchain has implications at every step of the life insurance process. As the blockchain provides inherent security with the distributed ledger, new clients are often quoted and on-boarded very quickly. Once the blockchain is fully integrated into life insurance, prospective clients will be able to unlock access to their own medical histories so that a carrier will generate a quote automatically. By this method, there will be no additional gathering of documents from numerous doctors and medical professionals. This information will be in the cloud, trusted, and more secure. In the United States, it is calculated to be $7.4 billion in unclaimed insurance money. This can result in individuals losing the papers in their busy lives, and sometimes it is impractical to seek out the right beneficiary for a claim. This problem can be simply solved with blockchain smart contracts. Through these smart contracts, funds would automatically be paid out supported by the news of death without the need for the beneficiary to come forward with a claim.

It is an open secret that life insurance policies can be traded and might be sold to others. If the insured person has paid the premium and no longer requires the insurance, they can sell the policy and benefits for immediate cash to the other. But, selling a policy is a sophisticated process that involves many intermediaries. So, adopting blockchain technology that moves with no intermediaries would benefit the insured people who want to sell their policies at their will and quickly.

5.5.4 BLOCKCHAIN IN HEALTH INSURANCE INDUSTRY

Many aspects of the blockchain are useful to this industry, and some aspects are uniquely provided to this industry.

5.5.4.1 MEDICAL RECORDS

Distributed ledger technology (DLT) will be very useful to medical professionals all over the world. It makes the patient's medical records immutable, secure, digitally accessible, and transparent. Generating quotes will be simple for insurance agents and carriers as there is immediate access to all the necessary records to supply at accurate rates. This helps to avoid medical error, medical fraud, and privacy violations will be slashed automatically.

Smart contracts enable the claims to be paid out quickly and automatically. Once a patient checks into the hospitals, treatment records will be automatically added to the blockchain and also the insurer will payout. This reduces the requirement for sophisticated forms and back-and-forth communication.

The massive efficiency boost can be seen in doctors, administration, and insurers. They will have access to the trusted and complete patient medical history and doctors can utilize the results of tests made at alternative facilities. They will be able to observe the result of past procedures and could eliminate the duplicated work that is common today. This way, treatments will take less time and medical prices will go down, which could profit everyone.

5.5.4.2 DATA STORAGE

The current trend set blockchain is used to make a new way for storing data with decentralized storage networks by planting the power of prime back in the hands of customers.

The utmost significant triumph in the internet era that is helpful for both private usage and industry is cloud data storage. Even though this is a recent invention, it is already underneath hazard of being perpendicular by incoming blockchain storage developers.

The example includes the threat of close future blockchain technology and how cloud storage sectors work to avoid the loss of information. As some huge firms depend on spreading data to various data centers to avoid intrusion, decentralization of data in blockchain technology would eliminate the risk of meaningful disruptions. This can result from data stored on a huge number of individual nodes across the world with no central entity that will manage access to user's files, which improves security through decentralized file storage. There is still a need for development in current network scalability to accommodate large-scale file blockchain storage infrastructure. We can surely expect an industry that is with fragmented and encrypted information that is supported by a network of decentralized nodes in a user-friendly and cost-effective way.

The other method that blockchain use cases improve the current file storage system is by using an "incentive layer." This helps once information is not truly held on within the decentralized ledger. The relevant storage network is using that to process the subscription payments by avoiding flat exchange rates and store access information. Using this ledger to move with the storage blockchain project would be useful to finish user to improve settling times, increasing privacy and reliability. These are due to the use of a decentralized network and transparent record keeping. By moving such user-centric storage networks to decentralized blockchain storage networks would facilitate the users to own a lot of agile and customizable systems. They will be able to manipulate metrics like the speed of retrieval or redundancy.

5.5.4.3   TOKENIZED BLOCKCHAIN STORAGE

With a blockchain storage tokenization system, the network economy is often leveraged to incentivize individual nodes to uphold the network and sharing little storage capabilities. Blockchain technology allows users to easily upload, share, and monetize their content, which is like storing for personal use while reducing the cost of intermediaries.

5.6   CHALLENGES AND SOLUTIONS OF BLOCKCHAIN TECHNOLOGY

Blockchain technology is poised to potentially address the critical challenges and issues to unleash economic benefits with advancements in the IT industry. The blockchain holistic depiction can be leveraged for secure transactions due to its consensus-driven, decentralized, and distributed ledger. It has blossomed to assuage many challenging issues across various domains. The recent explosion of blockchain technology has shaped a dazzling impact on stakeholders, business experts, industrialists, and researchers.

The distributed and decentralized nature of blockchain technology can provide users across the world with proactive resistor over their data. The emergence of blockchain and DLT has become a trend set component of the digital economy in the near future. The inconsistent and insecure nature exploded in traditional technology may stance further challenges for IT professionals and that gave rise to the prominent technology trend "blockchain technology."

There are numerous blockchain applications, in which the furthest of them influence decentralization, transparency, and persistence. Blockchain technology plays a vital role and feasibly be a silver bullet for IoT technology. The combination of blockchain with IoT technology can leverage the transaction processing between billions of connected devices effectively and can be used to create an optimal and cohesive functioning of IoT devices and networks. The decentralized nature of blockchain technology can eradicate single points of failure due to the transformation from a centralized infrastructure to a distributed and decentralized architecture. The integration of blockchain with IoT applications can influence and create a tamper-resilient ledger. The decentralized architecture helps to minimize the IoT Silos and improves the fault tolerance and scalability of the system. Blockchain offers trustworthiness using distributed authorization and authentication among devices in IoT applications. Device agnostic features can be achieved through the integration in which the devices can communicate with each other without the intervention of servers.

Another important challenging issue in blockchain is that it demands on large computation power and hence it needs a lot of energy in order to execute. Cost is another cause for concern in blockchain technology, where organizations must purchase dedicated hardware and software to create and maintain the blockchain. Many companies are working on issues to reduce the complexity and cost required for building blockchain networks and found a key solution technology called cloud computing. Blockchain as a service is the mantra for most of the issues by effectively using "templates" for building and running blockchain networks.

5.7 CONCLUSION

Industries widely use IoT for remotely monitoring resources and storing the sensed data in a database or cloud computing environment. Due to the complex operations and enormous data storage, a proper security mechanism is required in order to store and perform transaction processing in a secure way. Blockchain technology is hastily rising as a game changer and provides solutions to complex computing problems in various fields. This chapter presents the need for blockchain technology for e industry and how blockchain technology solves the research challenges and issues in Industrial IoT.

KEYWORDS

- **blockchain technology**
- **cloud computing**
- **heterogeneous environment**
- **IIoT**
- **IoT**
- **over-the-counter**

REFERENCES

1. Shruti, G. H., & Soumyalatha, (2016). Internet of things (IoT): A study on architectural elements, communication technologies and applications. *IJARCCE, 5*(9), 2278–1021.
2. Zhang, D., Wan, J., Hsu, C. H., & Rayes, A., (2016). Industrial technologies and applications for the internet of things. *Comput. Netw., 101*, 1–4.
3. Zhang, Y., (2016). GroRec: A group-centric intelligent recommender system integrating social, mobile and big data technologies. *IEEE Trans. Services Comput., 9*(5), 786–795.
4. Chen, X., Wu, X., Li, X. Y., He, Y., & Liu, Y., (2014). Privacy-preserving high-quality map generation with participatory sensing. In: *IEEE INFOCOM'14* (pp. 2310–2318).
5. Huang, X., *et al.,* (2012). Software monitoring with controllable overhead. *Int. J. Softw. Tools Technol. Transfer, 14*(3), 327–347.
6. Arora, D., Ravi, S., Raghunathan, A., & Jha, N. K., (2006). Hardware-assisted run-time monitoring for secure program execution on embedded processors. *IEEE Trans. Very Large Scale Integr. (VLSI) Syst., 14*(12), 1295–1308.
7. Gao, W., Hatcher, W. G., & Yu, W., (2018). A survey of blockchain: Techniques, applications, and challenges. In: *IEEE 27th International Conference on Computer Communication and Networks, ICCCN* (pp. 1–11).
8. Peters, G. W., & Panayi, E. (2016). Understanding modern banking ledgers through blockchain technologies: Future of transaction processing and smart contracts on the

internet of money. In *Banking Beyond Banks and Money* (pp. 239–278). Springer, Cham.

9. Wahab, J., (2018). *Privacy in Blockchain Systems*. arXiv preprint arXiv: 1809.10642.
10. Feng, Q., He, D., Zeadally, S., Khan, M. K., & Kumar, N., (2018). A survey on privacy protection in blockchain system. *J. Netw. Comput. Appl.*

CHAPTER 6

Using Blockchain in IoT for Pharmaceutical Drug Supply

P. SATHISH KUMAR, K. AJITH KUMAR, and R. SWATHI

School of Information Technology and Engineering,
Vellore Institute of Technology, Vellore, Tamil Nadu, India

ABSTRACT

Pharmaceutical companies face many challenges in eradicating counterfeit medicines. Due to high requirements and seamless transport, the supply chain plays an especially important role in reducing counterfeit medicines in life science companies. However, they face complex challenges. This chapter proposes a method and guidelines for implementing the IoT with blockchain in pharmaceutical drug supply chain management. Thereby we can reduce the number of counterfeit drugs in the market and save millions of lives.

6.1 INTRODUCTION

Multiple stakeholders are involved in the pharmaceutical drug supply, such as supplier pharmacies, wholesalers, and hospitals. There is no possibility that they all use the same information technology (IT) systems, and this makes the data hard to transfer. Even if they use the same IT system, there will be data redundancy or false records. The transport conditions like humidity, temperature, luminosity, and vibration make the medicine

Hybridization of Blockchain and Cloud Computing: Overcoming Security Issues in IoT.
M. Lawanya Shri, E. Gangadevi, K. Santhi, & Chiranji Lal Chowdhary (Eds.)
© 2024 Apple Academic Press, Inc. Co-published with CRC Press (Taylor & Francis)

unusable, which cannot be accessed in real-time for every medicine in-person [1]. Further, this makes them unable to find counterfeit medicine. Every year, millions of people's lives are in danger because of these counterfeit medicines are circulating in the market. In this chapter, we will compare the proposed solutions which are already using the blockchain and IoT for the supply chain in the pharmaceutical industry. We propose an efficient way of tracking the conditions of the medicine with temperature, vibration, humidity, and luminosity with IoT sensors. As we use blockchain technology, the data here is immutable, so we propose an idea that makes the data available for all stakeholders. So, every stakeholder in the process can check for counterfeit medicine.

In this chapter, we have proposed the method and guidelines for implementing the IoT with blockchain in pharmaceutical drug supply chain management. Thereby we can reduce the number of counterfeit drugs in the market and save millions of lives.

6.2   IDENTIFICATION OF PROBLEM

There are many disadvantages in the traditional supply chain management for pharmaceutical companies, and not every company is motivated to do good for people. Many companies focus on making more money than they invested. Sometimes, the problem occurs in unexpected ways.

6.2.1   COUNTERFEIT DRUGS

Counterfeit drugs or counterfeit medication is fake medicine. Counterfeit drugs are illegal and may be harmful to your health because they give the wrong dose of the drug. More counterfeit drugs are sold on the market and even on the internet [2]. Counterfeit drugs are more like original drugs; when we analyze only, we can find fake drugs. There are many illegal websites for counterfeit drugs through which people are buying them; using these causes more danger. We know that supply chain security is crucial in the fight against fake drugs and in protecting consumers and manufacturers.

6.2.2   DIVERSION OF DRUG

Diversion of a drug is the main problem in the pharmacy industry. Diversion of drugs is the illegal use of doctor-prescribed medicine with the help of an illegal market. Due to some money-seeking companies, it still exists in the market. Not only with them, but it also exists; it will even function with the help of the clinic staff, and pharmacy store. Due to this, many people lose their lives by taking medicine without any prescription.

6.2.3   DRUG SHORTAGE

Drug shortage can happen in many ways, like quality problems, delay of therapy, switch to a lower dose, rationing of drugs, production discontinuation, and increase in demand. Drug shortages affect how pharmacists and doctors care for patients and can lead to unsafe practices and potentially harmful errors, and unfortunately, these shortages are more common.

6.3   RELATED WORK

The supply chain is an interconnected network related to organizations and individuals involved in manufacturing and sales. It starts from the supplier to the end-users. It takes care of the movement and storage of medicine.

1. **Manufacturer:** The manufacturer gets the drugs from wholesalers or distributors. They ship produced drugs in enormous quantities to distributor warehouses.
2. **Wholesalers:** They take a key role in distributing manufactured drugs to pharmacies and hospitals. They save the time and effort of the manufacturer.
3. **Pharmacies:** Pharmacy and hospitals buy drugs from a wholesaler. They sell the drugs to the end-users or patients. The drugs should be in specific temperatures during transit and storage. The temperature monitoring follows the cold chain process.

In the process of the drug, supply could merge at any level in the supply chain. Some pharmaceutical industries use holographic to reduce this issue. This technique is more expensive. The cold chain process must monitor the vaccine throughout the supply chain, which is critical. Data stored in the blockchain is public. When the organization wants the data to be hidden from others, then it must go through some encryption [3].

6.4 MODULES

The main modules of the blockchain system are as follows:

1. **Blockchain Network:** This is the core component of the project where the data from the IoT sensors are stored immutably and given the privilege to authenticate stakeholders.
2. **Application Module:** In this module, the data upload process and data querying process are done. This module will be directly connected with the user interface for data querying and the block-chain network for uploading the data.
3. **IoT Module:** This module consists of the IoT sensors, which send the sensor data to the application module in a particular time interval.
4. **User Interface:** This module is used by all the stakeholders of the project where it is to view the smart contract and data in the blockchain.
5. **Smart Contract Module:** This module is for verifying the value of the sensor to the predefined values assigned for each medicine.

6.5 BLOCKCHAIN NETWORK

A block of nodes that are connected in a chained manner is called block-chain network. One single blockchain network has many blockchain in it. The blockchain network needs to maintain all the blockchain, and make sure that all the transactions in it are working correctly or not. Mostly the organization which takes care of this blockchain network lets it open to all, but some may not do that.

It all depends on the organization's policy. In our system's case, only authorized stakeholders or end-users can view the data present in the blockchain. This blockchain network allows us to make the data present in the blockchain more secure and makes the attack hard to tamper with the data. The services provided by the blockchain network will be applicable for all the blockchain that are present within the network.

6.5.1 NODE

We know that blockchain is a chain of blocks/nodes connected within the network. In general, a node is a computing device. All nodes in the blockchain network will exchange the data regularly, so all nodes will track other nodes' status. The main purpose of the node is to store immutable data, and if any new transaction arrives, they need to be verified by the present nodes, and they help us to keep the synchronized data of the blockchain network [4].

There exists a master node on which the blockchain will rely on that. The master node is also a computing device, but the main difference is that the master node should always be available as the respective blockchain will run correctly.

6.5.2 DISTRIBUTED LEDGER

A ledger is a file. In our real world, we keep track of all activities with the ledger. But it is extremely hard to search and find the needed data in the minimum amount of time. So, we go for the digital ledger. This digital ledger is most like the excel sheets, where the data can be stored in order or randomly. It is quite easy to search and find the required data in minimum time and manpower. But the main disadvantage in the digital ledger was if the computer or the storage device was damaged, we might not get the data back. So, to resolve this, we go with the distributed ledger, from this concept, all the data were stored in different systems or different storage devices on various locations. All the data newly inserted in the ledger will be updated and synchronized everywhere.

6.5.3 CONSENSUS ALGORITHM

The blockchain is stable and secured. It has privacy and transparency due to distributed decentralized networks. Every process and transaction are going to be done automatically, so no one is going to verify and validate any transitions, but still, blockchain is a well-secured and verified one. It's due to the consensus protocol presented in the blockchain and it is also known as the core part of blockchain.

It is known as a procedure where all the peers in the network will get a similar agreement about the current state of those distributed ledgers. Whenever a new node is added to the blockchain, consensus checks for the version. This is agreed upon by comparing all the nodes in the blockchain network.

1. **Proof of Work:** The consensus algorithm concept is used here for choosing the miner for assigning the next block creation. This POW algorithm is used in Bitcoin. The idea of this algorithm is to solve complex, critical mathematical equations and puzzles to give an easy solution. Because they need more calculations to be done, only then will it get to create a new block [5].

2. **Proof of Stake:** A new method is used to generate a new block in this concept, where the proof of stake and the proof of the work have some differences among them. Miner is the one person who can solve the puzzle, and only they can create a new block for the transition. In this concept, the one who can create the block can prove proof of the stake. Those people are known as validates.

3. **Proof of Burn:** There are many versions of this, wherein the miner will play the key role. In burn, the coins are used to represent the participants of the node, where it is used to check where the correct node is burned or some other one, and the end-user can find the correct value among the blockchain.

6.5.4   *VIRTUAL MACHINE*

To make our smart contract in our blockchain network for every single blockchain we need a virtual machine. They provide us with the basic level of abstraction among the program executing machine and code. The code mentioned here was the smart contract. This is needed to improve the portability of the system. This also acts as the node, in some cases, power-full, and the best virtual machine for the blockchain was the Ethereum Virtual Machine (EVM). This EVM can improve the blockchain network by maintaining the components of the blockchain network like a smart contract [6].

6.5.5   *MEMORY POOL*

It is a buffer memory for the unconfirmed transaction to be stored when a transaction is initiated. It does not directly place into the blocks in the blockchain network. We must verify whether that transaction is valid or invalid. We will verify the digital signature, hash value, and so on. If any transaction fails to satisfy those conditions, then that particular transaction will be rejected. The transactions which satisfy the conditions are only stored in the blocks as the blockchain.

6.6 COMPONENTS OF BLOCKCHAIN NETWORK

6.6.1 SMART CONTRACT

Smart contract programs, stored in a blockchain program, are created to satisfy certain conditions like true or false, if or else in blockchain are called smart contracts. In smart contracts, if a given condition has satisfied a course of action takes place, another set of even executions [7]. The data smart contract ensures that the database is up-to-date and secure and also prevents unauthorized access to the database. Any sort of data tampering would be impossible. A smart contract can be utilized for storing data of high network transactions like the transfer of cryptocurrencies or jewelry or blockchain-voting, in our case, the purchase of medicine. The negative side of a smart contract is that it cannot be utilized for a transaction involving micropayment; for example, when you transport the medicine with only a pair of medicine.

In that case, blockchain technology is not an economically viable choice because the consumer will have to bear the memory processing charge or operations charge for the use of smart contracts. The charge would be higher than the actual value of the item or net worth of the item. In this example, the charge could be higher than that of medicine that you have consumed. In their blockchain, the charges are broken in the smallest unit, known as gas smart contact. This can be utilized for processing and storage of assets that have high net worth and storing secure data like audit information. Also, private blockchains and cryptocurrencies can be created, so storage of data and trust transactions. An example of a private blockchain is a cat. If you have started a company and you want to attract customers to your company you could program a smart contract that could enable the customers the right to receive Ethereum for each visit. Thus, when a customer visit to your company, a smart contract get to transfer a certain unit of Ethereum to his/her wallet.

Ethereum is a platform for the creation of smart contracts. At the same time, it can be utilized as a cryptocurrency. Bitcoin blockchain can be used for storing transactions but not for smart contract; bitcoin is primarily a cryptocurrency. Smart contract is like normal contracts but the only difference is they are completely digital [8], where it is a computer code that is stored in the computer of the blockchain. The data which is going to be stored will not be done manually, so it is well secured. Some properties of the smart contract are:

i.   **Immutable:** If one contract is created, it cannot be changed again. So, no one can go back and call back your contract.
ii. **Distributed:** It is where your output of the contract is confirmed by everyone in the network. So, no single user can modify the details without knowing others in the network.

Smart contracts are used in banks, insurance, postal, and so on. Ethereum is specifically created and designed for smart contact. Smart contracts can be programmed in a special program called solidity. This language is specifically created for Ethereum and uses the syntax of JavaScript [9].

6.6.2   DATABASE

The data in the blockchain is stored as nodes or blocks. If a new transaction occurs, then all nodes must verify the transaction and then store that transaction, then that transaction will be added to the chain. Sometimes, the blockchain also acts as a database; in our case, we store the temperature, humidity, vibration, and luminosity. Not only that, but it also stores some predefined variables like previous block hash, current block hash, and time-stamp. They are all not stored in the form of a normal database. They are stored in the form of a distributed ledger, as we discussed above.

6.6.3   DEVICE

The device was used by the stakeholders or their end-users, who are also part of our system. It has the authority to register new shipments/logistics and track/send the records of the temperature as data to the server, which will be stored in the blocks for every interval of the time which is assigned by the end-users [10].

6.6.4   SENSOR

The sensor part focuses on the IoT device, and also, the data required is generated from the IoT sensors.

6.6.5   SERVER

There are many servers in the market. We choose the best blockchain server providing company listed in subsections.

6.6.5.1   MICROSOFT

Microsoft's Azure is one of the first companies to offer backend as a service (BaaS) and was launched as Azure Blockchain Service. It provides the users with the schema, logic, counterparties, external sources, ledger, and contract binding for constructing their blockchain services.

6.6.5.2   BITSE

BitSE works on VeChain, and it is a Chinese cloud product management platform built on a blockchain in collaboration with PricewaterhouseCoopers (PwC) to boost blockchain adoption in the Asia-Pacific markets.

6.6.5.3   PEER LEDGER

Peer ledger is an identity management blockchain. It uses the concepts of a public key infrastructure (PKI) system to certify identities from outside the blockchain before connecting them to blockchain accounts. The company is targeting trust-sensitive industries such as health care for their solution.

6.6.5.4   SAP CLOUD PLATFORM BLOCKCHAIN

Leonardo is a service that is based on hyper-ledger and resides in the SAP cloud service, so it can be accessed from any device and requires no on-premises hardware or software. Leonardo is a blockchain cloud service and machine learning (ML) service that supports the Internet of Things (IoT) in a single ecosystem.

6.7 SOME COMMON BLOCKCHAIN NETWORKS

6.7.1 ETHEREUM

Ethereum is a decentralized system, and it is an open-source blockchain. This works in the same principle as the basic blockchain concept itself. Ethereum has extra features like a smart contract which is an application. ETH (Ether) is commonly known as the cryptocurrency token of the Ethereum blockchain. The current transaction of Ethereum is about 15 per second, but they are planning to upgrade their speed to tens of thousands per second. The main difference between bitcoin and Ethereum is the concept, bitcoin is used for cryptocurrency, but Ethereum aims to build a world computing system.

6.7.2 NEO

Neo is the biggest rivalry for Ethereum. This is also working in crypto-currency and blockchain applications platforms. This is built for issuing digitized identities and creating digitized assets and smart contracts. Neo built these in a more secure platform and smart economy. Neo platform issues and manages two digital assets; Neo tokens and gas tokens. Neo tokens are used to block creations, network management, and any consensus requirements, and gas tokens fuel for more security.

6.7.3 EOS

Eos is aimed to support the industrial-scale decentralized application effectively. Eos claims that they can conduct millions of transactions per second, all without transaction fees. This is possible by solving the biggest problem in blockchain space scalability. Visa and bitcoin-like public blockchain currently require total consensus across nodes. The EOS solution for this is called delegated proof of steak. The major difference between Eos and other Dop platforms is Eos runs in an ownership model like an operating system. Other Dop-like Ethereum runs by renting out computation in exchange for the transaction fees. The number of votes we own on the Eos is equal to the number of tokens we have, and it is directly proportional to how much amount of network we own. This in the sense we can remove the transaction fees. In other words, the transaction fee is avoided because we use our network to do the transaction [11].

6.7.4   LISK

Lisk is a platform on which developers can build, publish, distribute, and then monetize their blockchain applications. Blockchain application looks and feels like a regular application, but it is built on top of a blockchain decentralized network rather than hosted by a single entity. However, the number of challenges associated with developing blockchain applications, such as a lack of tooling and frameworks, prevent it from being widely adopted. Lisk aims to remove these obstacles by providing developers with an easy-to-use side-chain development to build their blockchain applications. Each blockchain application runs on top of its side-chain, a fully customized blockchain that is connected to the Lisk main chain in the SDK is completely written in JavaScript, the most used programming language in the world, so list everyone can develop decentralized social networks, messengers, games, exchanges, storage platforms, and much more without the complexity of developing a blockchain from scratch [12].

In this concept, the devices are given to the end-users, and they are assigned with an interval time. The product supplier will get the medicines for delivery, and he will load all of them into the box and he will fix the sensors and IoT devices. The sensor will check for the temperature for every interval of time and sends the temperature to the blockchain which is connected through Bluetooth. The data can only be stored in the blockchain with hashes; they cannot be updated; only we can delete the entire blockchain. Only the end-users have the privilege to view or delete the data using internet-connected devices. While delivering the medicine, the details of the medicine will be verified. If it is in the correct state, it will be delivered, which is more beneficial for everyone.

1. **Block Hash:** It is calculated with the hash values of the data present in the block.
2. **Previous Block Hash:** This block consists of the previous block hash to maintain the chain link between the blocks.
3. **Timestamp:** It stores the timestamp of when the data is written into the blockchain.
4. **Data:** In our case, the data is provided by the sensors with the respective time interval.
5. **Merkle Root:** It consists of the hashes of all the nodes in the blockchain. It makes the searching easier with the Merkle tree.

6.8   SENSOR OVERVIEW

There are many sensors available in the market; we need temperature, humidity, vibration, and luminosity. And to make the data transfer, we need the Wi-Fi network where all the sensors are connected to the Wi-Fi router via Wi-Fi and the data must be sent to the blockchain network. To make the package compact and easy to transport, we should not use the three different sensors. We need an IoT sensor that will read all three values around it. Every sensor has a range, so it is difficult to have three separate sensors in every range. So, we must make the package accordingly.

The sensor which has all three sensors in it is "UbiBot-WS1" by the company UbiBot. This sensor can measure the light intensity as the arc flash with a fast response of 1 ms, the sensor has also designed to monitor the temperature using both analog and digital, which can also measure the light, humidity, temperature, and vibration; also, it can measure the pressure [13].

The sensor we have suggested was "UbiBot-WS1." Many sensors in the market give us all the required parameters, i.e., temperature, humidity, vibration, and luminosity but their cost was inadequate for the wide range of logistics. There are many cheaper sensors, but they fail to give us all the required parameters.

The main advantage of this sensor is it takes less space to set up (6.5 × 6.5 × 1.7 cm) which eventually increases the space to fill the medicines; it also weighs 31.8 g ± 3 g. It has the in-built power source of 2 × AA batteries/Micro USB (5V/2A). So, it can independently long last more than the normal sensors.

This sensor produces the values that have the accuracy for Temperature ±0.3°C, humidity ±3%, and ambient light ±2%, which is more efficient than other sensors. As we deal with human lives, we should consider this as the main factor. This sensor has an in-built Wi-Fi card, so it is extremely easy to connect to a Wi-Fi network and establish the connection to a blockchain network via a blockchain server [14].

6.9   SECURITY MEASURES

Blockchain technology is digitized and it encompasses decentralized ledgers in it. Every block is interconnected within the blockchain generation, so they may be secured tightly. Every transaction inside the blocks makes use of encryption techniques to comply with the transaction of some of the peers. The distinct protocol is used to discover if any fake operation happens inside the transaction at the same time as verifying.

6.9.1   BASIC TERMINOLOGY IN BLOCKCHAIN SECURITY

6.9.1.1   ENCRYPTION

In this idea, we use pocket protection, so each precise person might be furnished with a separate key known as "Hash." Where it is far a mathematically generated price to be assigned as a unique key for every block. The hash price might be done with the aid of using the constant output aggregate of the general public-key cryptography.

6.9.1.2   MINING

To hold the technology integrity the mining technique is used for its far steeply-priced and complicated technique. Miners inside the blockchain use to attach new blocks to the blockchain for the transaction. Its assessments for each transaction had been demonstrated or now no longer. Cryptocurrency rewards the miner technique.

6.9.1.3   IMMUTABILITY

Among each idea, it is by far one of the maximum critical additives in this blockchain generation. The different exchange significance is shipped ledger. The immutability approach had been as soon as the transaction is confirmed, it cannot be erased.

6.9.2   HOW FRAUDSTERS MANIPULATE THIS TECHNOLOGY?

Blockchain generation is going through many kinds and exchange manner of attacks, and shape while it is far launched. Exchanges and cryptocurrency wallets turned into the maximum attacked and centered component inside the blockchain. We have mentioned some security measures by which attackers or hackers can attack the blockchain system. We have also mentioned some of the countermeasures which help us to prevent the blockchain from those attacks.

6.9.2.1   DISTRIBUTED DENIAL OF SERVICE (DDOS)

Distributed denial of service (DDoS) attack is extremely hard to exploit on a blockchain network, but it can occur with less possibility. The main agenda of the hackers while performing this attack is to make the server down by consuming all its processing power, memory, and resources with an enormous number of requests. The attackers use the DDoS bot-nets to perform this attack.

6.9.2.2   SYBIL ATTACK

This is one of the serious attacks which need to be prevented before it happens. In this attack, the attacker pretends to be the data provider (in our case, the IoT devices) coinciding in time. The malicious node will have the capability to create many other nodes in the network. The malicious nodes will look like a large group of nodes that makes the original node unable to detect them, so the original nodes eventually accept them, believing that they are original data from various sources [15]. This attack can be prevented by implementing the Proof of Work (PoW) on every node.

6.9.2.3   *ECLIPSE ATTACK*

This attack targets the node from the peer-to-peer network, so the targeted node will not receive any information from the other original nodes in the network. Then the separated node will continually be on that incorrect blockchain network. There are many ways to reduce this attack:

1. **0-Confirmation Double Spends:** If a block accepts any transaction with no verification or confirmation then it may be attacked for the double spend. It may lead to the loss of the stored data.
2. **N-Confirmation Double Spends:** This is more expensive than the 0-Confirmation double spends, where it requires the attacker to be more prepared in this case. The original node waits for more confirmation, where the attacker needs to work for that with the botnets he included for this attack.

6.9.2.4   *ROUTING ATTACK*

This is one of the serious attacks, but this does not attack the blockchain network. It attacks the ISP's which provide the connection to the blockchain network. For example, imagine you sent some package via some courier company. If that courier company tries to take some part of the package, then the receiver will not be able to receive the tampered part of the package, even the receiver will not be able to know whether the package tampered or not. There are two types: partitioning attack and delayed attack; these two drop attack and append attack.

Blockchain generation has trusted the download and adds of the actual time records that are in a massive volume. Data and the records transferred to the Internet Carrier Company might be suffering from the hacker is referred to as routing assault. In this technique, wherein the transition appears to be stopped or like now no longer running with the aid of using it is going to be stolen with the aid of using the hackers [16].

6.9.2.5   *51% ATTACKS*

A high degree of computing strength is needed for mining due to the fact it is a far extra extensive technique. If 51% of the computing community will be an advantage with the aid of using the unmarried miner or a set of miners, then they may control and manipulate it. Without spending, they can upload new transactions to the blockchain where double-spend cash is used on this technique. An organization of coordinated movements attacked Bitcoin gold in May 2018, and it's one of the blockchains. Bitcoin gold has double-spent $70,000. The modern-day blockchain that is stricken by 51% assault is Ethereum Classic.

6.9.2.6　PHISHING

It is a form of fraud wherein the hackers ship out the e-mails from the faux e-mails of reputed companies. They ship the e-mails to the pocket's key owners, asking them to ship their confidential information to positive links. Some of the unlawful cryptocurrency mining had been completed with the aid of using the person's machine as a host. In 2017, first 1/2 of my extra than $225 million had been misplaced with the aid of using blockchain inventors inside the phishing frauds.

6.9.3　HERE WE'VE GOT A FEW MEASURES TO SAVE YOU FROM CRYPTOCURRENCY FRAUD

The counter and the discovery and the beyond fraud at the peer-to-peer networks is a critical idea which turned into found out with the aid of using the exchange, expected, tokens, and blockchain companies. Cryptocurrency funding may be blanketed with the aid of using a few measures [17].

6.9.3.1　TWO-ELEMENT AUTHENTICATION (2FA)

It is likewise referred to as two-step verification. In blockchain, 2FA is increasingly acquainted with the period. It is one of the layers supplied with inside the pockets protection, which gives the person a one-time password (OTP) for verification, at the same time as getting access to the foreign money pockets. If the fraudsters attempt to advantage any get entry to password to the pockets, they should want the OTP tool to get the authentication. This guarantee acts as a greater layer of safety and protects against important thing thefts and phishing frauds. 2FA software program is an unfastened Google useful resource that enables us to apply more than one tool to steady crypto wallets.

6.9.3.2 ANTI-PHISHING SOFTWARE PROGRAM

Malicious hyperlinks, faux websites, and e-mail threats may be recognized through the usage of anti-phishing software programs. It simply approves the right hyperlinks and websites. Metacert's anti-phishing is a software program, wherein it can assist in verifying one's net cope with the mass scale and has included each person from an unknown bureaucracy and acquainted with phishing threats.

6.9.3.3 COLD WALLETS

In cryptocurrency, there are varieties of wallets. A hot pocket is greater susceptible in comparison to bloodless pockets, and due to that fact, the bloodless pockets are not linked to the internet. In the shape of a tool, the bloodless pockets supplied had been its greater secured; however, even though the recent pockets are unfastened and maximum not unusual, it's much less secure.

6.9.3.4 BLACKLISTING

By figuring out the frauds that happen inside the phishing sample and services and key thieves and making them blacklist cryptocurrency businesses simplest they could themselves make a falling sufferer repeat the fraud sample once more.

6.9.4 PROBLEMS OCCUR BY FORK

It is a decentralized node settlement and model-associated hassle. It happens best while that software program is up to date. More quantity of the blockchain is concerned on this, so this hassle might be massive trouble here.

When the booklet of the blockchain is a new edition, the adjustments have occurred inside the nodes via way of means of the consensus rule because of the brand-new settlement. The old node and new node are the two components divided employing the prevailing nodes inside the blockchain [18].

The vintage node sends the transaction to the block to be perfect via means of the brand-new node. The vintage node sends the transaction to the block to now no longer be perfect via means of the brand-new node.

The new node sends the transaction to the block to be perfect via way of means of the vintage node. The new node sends the transaction to the block to now no longer be perfect via way of means of the vintage node. Getting consensus on those one-of-a-kind four styles of instances happens, so fork hassle has taken a region on this. And additionally, because of those four instances, we get hard fork and soft fork via a means of dividing the Fork hassle. By evaluating the brand-new node and vintage node, we will discover the computing electricity of the brand-new node is 50 more than the vintage node.

6.9.4.1   HARD FORK

It is an approach in which the machine involves the brand-new settlement or to the new edition; however, in which they are now no longer like-minded to the vintage model. The vintage nodes cannot receive with the extraction of the brand-new node, so in which an unmarried node is break up into nodes. Even though the computing electricity of the brand-new node is more potent than the vintage node, the vintage has the functionality to nonetheless keep the blockchain via means of the proper manner of the transaction.

When this hard fork takes region, the replacement manner of settlement should be taken region via way of means of all the nodes in that community, as a request via way of means of us. Those nodes which are not up to date cannot be capable of maintaining that painting like usual. If a greater quantity of vintage nodes is not capable of replacing then, it is going to begin running absolutely with some other chain in which the fork has divided as two chains.

6.9.4.2   SOFT FORK

Its approach in which the machine involves the brand-new settlement or to the new edition; however, in which they are now no longer like-minded to the new edition, the brand-new nodes cannot receive with the extraction of the vintage node. Where the computing electricity of the vintage node is much less in comparison to the brand-new node, so had been the mining nodes of the vintage nodes will now no longer be well-known via way of means of the brand-new nodes, however nonetheless, each of the brand new and vintage node chain might be running on the equal time.

When this soft fork takes place, the brand-new agreements are not required to be up to date via way of means of all the nodes within the blockchain community at a comparable time. They permit the updating separately gradually. Hard fork differs from Soft Fork, due to the fact while the node updating happens, it is going to no longer affect the effectiveness and balance of the machine. Somehow, the old nodes are made invisible by the soft fork so that the adjustments arise with inside the consensus. In place of that, verifying each node may be performed to a few make bigger via a way of means of the precept of nodes.

6.10 SCALABILITY OF BLOCKCHAIN

Data is developing greater and larger within the blockchain, and additionally, the manner of computing and storing has emerged as greater more difficult to more difficult. At equal time synchronizing the records take greater time consumption and offers the customers greater troubles while running the systems.

6.10.1 BLOCKCHAIN RECORDS' TIME CONFIRMATION

It is compared to credit score card transactions online in a conventional manner, and they take greater than one day to verify the transaction. But in the bitcoin transaction, it is going to no longer take greater than 1 hour to affirm it. However, they are now no longer sufficient to our expectations as we want them. There is a manner to resolve the hassle of the usage of Lighting Networks.

Hashed Time Lock Contract (HTLCs) is one of the bi-directional manner payment channels that is proposed to be applied via way of means of the Lightning Network. They permit the price technique to be greater secure throughout many peer-to-peer channels. The network formation is permitted to make a payment to many of the peers, even though they had now no longer opened any channels, among others.

6.10.2 CURRENT REGULATIONS PROBLEM

As the usage of Bitcoin as an example, decentralized system traits of the coins quantity and the coverage of the money that's managed via way of means of the significant financial institution is made weaker and it makes the authorities to be alert of the blockchain technology. Authority of the blockchain should appear in it, developing new coverage via means of new methodically should be performed, if now no longer they could have an excessive hazard on markets.

6.10.3 INTEGRATED COST PROBLEM

It will have a lot of fees which include money and time to extrude the present system while it is an infrastructure. We must make certain this modern era now no longer handily creates financial benefits and meet the necessities of supervision. However, additionally, the bridge with conventional enterprise and it usually comes across difficulties from the inner enterprise that is present now.

6.10.4 CONCLUSIONS

There's absolute confidence that blockchain is warm trouble in current years. Even though it has a few subjects, we want to notice, a few troubles have already been advanced at the side of new techniques growing on the software side, getting increasingly mature and stable. The authorities ought to make corresponding legal guidelines for this technology, and employers must prepare to embody blockchain technology, stopping it brings an excessive amount of effect to the modern-day system. When we revel in within the gain of blockchain technology delivered to us, within the identical time, we nonetheless ought to live carefully on its in hence and protection troubles that it may behave.

6.11 SENSOR TO BLOCKCHAIN DATA FLOW SECURITY

There is a high chance of tampering with the data in an intermediate way between the data provided by the sensor and blockchain network. So, to avoid that attack, we propose the method of encrypting the data right after it is provided from the IoT device and decrypting it right before it enters the memory pool of our blockchain network. To implement it, we need a strong and efficient encryption algorithm. Here, we describe some algorithms and their properties and compare them with one another, and propose the best among those algorithms.

6.11.1 TRIPLE DATA ENCRYPTION STANDARD (TRIPLE DES)

Triple-DES uses 56-bit keys rather than a stream cipher; it is a block cipher and it uses 64-bit blocks. In 1998 DES became correctly damaged while a DES-encrypted message became cracked in three days a year later a community of 10,000 systems around the world cracked a DES-encrypted message in less than a day and it has just gotten worse since then with modern computing power being what it is. Since DES was encrypted in the writing was on the wall for a little while we knew we needed something else so along comes to triple-DES isn't three times the strength of DES necessarily it's DES applied three times and what I mean by that, what we do is we take a plain text message and let's call that p and we're going to use a key that will call k1 and we're gone used that key to encrypt the message and that's going to result in the ciphertext and we'll call that 'c.' So with c1 the output of the first round of encryption we're going to apply a second key and we'll call that k2 with that second key we are going to go through a decryption process on c1.

Since it is the wrong key, we are not going to get the plain text out the other end what we are going to get is another round of cipher text and we will call that c2 with c2 we are going to apply the third key we will call that third key k3 and we are going to encrypt the cipher text c2 and that's going to result in another round of cipher text that we will call c3. So, we have three different keys applied in two separate ways. So, with key1 and key3, we do a round of encryption and with k2 we do a round of decryption.

So, it is an encrypt decrypt encrypt process with three separate keys while that does not yield a full 168-bit key size the three rounds of encryption yield an effective key size of a 168-bits because you must find three 56-bit keys. The main advantage of 3DES is the key size of 3DES is larger than DES and it has a 56-bit block size. The disadvantage is slower compared to the AES. So, speaking of the technical details for triple DES, we are still using the DES block cipher with 56 keys, but since we have three different keys, we get an effective key length of 168 bits. Triple DES is a stopgap measure however we knew that it was broken and if you could decrypt a DES message it would not be all that long but or decrypt triple DES message.

6.11.2   ADVANCED ENCRYPTION STANDARD (AES)

For an AES, the National Institute of Standards and Technology (NIST) requested a proposal that was in 1999, and in 2001 NIST published an algorithm RIJNDAEL as AES. AES consists of 128 bits long in a key that encrypts key can be 128, 192, or 256 bits. First, we must copy into a point for a square matrix that is known as a state. This state matrix is then modified in each step of encryption and decryption. The key is copied into a separate point for the matrix, and that key is expanded into words. The expanded keys are then used while encrypting and decrypting the message. Ordering within the matrix is by a column that is the first four bytes of 128 bit and occupies the first column of the matrix.

The cipher also consists of n runs where n depends on the key length that is 10 rounds for 128-bits encryption to well for 192 and 14 for 256 billion the first n minus 1 round consists of four distinct transformations that are sub bytes mix column and add round key the final run skills to mix column there is also a single round key before the first run the key that is used for encryption and decryption.

Our first expanded the same expanded key is used for both encryption and decryption. First, the key is copied into who informatics after which the extended growth includes three steps for the primary column rotation of phrase and a substitution byte adding the round constant the remaining column only uses XOR with the newly generated were in next column word in the previous matrix rotation reward perform a one-byte shock could have left seat of the fourth column the sub byte uses substitution from the mess box the air-ground constant exhausts the output of sub bytes with the first column word and run constantly the round constants is a predefined set of constants for each run listed here are 10 round constants for 128-bit encryption.

Some technical specs AES set of rules are distinctive variable block sizes and key lengths and so long as the ones block sizes and key lengths were multiples of 32 bits. So, 32, 64, 96, and so on you could use those block sizes and key lengths when AES was published an EES specified a fixed 128-bit block size and key lengths of 128, 192, and 256 bits.

So, we have AES. The advantage of AES is stronger and faster, supports the hardware and software, less susceptible to crypt-analysis, and 128-bit block size. The disadvantage is the costliest to implement, complex in encryption and encryption and simple algebraic structure.

6.11.3   BLOWFISH ENCRYPTION ALGORITHM

Blowfish is a symmetric key block cipher. It was developed in 1983 by Bruce Schneider. It was created to improve upon the data encryption standard or DES and algorithm known to be slow and insecure. The first secure block ciphers are blowfish. It is not subject to any patents and hence freely available for anyone to use. To work on the blowfish, 64-bits must be in block size. The key size should be 32-bits to 448-bits as variable size, the number of subkeys must be 18 [P1 to P18], several rounds contain 16, and several substitution boxes should be 4. Let's take a look at blowfish and how it works. First, we initialize our key-dependent p-box and s-box using the hexadecimal representation of pi for now we will skip over the details of their creation the p- box says in 18 entries as we look before and in the s-box is 256 next we take our 64-bit plain text and split it into the half we'll call the first half L the second half are we then enter a loop which we repeat 16 times we take L and then XOR with p1 the value in the p box at our current index we then take our and excerpt with a function of L.

So, the function we split out into four quarters, the value at quarter one is added to the s box value at quarter to then that sum is XY with the s box value at quarter three finally our results are added to the s-box value a quarter four lastly, we swap L and R. Then we repeat the loop all over again after going through the loop 16 times we swap L and R. Once more if you recall our p box had 18 entire, we went through the first 16 in the loop and we now have only two left. So, we XOR, R, and L with p 17 and p 18, respectively; we did not combine L and R to get our cipher text decryption that follows the same process but, in the loop, we would start at p 16 and go down from 16 to 1 blowfish has many pros it had a good encryption rate it was resilient against cryptoanalysis, was unpatented, and free to use at a time when most algorithms were patented. The main advantage of blowfish is good protection against Brute force attacks and it is one of the fastest block ciphers in widespread use today. Disadvantages are prophecies, the crucial process over other creatures which means it is time-consuming.

6.11.4   TWO FISH ENCRYPTION ALGORITHM

Two fish encryptions have 128 bits and key sizes as much as 256 bits. It changed into one of the five finalists of the superior encryption preferred contest; however, it changed into now no longer decided on standardization. Two fish is associated with the sooner block cipher Blowfish. Two fish specific capabilities are the usage of pre-computed keys – established s-boxes, and a complicated key time table. One 1/2 of an n-bit secret is used because the real encryption key and the alternative 1/2 of the n-bit secret is used to adjust the encryption set of rules. Two fish borrows a few factors from distinctive designs; for example, pseudo-Hadamard remodel from the more secure own circle of relatives of ciphers.

Two fish has a feistily shaped DES. On maximum software program structures, Two fish changed into barely slower the Rijndael for 128-bit keys, however, it is miles a few what quicker for 256-bit keys. Two fish changed into designed via way of means of Bruce Schneier, John Kelsey, David Wagner, Doug whiting, Chris corridor, and Niels Ferguson; the prolonged Two fish crew who met to carry out also cryptanalysis of Two fish and different AES contest entrants consist of Stefan lucks, Takayoshi Kohno, and mike stay. The Two fish cipher has now no longer been patented and the reference implementation has been positioned with inside the public domain. As a result, the Two fish set of rules is unfastened for anybody to apply with no regulations whatsoever. It is certainly considered one among some ciphers blanketed with inside the open Pretty Good Privacy (PGP) preferred. However, two fish has visibly much less been to be had longer. Crypt-analysis in 1999, Niels Ferguson posted as not possible differential assault that breaks six rounds out of 16 of the 256-bits key model the use of 2,256 steps.

The key period must be 128–192 and 256 bits. There are not any vulnerable keys in Two fish, it is miles performance and bendy in design. 128-bit block Feistel network. It includes 16 rounds. Key depends on s container. Key time table on computable "on-the-fly." First, we input the important thing into plain text. Plain textual content sends to the enter, and the enter sends the important thing to s container realizes it runs 16 rounds of a set of rules.

At last, it comes as an output that we bear in mind as cipher textual content. Input and output statistics are XOR with 8 sub key k0 to k7. 128 – a bit simple textual content is split into 4 components of 32-bit. Then its miles are given for the enter wherein it is miles XOR with 4 keys. R_0 and R_1 are exceeded thru function. Results are f_0 and f_1. The primary benefit of Two fish is drastically crypt-analyzed, unpatented, unfastened, and un copyrighted.

We have compared four encryption algorithms, and in those, we found that the blowfish algorithm is speed and occupies less space than others. Blowfish algorithm occupies the O(1) space and O(n) time, where n represents the number of blocks.

6.12 METHODOLOGY

The medicines should be tested in the laboratory, and they should be classified accordingly, the classified medicine must be kept inside the sensor container, after placing it into the container, the smart contract must be created for each container and packed for shipment or cargo. Before dispatching the details of the smart contract will be generated as the QR code.

By right authorization scanning of QR code, any stakeholder will be able to view the full immutable blockchain nodes, then the sensors will be activated after the dispatch then the sensor hub placed inside will encrypt the data and send the cipher text to the blockchain network. Before creating the node, we must decrypt and the sensor data will reach the memory pool and waits for node creation and if it is verified, then the node will be created within the blockchain network. After reaching the destination the smart contract is validated, when all the values from the sensor are within the smart contract range, then the medicine is not counterfeit so it is accepted, if not then the medicine must be given to the laboratory to check whether it is counterfeit.

6.12.1 BASIC IMPLEMENTATION

The main part of the blockchain is storing the sensor values into blocks, we implemented the simple blockchain system with python on the local server.

Then the core function of the blockchain is adding the digital fingerprint into the blocks; it can be done with the hashing, to implement it, we use the "SHA-256" encryption algorithm from the library "hashlib." The data in the blockchain is stored in the form of blocks, since there will be many blocks, it is mandatory to have the block ID to fetch the needed data.

In the blockchain, every node is linked with the previous block and has the calculated hash value from the previous block's hash value, if any previous block hash which makes the blockchain easy to find when any data is corrupted. The first node is called "genesis node" which has the previous block hash values as 0, and the initial sensor values are considered.

There is also a problem in the blockchain that if any intruder creates a new series of nodes with false values, to solve that Proof of Work (PoW), for this we introduce a new variable called the nonce. The nonce is an integer variable whose value keeps on changing until it provides the hash value that satisfies the constraint.

Adding a new node to the blockchain, to do that we need to check the proof of work, and the previous node's hash is referred to as the new node. Mining the nodes, all the requested nodes will be stored in the queue of unconfirmed transactions of nodes. Where the nodes hash verification and PoW verification is called mining of the nodes. In that code snippet, the data is considered as the values of temperature, vibration, and luminosity.

6.13 SUMMARY, CONCLUSIONS, AND FUTURE WORK

Due to the immutability blockchain will be the most suitable way to eradicate counterfeit medicine while transporting drugs. This can build more trust between the consumer and the pharmaceutical company. The basic implementation of the blockchain is everywhere, but there is also a problem in the blockchain that if any intruder creates a new series of nodes with the false values, to solve that we implemented PoW with the blockchain.

As we were given the steps and basic overview of the implantation, we had suggested the best blockchain network, suitable sensors, and best cloud server to maintain the data availability. The project can be implemented with Python, C#, or java. But we suggested the language python as it provides us to implement the front end also. Then the data usability, which can be done only by the authorized stakeholders of the system, will also be implemented in the future.

KEYWORDS

- **blockchain**
- **distributed denial of service**
- **information technology**
- **Internet of things**
- **PricewaterhouseCoopers**
- **public key infrastructure**

REFERENCES

1. Clauson, K. A., et al., (2018). Leveraging blockchain technology to enhance supply chain management in healthcare: an exploration of challenges and opportunities in the health supply chain. *Blockchain in Healthcare Today, 1*(3), 1–12.
2. Hackius, N., & Moritz, P., (2017). Blockchain in logistics and supply chain: trick or treat?. Digitalization in supply chain management and logistics: Smart and digital solutions for an Industry 4.0 environment. *Proceedings of the Hamburg International Conference of Logistics (HICL)* (Vol. 23). Berlin: Epubli GmbH.
3. Slim, P., et al., (2018). Blockchain technology for detecting falsified and substandard drugs in distribution: pharmaceutical supply chain intervention. *JMIR Research Protocols, 7*(9), e10163.
4. Alangot. W., & Krishnashree, A., (2017). Trace and track: Enhanced pharma supply chain infrastructure to prevent fraud. *International Conference on Ubiquitous Communications and Network Computing.* Springer, Cham.
5. Schöner, M. M., et al., (2017). *Blockchain Technology in the Pharmaceutical Industry.* Frankfurt School Blockchain Center: Frankfurt, Germany.
6. Ahmadi, V., et al., (2020). Drug governance: IoT-based blockchain implementation in the pharmaceutical supply chain. In: *2020 Sixth International Conference on Mobile and Secure Services (MobiSecServ).* IEEE.
7. Mohana, M., Gabriel, O., & Tze, E., (2019). Implementation of pharmaceutical drug traceability using blockchain technology. *Inti. Journal, 35.*

8. Botcha, K. M., & Chakravarthy, V. V. (2019, June). Enhancing traceability in pharmaceutical supply chain using Internet of Things (IoT) and blockchain. In *2019 IEEE International Conference on Intelligent Systems and Green Technology (ICISGT)* (pp. 45–453). IEEE.

9. Pandey, P., & Ratnesh, L., (2020). Securing e-health networks from counterfeit medicine penetration using blockchain. *Wireless Personal Communications*, 1–19.

10. Choi, J. B., Jamie, R., & Erick, C. J., (2015). The impact of a shared pharmaceutical supply chain model on counterfeit drugs, diverted drugs, and drug shortages. *Portland International Conference on Management of Engineering and Technology (PICMET)*. IEEE.

11. https://cointelegraph.com/news/blockchain-security-preventing-fraud-on-distributed-ledger-technology (accessed on 11 August 2022).

12. Bocek, T., et al., (2017). Blockchains everywhere-a use-case of blockchains in the pharma supply-chain. In: *2017 IFIP/IEEE Symposium on Integrated Network and Service Management (IM)*. IEEE.

13. Singh, R., Ashutosh, D. D., & Gautam, S., (2020). Internet of things based blockchain for temperature monitoring and counterfeit pharmaceutical prevention. *Sensors, 20*(14), 3951.

14. Moosivand, A., Ali, R. G., & Hamid, R. R., (2019). Supply chain challenges in pharmaceutical manufacturing companies: Using qualitative system dynamics methodology. *Iranian Journal of Pharmaceutical Research: IJPR, 18*(2), 1103.

15. Li, Z., Xiong, D., Dailiang, J., Wei, Z., & Chengqin, D., (2020). Management platform for second-use of retired power battery based on IPv6 and blockchain technology. In: 2020 *IEEE 5th Information Technology and Mechatronics Engineering Conference (ITOEC)* (pp. 1465–1469). IEEE.

16. ActiveState. https://www.activestate.com/ (accessed on 11 August 2022).

17. Singh, R., Dwivedi, A. D., & Srivastava, G., (2020). Internet of things-based blockchain for temperature monitoring and counterfeit pharmaceutical prevention. *Sensors, 20*(14), 3951.

18. Chowdhary, C. L. (2020). Growth of financial transaction toward bitcoin and blockchain technology. In *Bitcoin and Blockchain* (pp. 79–97). CRC Press.

CHAPTER 7

Financial and Banking Services Using Blockchain and Its Open Security Issues

SHIVAM KUMAR, VIKAS KUMAR, and PRIYANSHI SHARMA

Student, MCA Department, Vellore Institute of Technology, Vellore, Tamil Nadu, India

ABSTRACT

Blockchain has increased a lot of interest in the last decade in the techno-logical aspect as well as groundbreaking technology. This work system-atically reviews blockchain-based applications across the financial and banking domains. This chapter aims to investigate the use of blockchain across all the financial institutions and banking sectors. Earlier, in the past decade, the blockchain was considered to be a part of cryptocurrency, now it has grown beyond that. Blockchain is now considered to be one of the most secured techniques in cryptography which will decentralize data governance and remove the middle management involved in keeping the data. The fascinating peer-to-peer networking (PPN) in blockchain made us realize we can remove the middlemen involved in the transaction that we do in our daily lives, which will eventually lead us to cost-effective work. Also, the recent emergence of blockchain after 2008, in the past market made us curious, eventually encouraged us to explore more about it. This chapter unfolds the unexplored aspects of various blockchain tools and techniques/methods that are available in the market. However, the current understanding of the world is still insufficient and very few aspects are known yet. To verify the claims that are made in several research journals,

Hybridization of Blockchain and Cloud Computing: Overcoming Security Issues in IoT.
M. Lawanya Shri, E. Gangadevi, K. Santhi, & Chiranji Lal Chowdhary (Eds.)
© 2024 Apple Academic Press, Inc. Co-published with CRC Press (Taylor & Francis)

and reports on gray literature as a means to focus on our assessment and capturing the rapidly growing blockchain technology, are included in this review chapter.

7.1 INTRODUCTION

Blockchain came into existence in 2009, after the great recession that happened in 2008 when the world's 4th greatest investment bank Lehman Brothers failed. After the fall of Lehman Brothers, the world had lost confidence in the banking system and gradually started looking for an alternative solution where cryptocurrencies started becoming popular. An unknown person/group Satoshi Nakamoto [4] who is presumed to be the one who developed Bitcoin which was the first cryptocurrency that works on the concept of blockchain. Blockchain is the peer-to-peer linked structure where each node is carrying some data and is connected to adjacent nodes. Blockchain has high-security features due to the node-like structure and the cryptography techniques used to develop it. Also, the blockchain does not have any centralized authority due to which it was used in the past without any taxation. It was widely used in crypto-trading and financial markets in different financial institutions such as payment industries, cross-border money transfers, etc. Crypto-currency was assumed to be a single currency around the world for these reasons [5].

Blockchain is also called a distributed ledger, because of its distributed database. This technology is very much useful in the financial sector because it solves a lot of problems that the current system has like governance in which the central system is the supreme power, the centralized ledger which can be easily hacked, money laundering stilling the money in the international transfer. Blockchain is a technology that helps the financial system to remove all those drawbacks from the system. So, how does Blockchain solve these problems? [10–12].

Blockchain has some features like smart contracts which will be the new future of dealing, a cryptocurrency which will be the new form of currency in the future. It also uses cryptocurrencies like Bitcoin, Ethereum, and there are others too but these two are popular [17].

This chapter is divided into multiple sections viz; Section 7.2 is based on "Key Concepts of Blockchain;" Section 7.3 is based on "Use of Blockchain in Financial and Banking Sectors;" Section 7.4 is based on the "Security in Blockchain."

7.2 KEY CONCEPTS OF BLOCKCHAIN

Before proceeding to the chapter, there are a few terms that are needed to be discussed.

7.2.1 TYPES OF BLOCKCHAIN

There are mainly three types of blockchain that exist in today's world scenario, which are discussed in the following subsections.

7.2.1.1 PUBLIC BLOCKCHAIN

A public blockchain is an open-source permissionless network where anyone can join that network. A public blockchain is said to be the world's largest blockchain network in the world [9].

An example of a public blockchain is Bitcoin. Bitcoin is the first decentralized cryptocurrency that is the most popular and largely established in the market. In Public blockchain, participants join the network and begin participating in blockchain transactions and verifying by adding into the network. A public blockchain is good as anyone can join the network, but this could also lead to a problem when so many operations are going on the blockchain, it will slow down the transaction speed by little. Slow speed will not be easily seen but if compared to the old speed it will show you the difference [12].

7.2.1.2 PRIVATE BLOCKCHAIN

It is a private network that is closed and to join this network, permission is required that. A private key and public are so required to join this network. A private blockchain is just the opposite of a public blockchain. In a public blockchain, anyone can come and can start sharing and participating in the transaction and join the network but in a private blockchain, some sort of invitation is required. Without invitation, no one can go into the network [9].

For example, suppose a company named ABC Pvt. Ltd. wants to set up the blockchain network so they will go for the private blockchain and invite only the accounts department and higher officials of the company.

Another example supposes a bank needs to send money to another bank but they don't want to use the public blockchain as other members on the public blockchain can see the transaction so in this case, they will use the private blockchain and invite only the bank with whom they want to make the transaction.

7.2.1.3   FEDERATED BLOCKCHAIN

A federated blockchain is said to be a mixture (hybrid) of both private and public blockchain. It has the same security as private blockchain, but it partially allows the other users from the single point, i.e., leader nodes [2].

7.2.2   DISTRIBUTED LEDGER

Ledgers are the old way of keeping records as before the 20th century the transactions are recorded on the paper and it becomes very difficult if there are a lot of transactions. So, In the 20th century, when computers started taking over the market, a new way of record-keeping was introduced, but that was not accepted by the majority as all preferred the old way of keeping books.

Then in the 21st century when computers became more advanced and provided some great features and tools for record-keeping. Then it is accepted by everyone.

For example, suppose everyone has an account at ABC Bank. So, the bank is the central body of everyone's transaction. This is called centralized ledger technology which is being used by the current financial system.

Now comes the problem of a centralized ledger. Suppose if something happens to the ABC bank (previous example) like if the bank gets shut down, then all the money of every person will go away or if the bank turns into a fraud.

Giving so much power to someone is risky so Distributed Ledger comes into existence. Distributed Ledger is a technology used for recording the transaction assets in which the transaction and their details are stored in different locations. Distributed Ledger doesn't have a central database so no information is stored in a single place. In Distributed Ledger, every transaction is verified, and then it is assigned to a node that carries the information of the transaction. Distributed Ledger can store static data like registry and dynamic data like transactions.

So how does a distributed ledger solve the problem of the centralized ledger? So, in a centralized ledger, there is only one ledger or a database that can be easily hacked or manipulated, but in a distributed ledger, there are lots of ledgers that are stored in multiple places and every ledger shows the transaction of one entity.

1. **Working:** After every transaction, the details of the transactions are verified and then loaded into the blockchain nodes. Normally there are bundles of the transaction that are transferred to the blockchain and blockchain chains all the transactions together and after that, the blockchain process continues.

   If someone wants to see the transaction it is fast as for a particular person there is a particular node. Unlike a centralized ledger where all the information is in one place.

2. **Benefits:** No need for the middle man or the central authority which also slows the transaction. It is more secure than a centralized system as all the information is distributed and if someone tries to change anything they have to change all the other nodes also and changing a huge number of nodes is very difficult. It also reduces the transaction cost. It is also very transparent as any change that occurs is witnessed by all the other nodes.

7.2.3 CRYPTOCURRENCY

When we are talking about blockchain then there is an important term named cryptocurrency. Cryptocurrency is a type of currency that can be used as a type of currency that is accepted in the world. Cryptocurrency refers to digital currency which is used as money. In starting cryptocurrency is limited. It is like money that is being used online. There were many attempts to make a cryptocurrency, but all the attempts failed because of a lack of technologies at that time but in 2009, a group of developers or a developer-built Bitcoin using blockchain technology.

After all these benefits there are some questions also first is it possible to identify the actual value of the cryptocurrency as in the current system Kuwait dinar is the highest value currency in the world you will get 0.30 Kuwait dinar for 1 dollar and if in India you will see Rs. 240. So if we see creating a currency common to all is not that easy so for that some strategies need to be found [12].

Second, currently, blockchain tells about the amount but keeping track of the cryptocurrency is difficult [12].

Third, there is a question that all the cryptography, encryption, and other technology are used to create a cryptocurrency how accounting professionals and other professional audits or check the information with accuracy? [12].

If we have talked about the real-world comparison so now, we should also see if cryptocurrency is applied to how the government applies a tax on the cryptocurrency [12].

7.2.4 TAXATION OF CRYPTOCURRENCY

Internal Revenue Services (IRS) has issued a notice 2014–2021 on March 5, 2014, that taxpayers should consider digital currency (cryptocurrency) as a property, so any tax that includes on the property will also apply to the cryptocurrency.

IRS section 1.1001-1: if there is any property exchange like from property to cash or property to another property after doing that if any loss or gain happened, it will be considered as income or the loss [12].

If a taxpayer holds currency for more than one year, it is considered as a long-term capital gain which is taxed as 20% as per the income tax office. If the taxpayer holds the currency for exactly one year or less, it will be considered taxed up to height individual tax that is 30%. If a taxpayer does any activity like a sale or buy or exchange 1,000 times each time it is considered as an individual transaction and it will become 1,000 taxable events [12].

There are many types of cryptocurrencies:

i.   bitcoin;
ii. ethereum;
iii. lite coin;
iv. ripple, etc.

7.2.4.1 ETHEREUM

Ethereum is developed by Vitalik Buterin, who envisioned it as the most powerful currency exchange. Ethereum is a computer network that is used to exchange cryptocurrency. It is similar to bitcoin as its structure is likely similar to bitcoin. Bitcoin is the first and the largest established in the world and after that Ethereum came into existence and gained popularity and became second (next to bitcoin). Ethereum works on the Ethereum blockchain. Ethereum is different from Bitcoin only in that Ethereum provides two new features smart contract and crowdfunding.

Before creating the fully functional Ethereum, the application was limited to some basic operations like Bitcoin. For example, Bitcoin is considered an exclusive peer-to-peer network. Earlier Ethereum is also like that, but the owner of Ethereum thought of some new features and things like smart contracts, crowdfunding, and Ethereum virtual machine (EVM).

Vitalik Buterin thought that except for creating a new blockchain why don't we use the already existing blockchain and when he visualized Ethereum they using the term EVM but what does the machine mean?

EVM is an isolated network that is a runtime environment for smart contracts. An isolated environment means that its processes work away from the other processes of the host computer. Every node on the Ethereum blockchain runs the EVM implementation and all the operations done on the EVM are also done simultaneously on the host computer. This process is called 'gas' which is a transaction code that triggers read and writes and does some extensive computations. The transaction is measured in Ethereum in gas. Each time a gas unit is paid when the use of 'ether' happens. 'Ether' is nothing but the coin currency of Ethereum.

EVM is also used to test some of the operations as it is isolated from the main blockchain so any operation will not affect the blockchain operations. Some think that EVM is used to understand Ethereum but it is more of that it shows the decentralized feature or the Blockchain. We have seen smart contracts many times so what are these smart contracts?

7.2.4.2 SMART CONTRACTS

A smart contract is a line of code executed when the conditions are matched simply put that it is a program that is executed by the developers. The benefit of a smart contract is that it creates some kind of agreement through which both the parties have to do without any middleman [17].

➢ *What Does a Smart Contract Do?*

To explain this, we can use an example like suppose you want to buy a house so for that a complex process is there that first, you have to deal with the dealer then you have to finance yourself to buy a house for that you will take a loan from the bank and then there is a lot of paperwork you have to do.

Except for all this stressful work you have to wait for the loan to be approved from the bank and all the way, you have interacted with the bank, broker, and dealer.

But using smart contract banks can see the details of your and release the funds on the blockchain then those funds are accepted by the dealer and the house is purchased. As the dealer and bank can see all the details of the buyer on the blockchain and fill in all the necessary information of the user. In normal procedure, if the dealer does some fraud and doesn't give the house you can file a court case, but there is less than you will win but in a smart contract, all the information is stored on the blockchain and shared with everyone those who are on the network. So, it also solves the problem of fraud.

➢ *How Does a Smart Contract Work?*

Smart contracts work on simple if/else/when conditions like if this is done then do something else, do something or when something bad happens to do something else. A network of computers executes an action like a release fund, receives funds, registering a vehicle, etc., when all the conditions are met. The blockchain is then updated when the transaction is completed [17].

For example, suppose Amazon uses this blockchain smart contract. So, the buyer buys a product from Amazon and Amazon uses the shipper to ship the product to the buyer after receiving the product buyer puts the money on the network which is received by Amazon and the shipper. But what if the buyer didn't receive the product on time, then the transaction is canceled and the contract will close. After successful execution, Amazon tells the manufacturer to increase the supply. All this is done automatically.

So, if a smart contract needs to do all these things, how will it know what to do? So, for that, the stakeholder needs to tell the developer to set the terms and conditions to make the transaction successfully. It involves how transaction and their data is represented, agree on the rules that govern the transaction, exploring all the possible exception, defining framework of resolving disputes, usually this is the iterative process which requires both the developer and the stakeholder.

7.2.4.2.1 Benefits

1. **Speed and Accuracy:** The smart contract is a program so it will execute fast so users don't fill in the details manually or go through the complex and time-consuming process. A smart contract is also accurate as it is a predetermined code or rules or it will execute automatically if you don't use the smart contract then human errors are common.
2. **Trust:** The smart contract is code that is predetermined and executes accordingly it will not stop the work also the feature of encrypted data ensures that the data cannot go into the wrong hands but in any case, if it goes in the wrong hand no one can understand it but if we don't use the smart contract then another party can do fraud, we cannot trust humans.
3. **Security:** The smart contract is secured because of the encrypted data and it is not easy to hack. Every node on the blockchain is connected to the previous block and corresponding distributed ledger if someone wants to do any changes that they have to alter all the connected records which is kind of impossible.
4. **Savings:** The smart contract removes the middleman, as the user can trust the visual data and also can trust the code to execute the transaction. There is no need for a middleman to tell the user about the agreement completion because it is built into the code.

7.3 USE OF BLOCKCHAIN IN THE FINANCIAL AND BANKING SECTOR

7.3.1 CRYPTOCURRENCY TRADING

After bitcoin was introduced in 2008, public trading started in the year 2009. After the slow growth of cryptocurrency, the most famous cryptocurrency to be traded was Bitcoin. It was heavily traded and the valuation of it was calculated in dollars. Its value was USD 10 in 2009 and in June 2017, its value rose to USD 3000. After that, a lot of investors started investing in cryptocurrency. In the chapter, it is stated that the investment portfolio can be increased in two ways, first is to decrease the standard deviation to the minimum, and in a second way, it is proposed that to allocate 5% to 20% depending on the risk tolerance level of the investor [8].

7.3.2   BLOCKCHAIN IN FINANCE TRADE MODEL

In the day, business involves the practice of giving and take, the buyer has to pay the amount of money to purchase the goods from the seller which takes time to be confirmed from the seller side, and also it can be pretty risky if there is a lack of trust from both the parties, if there is no proper documentation about the transaction the seller can deny about the payment also. The trading system works on the promise system that the seller promises to send the goods as soon as they receive the payment from the buyer. So, in the chapter, it is discussed that if we use the blockchain technique which is known as smart contracting, where all the parties agree to the agreement and the and a single blockchain is implemented to store the data of the transactions, which increases the trust in the trade as well as accountability in the trade. Also, the invoices and the credit proof can be stored in it, which will be visible to both the parties, and the data stored are irreversible [7].

7.3.3   SUSTAINABLE KYC AND BLOCKCHAIN IN BANKING SECTORS

In the banking sector, one of the important factors is to store the data of the customers in the database. As we go to the bank for the account opening, the first step is to get the Know Your Customer (KYC) done in the bank. The KYC process involves getting the basic information of the customer, the biometric verification, and the document verification which is a very hectic task, yet a very important step. The KYC process is slow and time-consuming. There are many challenges faced by banks that are verification of the data provided by the customers, customer on boarding, tracking the credit/loan history, monitoring the transactions, etc.

This chapter [3] discusses that to overcome these challenges faced by the banking sector, blockchain can be used in many ways to fasten up the process of KYC, the blockchain technology that can be used to solve this problem is public blockchain which is open-sourced and hence contribution can be made by all the banks in the same network, but as we know in public blockchain the data is visible to every user and the presence of sensitive data, hybrid/federated blockchain can be used for this purpose. By using this it will be assured that the data will be irreversible and cannot be manipulated, the limited number of authorized users will only be allowed to use this blockchain system. This process will not only make the KYC process faster but more efficient as the data stored is very secured.

The data sharing can be governed by using the smart contract between the parties involved in this transaction/process. The secured KYC process will decrease the fraud happening in the bank nowadays. Many larger investment banks such as Goldman Sachs, Barclays have also joined the forces [2].

One more advantage of using blockchain for KYC is EMI or Loan Approval for the customers. Banks fail due to the non-performing assets (NPA) under them, the continuous failure in repayment of the loan increases the debts on the bank and hence smart contracting can help the banks in repayment of loans, to get the properties which are kept as collateral and sell them to recover the loan amount [6].

7.3.4   *MONEY TRANSFERS IN CROSS BORDERS USING BLOCKCHAIN*

In the global market, trade is not limited to a single country. Cross-border trade is very common nowadays. The same concept of Blockchain in the finance trade model applies here. So, there must be a proper pipeline for the trade to happen. The trust factor and transaction management can be managed by smart contracting, as discussed above, but the exchange of money is the issue as in different countries, the transactions happen in different currency notes. So, cross-border money exchange is one of the major issues that trade faces in day-to-day life. So, there is a need for a legitimate way to transfer money for the trade to happen.

A few of the challenges that are faced in cross-border money exchange are high transaction fees, high processing time, low availability of resources, and less transparency [5].

In the Ref. [5] paper, the methodology of sending money across the border is explained. In this chapter, the use of e-wallets to send cryptocurrency namely bitcoin or Ethereum is explained. The chapter explains by doing the KYC, the verification process will become very easy and the users will be fit-for-trade. The user can send the crypto token as per the demand of the trade and whereas the smart contracts will help to validate the transaction. A wallet is software that is used to store crypto tokens. The crypto tokens can be stored in the wallets where the public key and the private key are stored, and whenever a user wants to send money to the other user, they generally transfer the ownership to them, and hence the crypto token is reflected in the receiver's wallet. And due to this wallet transaction, it can happen in a decentralized manner and a secure manner.

7.3.5   TRACKING OF CURRENCY NOTES USING BLOCKCHAIN

In our daily life, we buy and sell to purchase goods according to our needs. The major portion of that is done in cash rather than digital currency. So, the question arises what if our currency notes get stolen or spoilt? In the chapter [1], the ideology of scanning the currency notes using the mobile phone which will give us the GPS location with the timestamp combined with the serial number of the notes using image processing and this recording of complete data in the blockchain ledger, so that in future the currency notes serial number can be tracked and local movement of currency notes can be tracked using this. The data stored in the blockchain will be secured and irreversible and so if the currency notes will be stolen the serial number will be marked and again when it will be used in the next location for scanning the amount can be traced back to the one who stole it.

In the chapter [1], they found out mean accuracy of 86.42% after testing it with 110 banknotes with 21 different users. The process of scanning money is very slow and less accurate as stated. Scanning every note before making a transaction can be a difficult task.

One of the major advantages according to me of tracking the currency notes is money laundering which is done illegally, the government does not have a record of the movement of money which can be used in funding the terrorists or bribing. The illegal money movement and the person/group who is supporting it can be traced and the wrong deeds can be suppressed.

7.4   SECURITY IN BLOCKCHAIN

Security in blockchain has a wide aspect to look at. As far as security is concerned, there has been much research about several kinds and types of attacks that hinder the mechanism of blockchain. However, the solutions to all have not been found out, but several remarkable research has been accomplished in coming up with suitable and appropriate solutions to several problems. This chapter lists some of those attacks and threats that are dealt with by using several different techniques developed across the globe.

Since blockchain is defined as a chain of blocks that store information and managed by a peer-to-peer network efficiently and in a verifiable way, there is a very high possibility that the peer or other mechanism help in attacking or breaking or in an alternative case bring information about the peer who handles the different accounts bring out or express the crucial and sensitive information used to manage the process. Also, the blockchain in finance is done through online transactions that have to rely on third-party financial institutions, but it may cause leakage of personal privacy and security threats.

7.4.1 SECURE CRYPTO-CURRENCY SCHEME BASED ON POST-QUANTUM BLOCKCHAIN

Besides, public-key cryptography plays a very fundamental role in the security of the blockchain. Currently, Elliptic Curves Cryptography (ECC) is used in blockchain. Its security is based on the intractability of the elliptic curve discrete algorithm problem. This technique uses lattice-based cryptography to increase the security in the post-quantum blockchain (PQB) [18]. It has been discovered and tried that if the combination of post-quantum cryptography with blockchain is used then it could give a more secure cryptocurrency scheme. It has been verified that such a scheme can even resist quantum computing attacks [18]. Besides the post-quantum cryptography, this scheme includes Hash function-based cryptography, lattice-based cryptography to make the signature, and other algorithms. Using these algorithms PQB can resist the quantum computing attack and assures a higher level of security. It is considered that only signing keys which use the hash functions are not up to the mark in playing the role of a secure scheme while protecting cryptocurrencies. That is the reason a new signature scheme based on lattice signature algorithm [18] is developed so that third parties which previously generated the secret keys are eliminated and secret keys are selected by the user by selecting a random value each time. Therefore, a combination of PQB and post-quantum cryptography is used to provide up-to-mark security. The exact scheme states that suppose Alice and Bob trade through a cryptocurrency scheme based on PQB and Alice transfers her crypt-currency to Bob. The scheme is processed in such a manner that if and only if Alice has generated the signature, the transaction takes place; otherwise it is rejected. There is effective and efficient communication between minors, who are responsible to add blocks in the blockchain and once Bob verifies the transaction, the cryptocurrency is transferred [18].

7.4.2 HYBRID BLOCKCHAINS

Public blockchains [19] have been used to manage several cryptocurrencies. This kind of blockchain allows every participant who is involved in the transaction to observe all the transactions and data stored in it. Now, this feature results in big privacy concerns as crucial and sensitive information get leaked. Also, private blockchains [19] have emerged as more privacy-preserving solutions but still face a lot of issues. In such a blockchain only the parties involved can see the transaction but if it is to be publicly announced, no way can be done. Therefore, a hybrid blockchain was developed in this chapter [19] so that the right aspects from both the blockchain can be taken into account and put into a hybrid version of it. These kinds are majorly used where accountability information is maintained while limiting the amount of sensitive information that is disclosed. It has been proposed this hybrid blockchain scheme for online auctions. They make the system secured as using public smart contract the cheating (if done) by the auctioneer can be detected using their studies [19]. Thought one aspect remains unsolved that is if there is a collision (whilst declaring the highest bidder the second-highest bidder shall also be disclosed, if not then the auctioneer's cheating cannot be caught) [19]. Though majorly this technique solves a lot of the problematic phase but still needs work to establish its perfect role in blockchain techniques. Also, this technique leaves many privacy control issues like who all should get the results and who all should be allowed to see the insider information that is who all are bidding for later research.

7.4.3 SMART CONTRACTING AND BLOCKCHAIN

Smart contract-based blockchain has been proposed already, but it adds to the additional cost and difficulty in deployment to developers and infrastructure builders. Therefore, a new scheme called ChainIDE [20] where IDE is Integrated Development Environment is developed so that blockchain-based smart contracts can become more efficient. A smart contract defines the rules between different organizations in executable code. Combining with blockchain systems, the smart contract will be invoked and a series of transactions will be generated to be recorded on the ledger with verification [20]. There can be issues regarding source codes [calling some unknown function or block, completing a transaction without ETH (Ether), and several coding hindrances like exception disorder, and field disclosure]. Also, Bytecode issues can come up when coding is not precisely taken care of. Bugs have been reported to be a great problem that results in an unpredictable state, stack overflow/underflow. Sometimes an attacker can take full control over the victim's network and find loopholes in block propagation and further doing practices like selfish mining, splitting mining power, etc., that will obviously in turn crash every data [21].

7.4.4 KYC WALLET SYSTEM

Cryptocurrency providers provide wallet services to store crypto coins or tokens. The wallet application undergoes a few steps like authentication, authorization, and access control mechanism [21]. This system has several issues à stolen key – the wallets do not store private key so the private key can be easily stolen and the amount could be used by any person to whom it does not belong, though this private key problem in explicit blockchain employment is solved by the new signature-based techniques [18] new techniques concerning these should be brought to be deployed in the KYC wallet systems. Also Ref. [22] gives a new model that helps to analyze the transitory states and parameters, this best enables an air-gapped wallet user to know the risks that are associated with air-gapped wallet and how to mitigate them as best as possible; lack of control in address creation à according to Ref. [21] there is a major blemish or defect in the design of blockchain that is no restriction on Wallet address creation and there is a lack of identity check or KYC. Anonymous users are supposed to be eliminated from this chain to get a very secure and highly dependable blockchain system regarding the Wallet Systems.

7.4.5 *DATA ACCESS AND SHARING APPROACH FOR TRADE DOCUMENTATION*

In every country trade across every kind of border, be it domestic or international, plays a major role in its development. Trade involves many kinds of documentation that have to be dealt with in a very specific and secure manner. Data and documents have to be shared with other businesses as well as the government for smooth business functioning. Now during these transactions, there could be any kind of malfunctioning or sensitive data leakage with the existing systems and protocols. That too India is popular for its big bureaucratic systems, it is quite natural and innate that such types of problems would be faced by both the businesses and the government. In Ref. [23], the authors have come up with a very secure and dependable attribute-based encryption (ABE) approach for trade document access and sharing using blockchain technology. The data access and control policy work on two bases: (i) data access control and sharing model which is proposed in this chapter; (ii) smart contract. The model deploys two main systems, i.e., blockchain and interplanetary file system (IPFS) that act as a storage device for critical information and a trusted network for cross-border trade platforms. Also, this scheme uses a permission blockchain which restricts access depending upon the specifications. Another very crucial aspect of using this technique is that it takes out transactions towards a more paperless world where things are transparent, quick, and there is no bureaucratic hindrance.

7.4.6 *DOUBLE SPENDING*

Although consensus mechanisms can validate transactions that take place using blockchain, it is not possible to avoid double-spending. Double spending [24] refers to the scenario when a customer uses its cryptocurrency multiple times for the same transaction. It is believed to be an unsolvable threat to the blockchain system. Here the attacker takes advantage of the intermediate time between two transactions' initiation and confirmation [24]. It quickly gets into that time, launches its attack, and gets the transaction of the first output. The time taken by two transactions can be made limited but not to any of the extent that an attacker cannot intervene in it. If we choose to get the address jumped from one to another, the dummy address will affect the reverse tracing of the transactions.

Therefore, to avoid such attacks we have to depend on the users to validate the legitimacy of the bitcoin used as an input to the transaction, using this information stored in the blockchain from previous transactions, the users validate the inputs of any new transactions to ensure it does not contain any previously spent inputs [25].

7.4.7 DENIAL OF SERVICE (DOS)

Denial of Service (DoS) attacks fill up the network with spurious traffic to play havoc with legitimate services and participating constituents connected to the bitcoin network. Some nodes preferably connect to bitcoin as a private network to restrict the possibility of getting into the trap of becoming victims of DoS attacks. Bitcoin developers are continuous without major gaps updating the Bitcoin implementation to decrease and take the chances of DoS occurrences to the lowest. The newer versions analyze the network connections with a closer approach to try to eradicate suspicious nodes so that they don't get connected. Here is also no assurance of the legitimacy of the eight outgoing connections each private node connects to. This means that even a private node can still be vulnerable to a DoS attack if it, unfortunately, enters into a connection with non-legitimate nodes. New transactions/blocks are given priority over less important ones such as orphan transactions/blocks [25].

7.4.8 ISSUES IN THE INTERNET OF THINGS

In IoT, chances of arising issues in several aspects is very likely to happen with ease. There are various areas to look upon like à security issues, privacy concerns, interoperability issues, legal, and regulatory issues, rights issues, emerging economic issues like infrastructure resources, technical, and industrial development. There can be several more issues that can come in the future which right now have not been even thought of. The blockchain could be a very efficient solution for all. Blockchain can provide inviolate data, trustless, and messaging possibility in peer to peer, robust, highly reliable, more private data, records the historic actions, documentation of transactions performed earlier in smart devices, allows the self-directing function, distributed file sharing (DFS) like distributed ledger, eradication of single control authority and all the middlemen, cost reduction in developing huge internet infrastructure, built-in trust, accelerate transactions. To maneuver the vast data processed in large-scale IoT systems, there is a need for escalating the internet infrastructure. An appropriate course of action to resolve this is to have decentralized or distributed networks where "Peer-to-Peer Networking (PPN), DFS, and Autonomous Device Coordination (ADC)" functions could be capable. Blockchain can carry out these three functions allowing the IoT systems to track the huge number of connected and networked devices [26].

7.5 CONCLUSION

We have conducted a comprehensive study on blockchain technology, its application in the financial and banking sectors, and its open security issues. Blockchain is a booming technology that holds a huge potential now. A lot of our issues can be solved using this technology. All the applications that we discussed above are only a few aspects of this huge domain. But there are many irregularities in this technology, for example, when the Government of India banned crypto trading and it portrayed a negative image on those citizens who were unknown to this technology and it made a bad name in the market. So rather than banning trading, there must be some rules to be made to regulate the usage of bitcoin in India. The industry has started adopting this technology slowly, but it requires active participation from the industry. There are a lot of aspects yet to be explored by the world, and it will be better if the security loopholes are fixed.

KEYWORDS

- **blockchain technology**
- **elliptic curves cryptography**
- **Ethereum virtual machine**
- **internal revenue services**
- **know your customer**
- **non-performing assets**

REFERENCES

1. Mohamed, K., Aziz, A., Mohamed, B., Abdel-Hakeem, K., Mostafa, M., & Atia, A., (2019). Blockchain for tracking serial numbers in money exchanges. *Intell. Sys. Acc. Fin. Mgmt., 26*, 193–201. https://doi.org/10.1002/isaf.1462

2. Casino, F., Dassaklis, T. K., & Patsakis, C., (2019). A systematic literature review of blockchain-based applications: Current status, classification, and open issues. *Telematics and Informatics, 36*, 55–81. https://doi.org/10.1016/j.tele.2018.11.006

3. Kulkarni, V., & Singh, A. P., (2019). Sustainable KYC through blockchain technology in global banks. *Annals of Dunarea De Jos University of Galati. Fascicle I. Economics and Applied Informatics, 25*(2), 34–38. https://doi.org/10.35219/eai1584040929

4. Nakamoto, S., (2008). *BitCoin: A Peer-to-Peer Electronic Cash System.* Retrieved from: https://bitcoin.org/bit coin.pdf (accessed on 11 August 2022).

5. Sood, A., & Simon, R., (2019). Implementation of blockchain in cross border money transfer. In: *4th International Conference on Information Systems and Computer Networks (ISCON)* (pp. 104–108). GLA University, Mathura, UP, India. Mathura, UP: IEEE.

6. Nir, K., & Jeffrey, V., (2018). *Blockchain in Developing Countries.* The University of North Carolina at Greensboro; Published by the IEEE Computer Society IEEE.

7. Somayaji, S. R. K., Alazab, M., Manoj, M. K., Bucchiarone, A., Chowdhary, C. L., & Gadekallu, T. R. (2020, December). A framework for prediction and storage of battery life in IoT devices using dnn and blockchain. In *2020 IEEE Globecom Workshops (GC Wkshps* (pp. 1–6). IEEE.

8. Chauhan, V., & Arora, G., (2019). A review paper on cryptocurrency & portfolio management. In: *2019 2nd International Conference on Power Energy, Environment and Intelligent Control (PEEIC)* (pp. 60–64). G. L. Bajaj Inst. of Technology and Management Greater Noida, U. P., India, Greater Noida, UP IEEE.

9. Kolekar, S., Bachal, S., More, R., & Yenkikar, A., (2018). Review paper on untwist blockchain: A data handling process of blockchain systems. In: *2018. International Conference on Information, Communication, Engineering and Technology (ICICET)* (pp. 1–5). Zeal College of Engineering and Research. Narhe, Pune, India. Pune, Maharashtra: IEEE.

10. Zachariadis, M., Hileman, G., & Scott, S. V. (2019). Governance and control in distributed ledgers: Understanding the challenges facing blockchain technology in financial services. *Information and Organization, 29*(2), 105–117.

11. Dozier, P. D., & Montgomery, T. A., (2020). Banking on blockchain: An evaluation of innovation decision making. *IEEE Transactions on Engineering Management, 67*(4),1129–1141. doi: 10.1109/tem.2019.2948142.

12. Smith, S. S., Petkov, R., & Lahijani, R., (2019). Blockchain and cryptocurrencies–considerations for treatment and reporting for financial services professionals. *The International Journal of Digital Accounting Research, 59*–78. doi: 10.4192/1577-8517-v19_3.

13. Peterson, M., (2018). Blockchain and the future of financial services. *The Journal of Wealth Management, 21*(1), 124–131. doi:10.3905/jwm.2018.21.1.124.

14. Bosco, F., Croce, V., & Raveduto, G., (2018). In: *Blockchain Technology for Financial Services Facilitation in RES Investments.* Institute of Electrical and Electronics Engineers. doi: 10.1109/RTSI.2018.8548505.

15. Jumde, A., Hazarika, I., & Cho, B. Y., (2019). In: *BlockChain Technology: A New Enabler of Financial Services*. Institute of Electrical and Electronics Engineers. doi: 10.1109/ITT48889.2019.9075091.

16. Ahmed, K. B., & Kumar, D., (2019). In: *Blockchain Use Cases in Financial Services for Improving Security* (pp. 1–5). Noida, UP Amity Institute of Information Technology. doi:10.1109/ICISC44355.2019.9036406.

17. Vinayak, M., dos Santos, S., Thulasiram, R. K., Thulasiraman, P., & Appadoo, S. S. (2019, October). Design and implementation of financial smart contract services on blockchain. In *2019 IEEE 10th Annual Information Technology, Electronics and Mobile Communication Conference (IEMCON)* (pp. 1023-1030). IEEE.

18. Gao, Y., Chen, X., Chen, Y., Sun, Y., Niu, X., & Yang, Y., (2018). A secure cryptocurrency scheme based on post-quantum blockchain. In: *IEEE Access* (Vol. 6, pp. 27205–27213). doi: 10.1109/ACCESS.2018.2827203.

19. Desai, H., Kantarcioglu, M., & Kagal, L. (2019, July). A hybrid blockchain architecture for privacy-enabled and accountable auctions. In *2019 IEEE International Conference on Blockchain (Blockchain)* (pp. 34-43). IEEE.

20. Wu, X., Qiu, H., Zhang, S., Memmi, G., Gai, K., & Cai, W., (2020). ChainIDE 2.0: Facilitating smart contract development for consortium blockchain. *IEEE INFOCOM 2020 - IEEE Conference on Computer Communications Workshops (INFOCOM WKSHPS)* (pp. 388–393). Toronto, ON, Canada. doi: 10.1109/INFOCOMWKSHPS 50562.2020.9163051.

21. Shrivas, M. K., Dean, T. Y., & Brunda, S. S., (2020). The disruptive blockchain security threats and threat categorization. In: *2020 First International Conference on Power, Control and Computing Technologies (ICPC2T)* (pp. 327–338). Raipur, India. doi: 10.1109/ICPC2T48082.2020.9071475.

22. Davenport, A., & Shetty, S., (2019). Air-gapped wallet schemes and private key leakage in permissioned blockchain platforms. In: *2019 IEEE International Conference on Blockchain (Blockchain)* (pp. 541–545). Atlanta, GA, USA. doi: 10.1109/Blockchain. 2019.00004.

23. Chen, T., Yu, Y., & Duan, Z., (2019). Data access & sharing approach for trade documentation based on blockchain technology. In: *2019 3rd International Conference on Electronic Information Technology and Computer Engineering (EITCE)* (pp. 1732–1736). Xiamen, China. doi: 10.1109/EITCE47263.2019.9095045.

24. Xiaoqi, L., Peng, J., Ting, C., Xiapu, L., & Qiaoyan, W., (2020). A survey on the security of blockchain systems. *Future Generation Computer Systems, 107*, 841–853. ISSN 0167-739X.

25. Zaghloul, E., Li, T., Mutka, M. W., & Ren, J., (2020). Bitcoin and blockchain: Security and privacy. In: *IEEE Internet of Things Journal* (Vol. 7, No. 10, pp. 10288–10313). doi: 10.1109/JIOT.2020.3004273.

26. Nallapaneni, M. K., & Pradeep, K. M., (2018). Blockchain technology for security issues and challenges in IoT. *Procedia Computer Science* (Vol. 132, pp. 1815–1823). ISSN 1877-0509.

CHAPTER 8

Scrutiny of Blockchain Technology

A. MURUGAN[1] and J. VIJAYALAKSHMI[2]

[1]Associate Professor and Head, PG and Research Department of Computer Science, Dr. Ambedkar Government Arts College (Autonomous), Affiliated to University of Madras, Chennai, Tamil Nadu, India

[2]Research Scholar, PG and Research Department of Computer Science, Dr. Ambedkar Government Arts College (Autonomous), Affiliated to University of Madras, Chennai, Tamil Nadu, India

ABSTRACT

Blockchain application is currently recommended in all financial and non-financial services fields. The decentralized infrastructure and peer-to-peer nature of blockchain make users interested in applying in all fields to avoid repudiation. The properties of blockchain, like decentralization, persistency, audibility, and anonymity, make blockchain broader acceptance in industries, health sectors, supply chains, and other sectors. The blockchain helps to store information, perform transaction execution functions, and create trust in an open environment. This research performs the analysis of blockchain in several aspects, like its history, generations, stack organization, architecture construction, storage structure, and the principle of working. Then, the research analysis is carried out in blockchain categories and their main components constituting blockchain. The security threat related to blockchain is analyzed in a deep manner.

Hybridization of Blockchain and Cloud Computing: Overcoming Security Issues in IoT.
M. Lawanya Shri, E. Gangadevi, K. Santhi, & Chiranji Lal Chowdhary (Eds.)
© 2024 Apple Academic Press, Inc. Co-published with CRC Press (Taylor & Francis)

Finally, the application of blockchain in several aspects is discussed. This research makes readers understand blockchain in concepts, system arrangement, security handling, and its use cases in multiple fields.

8.1 INTRODUCTION

In the early days, financial services are carried through banks and other intermediaries like fee-charging gatekeepers, financial traffic managers, security brokers, insurance agents, financial lawyers, credit card companies, etc. [1]. In 2008, the financial market faced a major financial crisis which made the entry of cryptocurrency into the financial world. The father of cryptocurrency was Satoshi Nakamoto, who introduced the first decentralized cryptocurrency named bitcoin [2]. The core mechanism behind bitcoin is blockchain, which Nakamoto first implemented in 2009 [3]. A blockchain is an immutable public ledger that holds all transactions that are shared among multiple participants on the bitcoin network. Blockchain holds a verifiable record of every transaction that happened previously. Blockchain creates trust among pseudonymous parties based on the following attributes: distributed and viable, private, indestructible, transparent, adaptable, consensus-based flexible, valid transaction support, and security [4].

The record-keeping technology behind the bitcoin network is blockchain. This is a special type of database that stores data in blocks and is arranged like a chain. Blockchain holds various types of information but is most commonly used to store transaction records. In the blockchain, all users collectively retain control rather than a single person or group has to control [5]. Blockchain gives guaranteed execution without a trusted third party by publishing the transaction history to all users in the network. The principle of blockchain is a distributed ledger system where the records are not kept on a single node; rather, it is distributed to each and every peer node on the network. Every node on the network keeps an updated copy of the blockchain. The records contain the transaction that specifies the transaction that takes place between any two nodes on the network, which ensures that the network structure is fraud-proof [6].

8.2 BLOCKCHAIN HISTORY

The idea of blockchain technology was introduced by Leslie Lamport in early 1990. He introduced a special model for reaching agreement among unreliable network of computers using distributed consensus model. In 1991, for generating digitally signed documents, a signed chain of information was used as an electronic ledger. Both these concepts were combined and applied to bitcoin in 2008 by Satoshi Nakamoto. The first blockchain application was bitcoin. The blockchain got popular by the use of distributed fashion principle. The primary benefit of blockchain is enabling direct transactions between users without a trusted intermediary. Another purpose is the issuance of new cryptocurrency based on certain principles like miners have to manage publications of new blocks and ledger copy maintenance. The application of blockchain and consensus-based approach ensure that only valid transactions and blocks are added to the blockchain [7].

8.3 BLOCKCHAIN GENERATIONS

8.3.1 STAGE 1

Blockchain was used as a shared public ledger which supports bitcoin cryptocurrency network. Satoshi used 1-megabyte (MB) blocks of information for storing bitcoin transactions. A complex crypto-graphic verification process was used for creating immutable chain of blocks.

8.3.2 STAGE 2

Ethereum symbolizes the second generation of blockchain technology. Blockchain cannot only store simple document transactions but also store assets and trust agreements. Ethereum has introduced a smart contract that can manage itself on a blockchain. The smart contract does not require the input of outside entities which can able to manage itself and make adjustments when there is an event triggering.

8.3.3 STAGE 3

The future of blockchain technology will be the improvement of the expansion of the network. Currently, bitcoin and other digital currencies are facing to solve the network enhancement issue through scalability features [8].

8.4 BLOCKCHAIN STACK

The technology stack of blockchain includes the following layers, which are shown in Figure 8.1 [9]:

- internet layer;
- blockchain protocol layer;
- application layer; and
- user experience layer.

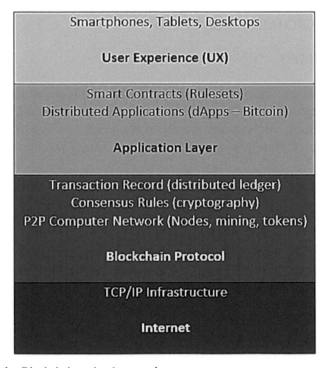

FIGURE 8.1   Blockchain technology stack.

8.4.1 INTERNET LAYER

The foundation layer behind blockchain is the Internet layer. This layer specifies how data is transmitted as packet, addressed, routed, and received among globally interconnected devices such as computers, smartphones, IoT devices, etc. Blockchain protocol works under the current version of the internet (Web3), where P2P interactions are completed without any intermediaries. One of the best-known blockchain applications today is bitcoin. Here, without financial intermediaries support, the values are transferred between any two individuals in a secure manner [9].

8.4.2 BLOCKCHAIN PROTOCOL LAYER

This protocol operates on the internet layer, which completes transactions based on a cryptographic consensus algorithm. This layer support open, shared, and trusted public ledger of transactions. The recorded transactions are immutable and can be verified by anyone on the P2P network [9].

8.4.3 APPLICATION LAYER

The most popular and first blockchain application is bitcoin. The bitcoin network facilitates the development of Decentralized Autonomous Organization (DAO). DAO supports the development of economic value through cryptographic tokens, which are generated in open networks that do not require formal contracts or agreements. Data storage techniques are also needed to develop complex blockchain-based applications beyond consensus algorithm. Another public blockchain, which support custom-built application is Ethereum. Here the tokens are issued as DAO or distributed application (dAPP) tokens [9]. dApps support more complex services through smart contracts.

8.4.4 USER EXPERIENCE LAYER

This layer supports the development of applications like smartphones, tablets, desktop, etc., that we use in our day-to-day activities [9].

8.5 BLOCKCHAIN ARCHITECTURE

The blockchain architecture consists of three layers namely which is represented in Figure 8.2 [10].

- application layer;
- decentralized ledger layer; and
- peer-to-peer network layer.

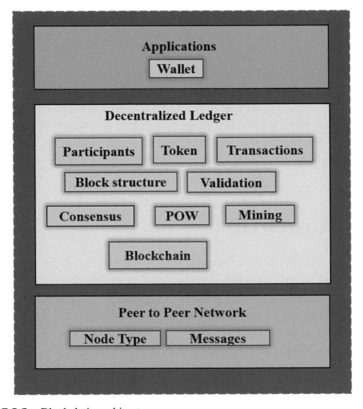

FIGURE 8.2   Blockchain architecture.

8.5.1 APPLICATION LAYER

This layer is based on the decentralized ledger layer maintained on a P2P network. This layer supports the exchange of bitcoins for e-commerce transactions through a wallet which holds user's unspent bitcoins [10].

8.5.2 DECENTRALIZED LEDGER LAYER

This layer consists of several components which ensure that ledger data are immutable and tamper-proof. In this layer, the transactions are arranged into blocks, and it is linked cryptographically to its parent block forming a blockchain. The exchange or movement of token between any two participants is called it as transaction. The network nodes perform the transaction validation which is done in the validation part of the blockchain. Mining is the process of adding transaction to the block of the blockchain [10]. Proof-of-work (POW) section ensures that the transaction is valid based on deriving mutual agreement among all participating nodes on the network.

8.5.3 PEER-TO-PEER NETWORK LAYER

This layer helps for updating and maintaining decentralized ledger based on exchanging various messages among P2P nodes [10]. This layer also specifies additional roles played by nodes in the network.

8.6 BLOCKCHAIN STRUCTURE

Blockchain is an organized data structure that links the blocks as a chain. Each block contains financial transactions that are shared and replicated among P2P nodes on the network. The blocks contain two sections namely block header and block body [3]. Parent blockhash or previous blockhash is included in the block header section. The block body section includes the set of transactions and its transaction counter. A block can hold only one parent block link. The current block contains parent blockhash value, which links the block to the parent block, i.e., previous block. Genesis block is said to be an initial block of blockchain which does not contain parent block hash value. Figure 8.3 represents the organizing structure of blockchain [11]. The blockchain data is written by certain participants and worldwide participants can read it. Blockchain applications' major benefit is that they support easy verification but are harder to modify because fraud data can be easily detected by the participating nodes [12].

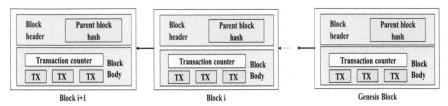

FIGURE 8.3   Blockchain structure.

8.7   BLOCKCHAIN WORKING PRINCIPLE

Figure 8.4 shows the blockchain working principle. Here the buyer generates transaction which is entered into the block. The transactions in the block are validated using cryptographic hashing and it is distributed among P2P nodes. Once the transaction is validated and verified by the miners, the transactions are committed and stored into the distributed database (blockchain) and the miners will get the rewards for their work through new cryptocoins addition to processing fee. The seller collects the amount from the buyer by receiving the transaction [11].

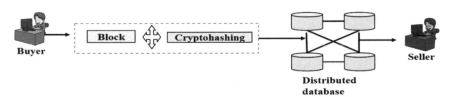

FIGURE 8.4   Blockchain working process.

Blockchain works based on three main concepts, namely [13]:

- blocks;
- miners; and
- nodes.

8.7.1   BLOCKS

A blockchain is constructed based on multiple blocks, and each block holds a block header and block body sections [11]. The block header part includes a coinbase transaction, block version, merkle root, timestamp, parent block hash/previous block hash, difficulty target, and nonce value. The block body part includes a set of transactions in that block and the transaction counter, which counts the transactions that are available in that block. Block version denotes the version of the block that is upgraded based on the validation rule. Merkle root represents the overall transaction hash value of that particular block.

Timestamp denotes the universal current time. Nonce value is a special value used by miners to determine the difficulty target. Parent block hash points to the previous block hash value, which is used to create a chain of blocks from the current block to the genesis block. Genesis block is the first block of the blockchain. The difficulty target signifies the valid block hash threshold value. The difficulty target value is adjusted for every 2016 blocks [14]. Figure 8.5 depicts the structure of bitcoin's block.

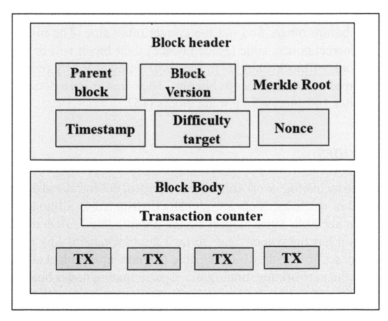

FIGURE 8.5   Block structure of bitcoin.

8.7.2 MINERS

The miner is a special node which is part of the bitcoin network creates new blocks on the blockchain through the mining process. The miner gathers the transaction that are already propagated by the users on the network, organize the transactions into blocks and adds them to the blockchain. To add a new block to the blockchain, the miner has to complete Proof-of-Work (POW) computation for his proposed new block. The proposed block is then broadcasted over the entire bitcoin network. The receiving node in the bitcoin network verifies the incoming blocks coming on the network and add it to the local blockchain copy as leading block [15]. Every block on the blockchain holds its own exclusive nonce, hash, and previous blockhash value. Hence block mining is not easy in larger blockchains like bitcoin.

For the mining process, the miners have to solve POW (amazing complex mathematical problem) for finding nonce value which generates a hash value which is accepted by the entire bitcoin network. This is not an easy work because nonce value takes 32 bits and hash value takes 256 bits their combinations take billion possible combinations that should be mined before others find out the correct one value. The miners who generate correct nonce value (golden nonce) their block will be added as current block of blockchain [13]. They will be awarded by rewards and summation of transaction fees as bitcoins. These rewarded amounts can be claimed after 100 successful mining blocks [15].

8.7.3   NODES

Blockchain technology works under the concept of decentralized distributed ledger where the ledger data are globally distributed to all nodes on the blockchain network. Since blockchain is a decentralized ledger no node or organization has the owner rights to hold the blockchain. Any electronic device can act as a node which capable of maintaining blockchain copy and keeps the network functioning. Each participating nodes holds unique alphanumeric identification number for their transactions. Every node holds its own blockchain copy and for updation of blockchain it needs trusted and verified network which must prove newly mined blocks algorithmically valid [13].

8.8   BLOCKCHAIN CATEGORIES

Blockchain systems are classified into three types, namely [3]:

1. **Public Blockchain:** This blockchain supports free and open access for anyone in the world. Participants are also very much active, e.g., bitcoin.
2. **Private Blockchain:** This blockchain supports limited access to the nodes within the organization. Only one organization node is active all other nodes will be doing their task based on organization node instructions.
3. **Consortium Blockchain:** This blockchain is similar to private blockchain but it can be applied to many business applications, e.g., Ethereum and Hyperledger.

All these blockchains are compared based on the following properties, namely consensus determination, read permission, immutability, efficient, centralized, and consensus process [3]. Table 8.1 shows the comparison of public, private, and consortium blockchain based on the above properties.

TABLE 8.1 Comparison of Different Blockchains

Properties	Public Blockchain	Private Blockchain	Consortium Blockchain
Consensus determination	All miners	One organization	Set of nodes selected
Read permission	Public	Public/restricted	Public/restricted
Immutability	Impossible to tamper	Possible to tamper	Possible to tamper
Efficiency	Low	High	High
Centralized	No	Yes	Partial
Consensus process	Permissionless	Permissioned	Permissioned

8.8.1 CONSENSUS DETERMINATION

Each node will perform the validation part of the consensus process in case of public blockchain. In case of private blockchain, validation of consensus process is fully carried out by an individual organization. In consortium blockchain, only selected set of nodes will perform the validation part of the consensus process [3].

8.8.2 READ PERMISSION

In public blockchain, the transactions can be easily read by all participants on the network whereas write and update permissions are restricted. The read permission is restricted in case of private and consortium blockchains where the organization has to decide about giving read permissions to the participants [3].

8.8.3 IMMUTABILITY

In public blockchains, the transaction data are distributed and stored in multiple nodes. Hence data tampering and modification is impossible. In case of private or consortium blockchain, data tampering and modification is quite easy and it solely depends on the dominant organization [3].

8.8.4 EFFICIENCY

In public blockchains, a large amount of time is needed for transferring blocks and high network safety is needed, which results in the limitation of transaction throughput. In private and consortium blockchains, fewer time, safety, and validators are needed [3].

8.8.5 CENTRALIZED

The public blockchain is a decentralized one where all the data are publicly shared and distributed. In case of private blockchain, the blockchain is fully centralized and it is controlled by a single organization. In case of consortium blockchain, the blockchain is partially centralized [3].

8.8.6 CONSENSUS PROCESS

Any node in the network can join the consensus process of public blockchain. In case of private or consortium blockchains, the organization node needs to certify for joining the consensus process of blockchain [3].

8.9 BLOCKCHAIN COMPONENTS

The blockchain technology is successfully built based on the following components namely [7]:

- Cryptographic hash functions;
- Transactions;
- Asymmetric key cryptography;
- Addresses;
- Ledgers;
- Blocks;
- Blocks chaining.

8.9.1 CRYPTOGRAPHIC HASH FUNCTION

A cryptographic hash function is applied to data from the sender as well as receiver side to prove that the data is valid. The process of applying a cryptographic hash function is called hashing. This proves that there is no change in unique output data (message digest) for given input of any size. Even a single-bit change in input will result in a completely different output. The cryptographic hash function has the following set of properties like preimage resistant, second preimage resistant, and collision resistant. Preimage resistant specifies that from the given output one cannot identify the computation of given input, i.e., input → digest given, finding x such that hash(x)=digest.

Second preimage resistant specifies that the correct input cannot be determined based on the given specific output hash, i.e., input → x given, finding y such that hash(x)=hash(y). Collision resistant specifies that no two inputs hash to the same output, i.e., finding 'x' and 'y' such that hash(x)=hash(y). Cryptographic hash functions are used in blockchain network for a variety of purposes, namely address derivation, unique identifiers creation, block data security, and block header security. Several cryptographic hash functions like SHA256, SHA 3, and RIPEMD-160 are used in blockchain technology. Of this SHA256 is popularly used.

8.9.2 TRANSACTIONS

Transaction is the basic part of the bitcoin network. In the bitcoin network, transferring of bitcoins from one owner to another owner is called a transaction. The wallet generates the bitcoin addresses which is used by the owners during transaction [16]. There may be zero or more transactions inside the block of blockchain. A transaction requires the following information namely inputs and outputs. Inputs represents the transferring list of digital assets. Input of a transaction is a reference to past events where the digital assets won't change.

In Input, a single digital asset can be split into multiple new digital assets, each of having lesser value or multiple digital assets can be combined to form new digital assets of greater value. In the transaction output part splitting or joining of assets will be declared. Outputs are the recipient digital assets account that specify the receiving digital asset value. This output part specifies transferring to digital assets to new owners, the owner identification, and the set of conditions the new owners must satisfy to spend that value. If extra digital assets are received then it is explicitly sent back to the sender as change [7].

8.9.3 ASYMMETRIC KEY CRYPTOGRAPHY

Asymmetric key cryptography uses two keys namely public key and private key that are linked to each other. Public key is kept open and everyone can able to access it whereas private key is kept as secret. These two keys are used for encryption and decryption process. For digital signing of transactions private keys are used. For deriving addresses public keys are used. Public keys can also be used to verify the digital signatures generated using private keys [7].

8.9.4 ADDRESSES

In blockchain network from the user's public key and cryptographic hash function, addresses are derived. These addresses are required for transaction sender and receiver. Addresses are kept public. To generate address, create a public key then apply the cryptographic hash function and converting the hash to text [7].

8.9.5 LEDGERS

The collection of transactions is said to be a ledger. Today, ledgers are stored digitally, owned, and operated by centralized trusted third party or it provides distributed ownership. Blockchain technology enables distributed ownership and distributed physical architecture [7].

8.9.6 BLOCKS

The block contains a list of validated and authentic transactions that are submitted to the blockchain network. The block consists of block header and block body which specifies block version/block number/block height, previous block header's hash value, block hash representation, timestamp, block size, nonce, transaction list and ledger events.

8.9.7 BLOCKS CHAINING

The chaining of blocks is done with the help of previous block hash value, thus forming a blockchain. If there is a change in previous published block hash value, then it would have a different hash value in all subsequent blocks. This makes to identify whether the blocks are altered or not [7].

8.10 BLOCKCHAIN SECURITY

Today, blockchain is most secure because to move any value over blockchain the network nodes must agree that the transaction is valid. To hack it, you can't hack just one system except you have to hack every single computer on that network. According to Bruce Schneier, a cryptographer and security said blockchains are secure whereas the application running on top of the application layer may not be safe [17]. Table 8.2 shows the list of security threats and its reason for that risk occurrence [18].

8.10.1 51% VULNERABILITY

If the hash power owned by a single miner acquires more than 50% of the total blockchain, then 51% vulnerability occurs in blockchains. By firing 51% attack, an attacker can immediately manipulate and modify the blockchain information. The attacker can create vulnerability by creating the following attacks namely [18]:

- Transaction reversible and double-spend attack initiation;
- Ordering of transactions may be modified or excluded;
- Restrict normal mining operations of other miners;
- Hinder the normal transaction confirmation operations.

TABLE 8.2   Blockchain Risk Categories

Risk	Reason
51% vulnerability	Consensus mechanism
Private key security	Public key encryption scheme
Criminal activity	Cryptocurrency application
Double-spending	Transaction verification mechanism
Transaction privacy leakage	Transaction design flaw
Criminal smart contracts	Smart contract application
Vulnerabilities in smart contract	Program design flaw
Under optimized smart contract	Program writing flaw
Underpriced operations	EVM design flaw

8.10.2   PRIVATE KEY SECURITY

In blockchain, the user's private key is kept as identity and security credential which is generated and maintained by users rather than third party agencies. Once the private key is lost or stolen by criminals on the blockchain network the user's blockchain account will face the risk of tampering information by others. Once the private key is stolen, the criminals' behaviors are difficult to track and tedious to recover from the modified blockchain information [18].

8.10.3   CRIMINAL ACTIVITY

The users of bitcoin can have multiple addresses, and the addresses are not linked to any real-life identity. Hence, bitcoin can be used in illegal activities. Some illegal activities include ransomware, underground market, and money laundering [18].

8.10.4 DOUBLE-SPENDING

The process of spending the same bitcoin multiple times in multiple transactions is called double-spend transaction or multi-spend transaction, or irreversible transactions. This attack is very much easy to implement in the bitcoin network because the bitcoin network uses digital money in the form of bits. Bits can be easily stored, replicated, and easily distributed across multiple situations. Figure 8.6 shows the double-spend attack situation [6].

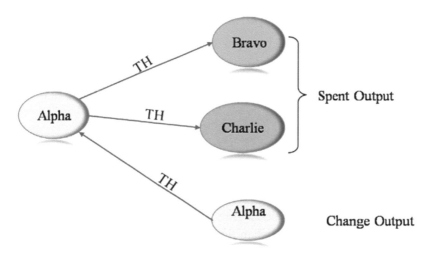

FIGURE 8.6 Double-spend attack.

Here the sender Alpha spends the same input amount (transaction hash: TH) to multiple recipients namely Bravo and Charlie. Here Bravo is the original recipient and Charlie is Alpha's friend. This is the category of double-spend attack. This attack happens when miners behave dishonestly or vendors or client may behave improperly or due to network propagation delay or through bitcoin exchange services. Attacks like race attack, gold finger attack, selfish mining attack, Finney attack and fork after with-holding will easily create double-spend attack [18].

8.10.5   TRANSACTION PRIVACY LEAKAGE

In blockchain user's behaviors are traceable hence it takes protective measures for the user's transaction privacy. In the case of bitcoin, one-time accounts are used to store the received cryptocurrency. In addition to it, the user has to assign a private key for each transaction. By the usage of this technique, the attacker cannot identify whether the cryptocurrency in different transactions is received by the same user or not. Miserably the protective measure of blockchain is not robust because the newer transaction outputs are used frequently as well a greater number of times which tends to security issues like double-spending attack [18].

8.10.6   CRIMINAL SMART CONTRACTS

The smart contracts may be used by the criminals for doing a lot of mischievous activities. The mischievous activities include the leakage of confidential information, stealing of cryptographic keys and doing numerous real-world crimes like murder, terrorism, etc., which may create a threat to our daily life [18].

8.10.7   VULNERABILITIES IN SMART CONTRACTS

Smart contracts may create security vulnerabilities due to program defects. Program defects occur due to transaction ordering dependence, timestamp dependence, mishandled exceptions, or through reentrancy vulnerability [18].

8.11   BLOCKCHAIN UTILIZATION

The application of blockchain technology improves the human lives quality with smart value based on money and rights. Improve the transactions based on smart contracts. Provides smart mobility with driverless and shared vehicles. Allowing smart energy grids based on the power of sustainable energy sources like solar, wind, wave, nuclear, etc. Constructing the smart building with the Internet of Things (IoT) using a network of sensors. Improving the planning, quality, and governance of blockchain applications. Following are the few uses cases of blockchain applications:

- Cryptocurrencies;
- Law enforcement;
- Insurance;
- Banking;
- Capitalism;
- Digital marketing and advertising;
- Assets and right ownership;
- Credit cards;
- Supply chain;
- Voting and governance;
- Health records;
- Crowdfunding via ICO.

8.11.1 CRYPTOCURRENCIES

The application of blockchain to bitcoin cryptocurrency aims to support open access data reading, writing, and lack of centralized power or control. In Bitcoin systems, the blockchain is used to store data and it is distributed through Peer-to-Peer network. Data validation and addition to block is done using a consensus mechanism. Data is stored and retrieved in blockchain using anonymous name. The misbehavior in the bitcoin network is identified through Proof-of-Work (POW) consensus mechanism [11]. Distributed ledger technology (DLT) (blockchain) eliminates the central authority need for verifying property possession and clearing documents [10].

8.11.2 LAW ENFORCEMENT

Law enforcement agencies are working for identifying and preventing the usage of blockchain in various applications. They work as part of Anti-Money Laundering (AML) process. They track the blockchain activities, their accuracy, and criminal activities through blockchain analysis [19], e.g., the US government used blockchain analysis for detecting fraud carried out by Silk Road trading platform.

8.11.3   INSURANCE

In future, insurance transactions will be based on blockchain storage and involve more direct transactions between insurers and consumers. Insurance agent's intermediation, their expenses and inferior services will be minimized. Consumers will get more benefits from insurance like lowering costs, more expedient services and customer focused solutions will be available. Insurers will be benefited like offers wider customer base solutions, fraud detection and removal, and the application of new IoT services [19].

8.11.4   BANKING

There is a huge impact on banking sector due to the application of blockchain. Part of this impact was created by bitcoin. Initially, several bankers try to downplay the impact of cryptocurrencies. Blockchain was accepted by global financial institutions like World Bank, national central bankers and some large bankers had tried to apply the blockchains in their applications [19].

8.11.5   DIGITAL MARKETING AND ADVERTISING

Today social media like Google and Facebook connect advertisers with content generators. Suspicions of fake clicks drive costs for advertisers which create negative impact on the user experience. With blockchain, advertisers can promote their ads directly to users if they permit. There will be identity verification for ads and the ad targeted users can be benefited from these ads. Ad fraud is greatly reduced by these blockchain applications [19].

8.11.6   CREDIT CARDS

A credit card company named Mastercard has launched its own blockchain network to do cross-border payments faster and with high security. This blockchain service uses smart contract to clear credit card transactions and eliminate administration task [20]. Mastercard build blockchain-based settlement networks to create solutions that are auditable, secure, scalable, and safe [21].

8.12 CONCLUSION

This research has made a deep inspection of various fields of blockchain usage. First, it explores about the blockchain then it starts to discuss about how the concept of blockchain arrival in the financial world. Next, this research analyzes the different generations of blockchain-based on various stages. Research starts to inspect the blockchain stack and its purpose of arrangement. Then, auditing starts on the architecture construction of blockchain, its elements, arrangements, and purposes are elaborated. Then its inquiry about the storage structure of blockchain and its working principle. Then it starts with the surveillance of blockchain categories and its components. Then the research moves to the reviewing of security aspect of blockchain. Finally, inspecting the blockchain applications in multiple fields are done successfully.

8.13 FORTHCOMING BLOCKCHAIN IMPROVEMENTS

Currently, blockchain systems mainly focus on consensus mechanisms for performing validation. This POW uses a lot of computing resources. Improvements in consensus mechanisms will develop blockchain usage in wider acceptance of all fields. Another serious issue of blockchain is the privacy leakage problem. Techniques like code obfuscation and application hardening will reduce this privacy leakage problem. Improvements in the usage of data cleanup and detection mechanisms will increase the efficiency of blockchain (a survey on the security of blockchain systems). Blockchain can be applied to all fields if it enhances the development of lightweight cryptographic algorithms (security and privacy of blockchain). Blockchain application will restructure the politics and entire society. Wealth can be protected by applying blockchain. Threats to wealth can be controlled by associating land titles with wealth storage in the blockchain.

KEYWORDS

- **anti-money laundering**
- **blockchain technology**
- **code obfuscation**
- **decentralized autonomous organization**
- **proof-of-work**
- **transaction hash**

REFERENCES

1. Vijayalakshmi, J., & Murugan, A., (2019). Revamp perception of bitcoin using cognizant Merkle. In: *Proceedings of Springer Conference on Emerging Research in Computing, Information, Communication and Application* (Vol. 882, pp. 141–150).
2. Vijayalakshm, J., & Murugan, A., (2017). Crypto coin overview of basic transaction. *International Journal of Applied Research on Information Technology and Computing, 8*(2), 113–120.
3. Zheng, Z., Shaoan, X., Hong-Ning, D., Xiangping, C., & Huaimin, W., (2018). Blockchain challenges and opportunities: A survey. *International Journal of Web and Grid Services, 14*(4), 352–375.
4. Crosby, M., Pradan, P., Sanjeev, V., & Vignesh, K., (2016). Blockchain technology: Beyond bitcoin. Applied *Innovation, 71*(2), 6–10.
5. *Blockchain Technology*. (2022). https://www.investopedia.com/terms/b/blockchain.asp (accessed on 11 August 2022).
6. Murugan, A., & Vijayalakshmi, J., (2020). Detecting multi-block double spent transaction based on B-tree indexing. *International Journal of Scientific and Technology Research, 9*(2), 743–749.
7. Yaga, D., Peter, M., Nik, R., & Karen, S., (2019). *Blockchain Technology Overview*. arXiv,1906(11078).
8. *Blockchain Technology Three Generations*. (2021). https://www.investopedia.com/tech/blockchain-technologys-three-generations/ (accessed on 11 August 2022).
9. *Blockchain Technology Stack*. https://arun-devan.medium.com/the-blockchain-technology-stack-cde66abad791 (accessed on 11 August 2022).
10. *Understanding Blockchains and Bitcoin: Part 2 Technology*. (2017). https://luxsci.com/blog/understanding-blockchains-and-bitcoin-technology.html (accessed on 11 August 2022).
11. Zheng, Z., Shaoan, X., Hongning, D., Xiangping, C., & Huaimin, W., (2017). An overview of blockchain technology: Architecture, consensus, and future trends. In: *Proceedings of IEEE International Congress on Big Data (BigData Congress)* (pp. 557–564) Honolulu.

12. Nofer, M., Peter, G., Oliver, H., & Dirk, S., (2017). Blockchain. *Business and Information Systems Engineering, 59*(3), 183–187.

13. *How Does Blockchain Work*, https://builtin.com/blockchain (accessed on 11 August 2022).

14. Campbell-Verduyn, M., (2018). *Bitcoin and Beyond (Open Access): Cryptocurrencies, Blockchains, and Global Governance.* ISBN: 978-0415792141, Routledge.

15. Bashir, I., (2018). *Mastering Blockchain: Distributed Ledger Technology, Decentralization, and Smart Contracts Explained.* ISBN: 978-1787122147, Packt Publishing Ltd.

16. Askitis, N., & Ranjan, S., (2007). HAT-trie: A cache-conscious trie-based data structure for strings. In: *Proceedings of the Thirtieth Australasian Conference on Computer Science, Australian Computer Society* (Vol. 62, pp. 97–105).

17. *What is Blockchain*, https://www.computerworld.com/article/3191077/what-is-blockchain-the-complete-guide.html (accessed on 11 August 2022).

18. Li, X., Peng, J., Ting, C., Xiapu, L., & Qiaoyan, W., (2020). A survey on the security of blockchain systems. *Future Generation Computer Systems, 107*(2007), 841–853.

19. *Emerging Use Cases of Blockchain Part 1*, https://arun-devan.medium.com/emerging-use-cases-for-the-blockchain-part-1-d5da793753ca (accessed on 11 August 2022).

20. What is blockchain, https://www.computerworld.com/article/3191077/what-is-blockchain-the-complete-guide.html?page=2#toc-5 (accessed on 11 August 2022).

21. *Emerging Use Cases of Blockchain Part 2*, https://arun-devan.medium.com/emerging-use-cases-for-the-blockchain-part-2-f47ccfca8bab (accessed on 11 August 2022).

## CHAPTER 9

The Big Picture of Blockchain Technology for Healthcare Applications

T. VIMALA[1], N. RAJEEV REDDY[1], and R. SHOBARANI[2]

[1]Department of Electronics and Communication Engineering, Dr. M.G.R. Educational and Research Institute, Chennai, Tamil Nadu, India

[2]Department of Computer Science Engineering, Dr. M.G.R. Educational and Research Institute, Chennai, Tamil Nadu, India

ABSTRACT

A blockchain is an appropriated, public record, recording exchange, and following resources, and of which unchanging nature is ensured by a shared organization of PCs, not by any incorporated power. A blockchain comprises of requested records organized in a square structure. Every information block contains a hash (advanced unique finger impression or remarkable identifier), timestamped clumps of ongoing exchanges, and a hash of the precedent square [1]. With this plan, each square is associated with a sequential request, and the associated blocks are considered in this chapter. It is basically difficult to change any particular squares in the blockchain, while the entirety of the squares after the altered square should be adjusted simultaneously. With this system, the information on the blockchain network is unchanging. With this emerging technology, patients can edge with diverse crisis services and accumulate their clinical

Hybridization of Blockchain and Cloud Computing: Overcoming Security Issues in IoT.
M. Lawanya Shri, E. Gangadevi, K. Santhi, & Chiranji Lal Chowdhary (Eds.)

data normally. Many accept that blockchain innovation can change medication and the past.

9.1 INTRODUCTION

Blockchain is a common, invariable record for recording trades, following resources, and building trust. Find why associations in general are accepting it. A blockchain controlled well-being data trade could open the genuine estimation of interoperability. Blockchain-based frameworks can possibly decrease or dispose of the contact and expenses of current go-betweens. The guarantee of blockchain has broad ramifications for partners in the medical services biological system. Misusing this development can interface separated systems to make encounters and to all the more promptly review the assessment of care. Eventually, the electronic clinical record that utilizes the cross country blockchain technology may improve the performance and maintain better prosperity results for patients [4].

Blockchain innovation makes remarkable occasions to diminish unpredictability, empower trustless joint attempt, and makes the data secure and permanent. To shape blockchain's future, HHS should consider arranging and gathering the blockchain natural framework, setting up a blockchain construction to sort out early users and supports a consortium for talk and disclosure.

Blockchain development licenses patients to give out access rules for their clinical information, for instance, allowing express specialists with portions of the data at a fixed time that is all. With blockchain development, the patients can edge with diverse crisis services and accumulate their clinical data normally [5].

Blockchain advancement is one of the most noteworthy and challenging progress on the planet. Various businesses are receiving the blockchain innovation to advance the manner of working. One of the fields that are eager to embrace of the emerging blockchain technology is the medical care industry. Resources can be substantial, for example, homes or money, or they can be immaterial, for example, licenses or copyrights. Numerous parts of blockchain innovation, for example, the permanence of the information set away and, are seeking the deliberation of the medical care division, and ruddy possibilities for some, accessible cases are being talked about. Blockchain innovation is required to improve clinical record the executives and the protection guarantee measure, quicken clinical and biomedical exploration, and advance biomedical and medical care information record [2]. These yearning rely on the significant pieces of blockchain trend set in decentralized organization, constant survey trail, data attribution, potential, and improvised security and insurance. Blockchain development can support the advancement from association with integration of services and to understand the focused interoperability [3]. Blockchain advancement licenses patients to consign access rules for their clinical information, for instance, allowing express experts to will portions of their information for a fixed time span.

Patients often lounge around coating and balancing reasonable designs. That is the explanation blockchain associations like Kalibrate Blockchain are expecting to improve things. The firm has built up a blockchain-filled motor called "Universal Patient Index for its Form Drop adaptable application." What this flexible application does is engage clinical facilities to utilize a blockchain course of action that grants new patients to fill in tireless constructions before taking off to the center to keep away from lines and lounge around. It's really an unmistakable benefit for clinical benefits foundations expecting to clean up work interaction and office efficiency.

There are a ton of agreements in medical care, like among patients and emergency clinics, between different medical care suppliers, between well-being associations and sellers, and so forth. Presently, savvy contracts execute on top of emerging technology.

9.1.1 B2B SMART CONTRACTS

Keen agreements can help measure, get asserts, and send installments. That is the place where keen blockchain organizations become an integral factor, helping draw brilliant agreements between well-being associations and protection suppliers. The blockchain-driven brilliant agreement framework made by TIBCO Software in a joint effort with Change Healthcare is a genuine model.

This first-of-its-sort framework empowers medical services payers to computerize measures over all cases and conditional lifecycles. Suitably called Project Dovetail, the keen agreement stage utilizes Astute Healthcare Network blockchain innovation and TIBCO's shrewd agreement venture to convey bother free, secure, and unquestionable medical services exchanges.

Another extraordinary occasion of B2B Smart agreements in medical services is the cooperation of Minute Clinic, PBM, and Caremark. The CVS Minute Clinics savvy contract framework was intended to make drug apportioning, remuneration, and installment handling a breeze.

"The new CVS-Aetna organization would have the option to make medical care plans with impetuses for individuals to use the CVS Minute Clinics, with disincentives for more costly visits to doctors' workplaces. The consolidated organization would have the option to use the immense measures of customer information it claims to increase better understanding and improve its oversaw care results. This would likewise essentially help with the organization's income cycle the board," says Prithvi Srinivasan, the Global Head of Digital of Prolifics on CVS utilization of brilliant agreements.

9.1.2 TOLERANT HOSPITAL CONTRACTS

For a long time, agents have existed in the medical services biological system basically on the grounds that there's an absence of trust among patients and well-being foundations/suppliers. These two gatherings can't believe each other with regard to leading exchanges. With blockchain-based keen agreements like the one created by Robomed Networks, it turns into a relic of past times.

Presently, clinics must utilize various complex business and custom frameworks to computerize a few parts of medical services exchange handling.

A portion of these frameworks are at present filled with holes and now and again need manual/human intercession. This lounges around, yet it can similarly be expensive. Shrewd patient-crisis facility contracts, of course, present a more gainful, canny, and more clear game plan in which self-executing contract concludes that underwriter and various social affairs should develop top of the blockchain. In like manner, at the point when a patient visits the subject matter expert, for example, the blockchain record is invigorated (which is constant).

9.2 KEY PARTS OF A BLOCKCHAIN

Blockchain development is presently getting colossal thought in clinical benefits. As mentioned, 40% of prosperity heads see blockchain as the top

5 requirements. Also, the overall clinical benefits market spends on the blockchain is dependent upon hitting $5.61 billion by 2025, as demonstrated by a report by BIS Research. The gathering of the blockchain development could save the clinical benefits industry up to $100–$150 billion consistently by 2025 in information enter related expenses, IT costs, exercises costs, maintenance of work and staff costs, and through a decline in cheats and phony things.

Picture an accounting page record imitated over and over on an association of thousands of PCs, and that is on a very basic level what blockchain does. It's a decentralized, passed on cutting edge record that contains a lot of unendingly revived, time-ventured, and significantly encoded virtual records. Without blockchain advancement, there would be no cryptographic types of cash, for instance, Bitcoin or Ethereum. Every unit of the said modernized record is known as a square.

Of more significance is that the squares of the virtual record are associated together through cryptography all together in which they were made. Believe it or not, blockchain centers are integrated by crypto development in a manner that is from a genuine perspective constant. That makes blockchain quite possibly the most secure headways known to man.

How unequivocally achieves it work? An individual regularly begins a change to the blockchain, making another "block." Interesting that this "block" is imparted all through the decentralized association. Once "seen" by each PC on the association, the record of the square or then again change is forever added to the chain. Over the long haul, all of these PCs confirm of the change, and it is irreversible.

9.2.1 SCATTERED RECORD DEVELOPMENT

All association individuals approach the scattered record and its perpetual record of trades. With this regular record, exchanges are recorded just a single time, disposing of the duplication of exertion that is ordinary of standard business affiliations.

9.2.2 RECORDS ARE CONSTANT

No part can change or alter an exchange after it's been recorded to the basic record. In the event that an exchange record joins a stumble, another exchange should be added to turn the mess up, and the two exchanges are then detectable.

9.2.3　SPLENDID PLANS

To speed exchanges, a ton of rules–called an insightful agreement–is dealt with on the blockchain and executed consequently. A marvelous arrangement can portray conditions for corporate security moves, combine terms for experience out confirmation to be paid and extensively more.

9.3　KINDS OF BLOCKCHAIN NETWORKS

There are four different ways to deal with fabricate a blockchain network [4].

9.3.1　PUBLIC BLOCKCHAIN NETWORKS

It is the one that anybody can join and take part in, for example, Bitcoin. Downsides may join critical computational force required, basically zero affirmation for exchanges, and slight security. These are tremendous contemplations for huge business use instances of blockchain.

9.3.2　PRIVATE BLOCKCHAIN NETWORKS

It is like a public blockchain network, is a decentralized shared relationship, with the essential separation that one connection deals with the affiliation. That connection controls who is permitted to investigate the affiliation, execute a course of action show, and keep up the ordinary record. Reliant upon the utilization case, this can on an essential level help trust and conviction between people.

9.3.3　PERMISSIONED BLOCKCHAIN NETWORKS

Affiliations who set up a private blockchain, will routinely set up a permissioned blockchain network. Note that public blockchain affiliations can in addition be a permissioned. This spots requirements on who is permitted to look at the affiliation, and simply in unequivocal exchanges. People need to get a greeting or consent to join.

9.3.4 CONSORTIUM BLOCKCHAINS

Different affiliations can share the commitments of keeping up a block-chain. These pre-chosen affiliations sort who may submit exchanges or access the information. A consortium blockchain is ideal for business when all people should be permissioned and have an ordinary responsibility concerning the blockchain.

9.4 CHANGE MEDICAL CARE RESULTS

Blockchain will change medical care endeavors and increment the nature of care by empowering new biological systems and new plans of action to develop. Medical services data put away on a blockchain can change the manner in which you store clinical data just as how you share data inside your association, with medical care accomplices, payers, and above all, with patients.

Blockchain decentralizes medical services data, expanding information accessibility, proficiency, straightforwardness, and trust; however it likewise requires cautious intending to benefit as much as possible from the focal points it brings [5].

9.4.1 QUIET ASSENT AND WELLBEING INFORMATION TRADE

Dissimilar record-keeping systems can achieve patient consent structures and clinical stories that are deficient, conflicting, or unclear. Blockchain-set aside records can be used to give complete longitudinal prosperity records to individuals, giving all patients more control over their own information through certain consent. With blockchain, every understanding record reflects the most well-known clinical real factors – from genomics data to illustrative clinical imaging – and can be constantly moved when needed, with no necessity for a central watchman.

9.4.2   CLINICAL PRELIMINARY ADMINISTRATION

Clinical starter organization makes stores of data, requiring clinical consideration administrators to keep strong, solid records for peer review and to meet authoritative necessities. Blockchain gadgets, cooperating with electronic data get (EDC), can allow clinical data to be normally aggregated, rehashed, and flowed among researchers and specialists with more unmistakable auditability, provenance following and control appeared differently in relation to puzzled, standard structures.

9.4.3   RESULT-BASED AGREEMENTS

Measuring the value of clinical consideration is troublesome. Representing the genuine expenses of all parts of medical services can baffle suppliers and patients the same. Blockchain-upheld, result based agreements attach clinical results to costs. Suppliers going from drug stores to medical clinics can offer medical services to customers with a fee for-esteem model rather than expense for services, and diminish the unpredictability of records.

9.4.4   OPEN DOORS FOR MEDICAL CARE

Blockchain advancement can change clinical benefits, setting the patient at the point of convergence of the clinical benefits organic framework and extending the security, assurance, and interoperability of prosperity data. This advancement could give another model to prosperity data trades which further makes the electronic clinical records more valuable, disintermediated, and secure. While it's definitely not a panacea, this new, rapidly propelling field gives prolific ground to testing, adventure, and check of-thought testing.

9.5   IMPLEMENTATION

That is a tremendous proportion of privileged information that can be ominous in the event that it falls in some unsatisfactory hands. For example, if your contraption shows that you are most certainly not rehearsing furthermore, your heart is coming up short, you can wind up noticing your prosperity consideration go up if your security net supplier discovers the data.

Hence, the security, transmission, and insurance of this pressing data should be guaranteed regardless. One of the fruitful approaches to deal with so is to use a blockchain approach that engages for safe record, transmission, and sharing of this data between your device and your prosperity expert center.

This style incorporates making proof of data dependability. Furthermore, using this "proof," clinical consideration suppliers (and the patient) can check the information timestamp without truly trusting upon pariahs that can include the security of the data and insurance of the customer. It's a common advantage.

It is a development that is proper for getting each piece of the prosperity course chain. Besides, there are a couple of utilization cases that have recently arisen on utilizing blockchain to improve prosperity deftly chain, similarly as upgrading the effectiveness of the Internet of Healthy Things (IoHT), securing web related clinical equipment, battling counterfeit prescriptions, and extensively more. Whenever executed well, blockchain innovation can be a brilliant answer for improving information provenance, honesty, usefulness, and, obviously, security of a pharma flexibly chain [8].

Perhaps the greatest test that influence the drug flexibly chain is uncontrolled fake or adulterated prescriptions. These phonies or traded off medications are the aftereffect of helpless assembling rehearses and procedures, insufficient capacity, burglary of medications, of prescriptions, and the market infiltration of inferior quality or fake items into the purported dark business sectors.

Indeed, the World Health Organization (WHO) says that this "bootleg market" or fake drugs market merits an astounding $75 billion, yet the figure could be considerably greater in all actuality. This is particularly evident in nations like Bangladesh where by far most of medication uses go to import providers. Obviously, the pharma gracefully tie is defenseless to fake medications in low-pay and agricultural countries, yet in addition here in the US.

In 2012, for example; the FDA cautioned around 1,000 medical services associations and well-being experts in a few expresses that they may have succumbed to counterfeit medication rings. Even more unequivocally, they were exhorted that they may have been sold phony Avastin, quite possibly the most looked after foe of danger drugs accessible. That is the explanation US Food and Drug Administration began supporting for the authorization of the Drug Supply Chain Security Act (DSCSA), which has recently been embraced into law.

In the event that you delve somewhat more profound into the quick and dirty of blockchain, you'll understand that the innovation fulfilled essentially every model required for DSCSA consistency. These models incorporate medication/item recognizable proof, item following confirmation, fake medication recognition and reaction, notice important offices like FDA, and sharing required data, e.g., licensure data.

Notwithstanding what you resemble at it, blockchain, and clinical benefits are a match made in paradise. First of all, medical services players ought to truly consider blockchain in the time of well-being information uncertainty. Given that the medical services industry experiences security breaks nearly on a regular schedule, it's an easy decision to fuse an innovation that vows to seal all the escape clauses. All things considered, there's significantly more to blockchain than just value-based exercises. It's about safely sharing information recently considered difficult to separate.

9.6   HEALTH CARE INDUSTRY USING BLOCKCHAIN TECHNOLOGY

An examination distributed by Johns Hopkins quiet security specialists recommends that in the United States, more than 2,50,000 individuals kick the bucket each year because of clinical blunders. This is especially disturbing while thinking about the main source of death in the U.S. – coronary illness – which is answerable for around 6,47,000 passings yearly.

Blockchain information must be added, not eradicated. This is decisively how well-being data ought to be put away. Doctors can get to the chronicled clinical records of their patients from their absolute first emergency clinic visit. Dr. David Classen, a main clinical data official at Pascal measurements, conceded in a meeting that the arrangement of care is divided. He proceeded, "Any devices that empower patients to deal with their medical care needs will be a distinct advantage." Blockchain has come to adequately disintegrate the predicament of blunders and digitize understanding well-being records.

Medication is, undoubtedly, an immensely unique field. Consistently, a great many well-being experts look for better approaches to improve quiet consideration and fulfillment. This is the essential inspiration driving the many examinations works and clinical preliminaries in medication today.

Shockingly, there is no successful focal framework for sharing exploration information. A large part of the exploration information has been isolated and, albeit numerous specialists couldn't imagine anything better than to contrast preliminary outcomes and individual scientists, there is actually no computerized framework to do as such.

Grasping the blockchain business can stop this polarity. In a protected advanced framework, analysts worldwide can, with patients' authorization, access a broad information base of data that would help quicken improvement in medical care and make the world a superior spot. Who knows? Blockchain may even assistance shut down malignancy [7].

Regardless of what we state, it will be inconceivable for us to overstate the implication of the medical industry. This is effectively one of the slowest developing enterprises in the whole space. We understand that this is an extremely disputable comment, notwithstanding, the truth will eventually come out. Contrasted with 20 years back, clinics, generally, still capacity practically a similar way. The explanation, as Richie Etwaru says, states is its absence of development. This is in reality pretty astonishing when you consider the way that this space, specifically, has probably the most astute and accomplished individuals in the whole world [5].

In any case, saying that no advancements have been made in the clinical field is a truly off-base comment. Simply take a gander at how much the normal future has expanded gratitude to drugs. In this way, we should burrow somewhat more profound to comprehend what is implied by saying "absence of advancement." In the event that you investigate somewhat more profound, at that point you will see that this space is overflowing with vertical development, in any case, it generally lingers behind with regards to flat advancement. So, I'm not catching our meaning by vertical and even advancement?

9.6.1 *VERTICAL INNOVATION VERSUS HORIZONTAL INNOVATION*

Vertical headway is advancement that is done unequivocally in a particular field while level improvement is something that can be embraced by everyone. Penicillin, Polio inoculation, and refined working procedures are through and through occasions of vertical advancements since they are express to a particular field. Force, Internet, and Cloud Computing, of course, are level progressions that have been embraced by items fields and dares to make their handiness more capable. The way that most centers really use papers and archives to do their records exhibits that they wait far behind with respect to even headway.

9.6.2   THE NEXT HORIZONTAL INNOVATION

We have talked about blockchain fundamentals a lot of times on this site already. Along these lines, to give you an extremely short depiction. A blockchain is, at all complex of terms, a period ventured game plan of constant record of data that is administered by a lot of PCs not controlled by any single substance. All of these squares of data (for instance, block) are ensured about and bound to each other using cryptographic norms (for instance, chain).

The inspiration driving why the blockchain has gotten such a lot of respect is that:

- It isn't possessed by a solitary substance, henceforth it is decentralized;
- The information is cryptographically put away inside;
- The blockchain is everlasting and no one can mess with the information that is within the blockchain;

The exact thing a medical clinic needs is to enlist quacks or unlicensed doctors, one more critical part of medical care blockchain can help comprehend.

Hashed Health is an association utilizing blockchain to guarantee that singular real specialists make to the clinical consideration climate. They created a capability affirmation structure for specialists to show they're undoubtedly approved to work. Hashed Health joined along with Accenture, WellCare, Spectrum Health, National Government Services, Hardenbergh Group, and HealthLink Dimensions to make a blockchain-energized credentialing structure.

The arrangement is really a trade stage that furnishes medical clinics and other medical care foundations with admittance to checked certifications data, just as a method for them to contribute confirmed data that is shareable with all other medical care associations.

The taking an interest clinical consideration affiliations are allowed to portray explicit norms, doodads, information, and endorsement checks for credentialing any sort of specialist, from AHPs and chaperons to specialists and various experts. At last, the blockchain-based stage eases specialists and medical care associations the same spare time and be agreeable with different solicitations.

9.7   MEDICAL CARE AND INTEROPERABILITY

Interoperability is a colossal issue in the medical services industry. Indeed, improved medical care interoperability is been a main concern for suppliers, policymakers, and patients for a long while now. The two significant territories with regards to ineffectual interoperability?

- the inconvenience of recognizing patients;
- information obstructing.

Envision an organization on medical care establishments where they don't claim a patient's very own information. The information all have a place in the blockchain. The patients are distinguished by means of their hash ID which will be their special identifier. The hashing permits the ID to be one of a kind and gets the security of the client. The blockchain can likewise help in the making of a patient data sharing commercial center. Along these lines, it will be feasible to really boost data dividing among the various establishments to forestall any sort of information hindering [6].

Be that as it may, imagine a scenario in which we actually have some malevolent entertainers who endeavor to do data hindering or altering.

All things considered two of the blockchain's most huge highlights will venture up and handle the present circumstance.

The blockchain is a simple medium. Anybody, who is important for the organization, can investigate the blockchain and take a gander at how every exchange happens and whether all the pertinent data is getting gone through or not. Furthermore, we have against altering.

In the event that anybody attempts to hinder the information, through the compounding phenomenon, it will change the hash radically. Presently, recall, that the squares in the blockchain are connected to each other through a hash pointer. Each square in the blockchain stores the hash of the information that is put away in the past block. On the off chance that the information inside any of the squares changes, it sets up a chain response which could freeze up the entire blockchain. Since this is a hypothetical inconceivability, it is difficult to alter any information that is inside the blockchain.

Blockchain modernism can actually modify the drug area all in all, just as medication disclosure, improvement, and circulation measure. That all by itself isn't unexpected in any way. As of now we surveyed that 9 out of 10 new prescriptions disregard to make it to clinical starter, and essentially more don't show up at the FDA-support stage. The gigantic issue for pharma associations is obtaining basic patient information in a period at the point when they are definitely not for the most part trusted by people [8]. Clearly, there are a great deal of information challenges big pharma is wrestling with. They are discussed in subsections.

9.7.1 DISSIMILARITY IN PHARMA DATA

Maybe the most disturbing information issue looked in accordance with the drug organizations, particularly with regards to sedate turn of events, constitutes a grave dissimilarity of information. Recollect pharma information is regularly documented and concealed in storehouses, and it is gotten to all through a few unique stages.

What's surprisingly more terrible is that every division regularly utilizes a different information structure and model. Thusly, gaining admittance to exceptionally significant information at whatever point required is critical for pharma organizations for enormous information investigation.

This is a region where man-made brainpower, large information investigation, and blockchain can work pair to convey effectiveness and precise outcomes for pharma firms. Luckily around 61% of pharma associations are currently getting a handle on AI, with blockchain execution underway.

9.7.2 INFORMATION ANALYTICS IS TIME-CONSUMING AND RESOURCE-HEAVY

Taking into account that pharma organizations have to manage, thus, numerous information sources, unmistakably there's an issue with regards to information social occasion, taking care of, and in the long run examination.

First off, some significant information may escape everyone's notice during the catching stage, watering down bits of knowledge about the inquiry.

As if that isn't awful enough, the entire cycle of orchestrating information from various sources can wind up becoming very tedious. Also, protracted examination cycle may really neglect to find experiences that may be useful to the pharma.

So, clearly the entire information dealing with measure for pharma organizations need to move. All things considered, overseeing enormous informational indexes is as of now a serious test for both little and huge drug organizations.

9.7.3   DATA IMPRECISION AND AMBIGUITY

Through the medication space, there's reliably dubiousness all over the precision of open data. Is the information examination article careful, as well as assuming without a doubt, constitute the encounters even pertinent?

It is routinely difficult for them to no doubt when all the data open is not yet new, as well as the watchful. Enter blockchain advancement. Once used fittingly, blockchain can empower pharma to record, store, and sort their information with the end goal that it yields encounters which are reliably pertinent and clear. Even more fundamentally, every game plan that may help pharma with taking care of information will eventually save stores of money, clean out the essential concern, and enhance prosperity results for everyone.

Against this foundation, pharma organizations should hold hands on developing blockchain tech firms to configuration, carry out, as well as to deal with their medication distribution chains.

Collaboration among the pharma worldwide monster GlaxoSmithKline and blockchain organization Viant is an incredible model. By using the positions of Microsoft, Imaginea, and GlaxoSmithKline ready, it merits watching out for.

Obviously, further exploration, arrangement with consistency and well-being strategies, and assessment must be completed to work with the selection of blockchain in the pharma store network. All things considered, most blockchain activities in pharma and medical care remain as yet stuck in pilot or verification of -idea stages.

Managing and having the opportunity to quiet fundamental information is a hot-button issue in the prosperity business, as well as, even more so for pharma associations. The Situation for the most part feels like a tradeoff between security and sharing information, which presents a giant issue for pharma IT.

In all actuality, most pharma organizations maintain their medication preliminary information in brought together information bases which must be agreeable with HITRUST, ISO, HIPAA, secrecy, as well as other moral and administrative prerequisites.

The difficulty is that these unified information bases make it hard for scientists and medication preliminary pioneers to impart the information to the correct individuals. That is the place where blockchain becomes possibly the most important factor. Blockchain in medical care assists pharma with making auditable, unalterable, and circulated information bases for putting away and getting to sedate preliminary information.

Take MIT Enigma structure, for example. It's a totally feathered blockchain movement that uses two focus cryptographic squares which work pair on top of a dispersed association of center points. In basic terms, this framework is a mystery sharing stage that permits specialists to keep up an elevated level of protection and protection in managing clinical investigations information.

Keeping steady over bookkeeping and expenses during clinical investigations/preliminaries, particularly those that keep going for significant stretches, is a notable test to drug organizations.

Accounting instruments right now accessible are unreasonably convoluted and will not catch the comprehensive cost image of the clinical preliminaries. If you want to do an already difficult situation even worse, assessed clinical preliminaries money related accumulations can immediately turn into a benevolent cycle, particularly when you need to fit frivolous books with yearly budgetary reports.

Fortunately, blockchain innovation can be executed to monitor clinical preliminaries financials just as make accounting proficient, exact, and simple.

Due to the inborn diverse nature of clinical starters financial statements, associations like Boehringer Ingelheim have pronounced working with blockchain firms to smooth out their accounting and budgetary uncovering works out. The Canadian-based unit of Boehringer Ingelheim similarly actually attained IBM to arrangement, make, and send a blockchain-filled bookkeeping system for the clinical fundamental test adventure.

The first of a sort in the pharma business, this joint effort will yield another blockchain answer for enhancing the idea of clinical starter cycles and record keeping. "The clinical preliminary biological system is profoundly unpredictable as it includes various partners, bringing about restricted trust, straightforwardness, and cycle failures without genuine patient strengthening," said UliBrödl, VP of clinical and administrative issues for Boehringer's Canadian division, clarifying the requirement for the blockchain-fueled arrangement.

Pharma and clinical benefits workplaces go through an enormous proportion of cash and loads of time discovering, qualifying, and onboarding the privilege competitor for their clinical primers. Disastrously, the specialists don't by and large ID the right patients, thus the necessity for blockchain advancement. Besides, assuming that solitary 10% of new prescriptions make it to the market, it's fundamental to perceive and choose undeniably a perfect contender. As of now, there are a couple of different programming and advances used by pharma to do this.

From one shopper and pharma perspective, two viewpoints of different blockchain commercial centers have been dispatched. While blockchain innovation itself probably won't do a lot to fix persistent distinguishing proof, it can help bring a portion of the information uprightness, availability, safety, protection, and interoperability required by pharma. The entire cycle can be hard, repetitive, and wasteful, also the powerful expenses related with this. Truth be told, as per a study led by KPMG, 38% of top medical services CIOs state improved management of electronic well-being records (EHR) is top of their plan and planning requirements.

Groundbreaking well-being offices, practices, and suppliers can make way for assent the executives by utilizing the intensity of blockchain.

Right now, the entire cycle of assent securing and the executives is an all-out wreck. You need every one of these authorizations, select ins and educated assent from patients. You have to remain agreeable with how you handle ensured well-being data. In addition, medical services associations must ensure information and patient security. It is a region where blockchain firms like HealthVerity bring their A-game.

HealthVerity is changing the way current medical care organizations settle on basic and characterizing choices, particularly with regard to taking care of patient information. HealthVerity has built up a blockchain-based stage which fills in as the stage for a quick age, sharing, and the executives of patient and medical services information.

All the more vitally, the cutting-edge innovation stage ensures administrative consistence is seen by building up a common, unchangeable record of all patient assent exchanges that occur inside a medical care office. Thusly, just gatherings with express consent can get to quiet information on the fly without trading off its safety and shopper protection. Notable likewise is that HealthVerity stage takes out different difficulties like information irregularity, vagueness, and fracture.

The outcome is a hearty assent to the board framework that makes it easy for important and allowed gatherings to gather understanding information for HIPAA consistence, showcasing, and a plenty of other medical care purposes.

9.7.4   DIFFERENT ADVANTAGES OF BLOCKCHAIN IN MEDICAL INDUSTRY

All in all, the interoperability feature can be addressed, what other astonishing benefits in which blockchain carry to the clinical medical services establishment? Since the blockchain is Immutable and detectable, patients can undoubtedly send records to anybody without the dread of information defilement or altering.

Essentially, a clinical record that has been created and added to the blockchain will be totally secure. The patient having the authority over their clinical information gets utilized and shared by the establishments. Any gathering which is hoping to get the clinical information about a patient could check with the blockchain to get the fundamental permission. The patient can likewise be boosted for appropriate conduct by means of a prize component, e.g., the persons can avail tokens that follow a consideration plan or for remaining sound. Likewise, they can be remunerated by tokens for giving their information for clinical preliminaries and examination [6].

Pharma organizations need to have a very secure store network in view of the sort of item they convey. Pharma drugs are reliably taken from the store network to be sold wrongfully to different shoppers. Additionally, following of medications to their starting place and subsequently help kill misrepresented medication. According to a statement by BIS research, by 2025, the medical services industry can set aside to $100 billion every year by 2025 in information penetrate related expenses, IT costs, activities costs, support capacity and staff costs, fake related fakes, and protection fakes on the off chance that they join the blockchain innovation [6].

Arising advances, for example, blockchain can help both clinical specialists and patients, who remain to pick up the best from its usage.

Prior to 2009, digital currency and blockchain were not mainstream terms. Nonetheless, since their delivery as open-source programming that year, the basic innovation has become a pivotal driver for different businesses, including money, gaming, medical services, designing, and farming. The size of the blockchain business is required to arrive at a dazzling $23.3 billion out of 2023 [7].

Blockchain innovation is a decentralized, digitized record or data set for putting away "blocks" of data. It takes into account the exchange of responsibility for utilizing an encryption framework without requiring control by the public authority or a national bank. In this chapter, we will examine how blockchain will change the medical services industry.

The episode of the novel Covid, COVID-19, is no uncertainty the greatest occasion of the year. At last, the medical care framework is being put to its greatest test in almost a century. The WHO is going under expanded investigation, bogus data is on the ascent day by day, and creating and sharing emergency techniques has been drawn-out—one of the serious issues in this being the satisfactory stockpiling and quick course of information continuously.

The Center for Disease Control, in association with the WHO and IBM, has effectively set up an undertaking to utilize blockchain to track, store, and dispense touchy data continuously to well-being communities for viable and uniform administration of pandemics. With this device, assaulting pandemics like COVID-19 can be halted sooner than anticipated.

As indicated by a report distributed by BIS research, the selection of blockchain in the medical care industry is assessed to set aside to $100 billion yearly by 2025. Through tokenization, accordingly killing avoidable outsider customers, fake drug items and noxious programming, the business would take an enormous float toward complete straightforwardness and responsibility, and at last set aside cash for the two patients and medical services organizations.

While it tends to be contended that digitizing and moving well-being data in squares can be very awkward, the certainty of blockchain in each industry is step by step finding the medical services industry. Beyond question, both the clinical expert and the patient remain to pick up the most from this insurgency.

9.8 CONCLUSION

We have discussed the different benefits that the blockchain can possibly confer to the medical care industry. What we can state as a reality is that different foundations and spaces have effectively begun testing and utilizing blockchain technology. The blockchain is being received by different areas, it unquestionably appears as though the eventual fate of the medical services industry is for sure decentralized. We should trust that blockchain innovation gives the level of advancement lift to this industry that it frantically needs.

KEYWORDS

- **artificial intelligence**
- **blockchain development**
- **Center for Disease Control**
- **COVID-19**
- **medical care industry**
- **World Health Organization**

REFERENCES

1. Gupta, M., (2018). *Blockchain for Dummies*. 2nd IBM Limited Edition. Hoboken (NJ): John Wiley & Sons.
2. Kuo, T. T., Kim, H. E., & Ohno-Machado, L., (2017). Blockchain distributed ledger technologies for biomedical and health care applications. *J Am Med Inform Assoc., 24*(6), 1211–1220.
3. Gordon, W. J., & Catalini, C., (2018). Blockchain technology for healthcare: facilitating the transition to patient-driven interoperability. *Comput. Struct. Biotechnol. J., 16*, 224–230.
4. https://www2.deloitte.com/us/en/pages/public-sector/articles/blockchain-opportunities-for-health-care.html (accessed on 11 August 2022).
5. https://blockgeeks.com/guides/blockchain-in-healthcare/ (accessed on 11 August 2022).
6. https://cointelegraph.com/news/how-blockchain-will-revolutionize-healthcare (accessed on 11 August 2022).
7. https://healthcareweekly.com/blockchain-in-healthcare-guide/ (accessed on 11 August 2022).

CHAPTER 10

Advanced Technologies for Precision Agriculture and Farming

C. NAVANEETHAN, S. THANGAPRASATH, M. BALASUBRAMANIYAN, and S. MEENATCHI

School of Information Technology and Engineering,
Vellore Institute of Technology Vellore, Tamil Nadu, India

ABSTRACT

It appears that all of the world's countries are now aware of the critical need for food; because the Corona epidemic shocked the world two years ago and made all countries aware of the people's critical needs (food). Consequently, every government pays special practical attention to agriculture and prioritizes improving agricultural productivity because traditional agricultural methods are incapable of meeting the population's food needs. The government urges farmers to employ cutting-edge technologies to increase yields. Smart farming allows farmers to manage their farmland in virtually any place and at any moment employ wireless sensor networks and the Internet of Things to constantly monitor crops on farmland without the need for human involvement. Smart farming uses field sensor nodes to collect soil nutrients, temperature, water level, and humidity. These details are forwarded to a remote server through a wireless gateway to distribute water and nutrients to crops at the right time to increase yield. Through this, everything needed by the crops reaches them at the right time. Researchers and scientists are constantly working hard to introduce various innovative agriculture technologies to improve farmers' productivity, quantity, and quality.

Hybridization of Blockchain and Cloud Computing: Overcoming Security Issues in IoT.
M. Lawanya Shri, E. Gangadevi, K. Santhi, & Chiranji Lal Chowdhary (Eds.)
© 2024 Apple Academic Press, Inc. Co-published with CRC Press (Taylor & Francis)

10.1   INTRODUCTION

In the globe, the majority of nations soul depend on agriculture only. We could not demand the salary to do agriculture because it is not work based on timing. Agriculture plays a vital role in society, producing food, grains, and raw materials [1]. Food is a significant issue for all humans, and most food is only from agriculture [2]. Every year, millions of people lose their lives because of food scarcity. The food production and cultivation method may vary based on the land type, soil type, moisture level, and climate. Agriculture is a science-based art of increasing the soil's nutrient level, growing healthy crops, and reducing pesticide usage in farming land. Hence using these techniques in land cultivation will significantly increase food production. It is the responsibility of all countries to feed all citizens without discrimination. Thus, our responsibility is to increase food production to provide for all. Unfortunately, instead of going upwards, we are currently moving downwards. Water shortage, diminishing agricultural labor, sudden pest attacks, rising harvesting costs, lack of technical knowledge, and declining arable lands are already worrying [3]. As a result, we are not achieving our full yielding potential. It is difficult to feed the ever-increasing population in these desperate circumstances. Thus, we must assist farmers in increasing their production. The time has come to take agriculture to the next level [4].

Nowadays, technologies are growing exponentially day by day. Rapid development in the field of artificial intelligence and cloud computing will significantly help take agriculture to the next level. Hence, have to improve traditional agriculture into precision agriculture (PA). Precision agriculture is used to minimize water usage in agricultural land and maintain the soil minerals. This change is made possible by the latest developments in technologies like geographic information systems (GIS), sensor automation techniques, data management and processing technology, and information and communications technology (ICT) environment-friendly farming through flexible fertilization technology [5]. Recent development in information technology (IT) and wireless communication techniques helps to upgrade agriculture smartly. All networks are based on Wireless Sensor Network (WSN) techniques, consisting of a series of sensor nodes that exchange information. Each sensor node senses unique information like temperature, air, humidity, moisture, and land irrigation level and stores it in its databases. The agriculture sector utilizes Fog computing technics and Long-distance communication methods to share information in a wide range [6, 7]. The scalable network architecture is used for monitoring and controlling the farms. The above technologies are used in agriculture to optimum production and maximize profit and reduce fertilizer usage. Here various techniques are using wireless communication, IoT, and artificial intelligence to ensure PA.

Wireless communication agriculture typically has two sections field agriculture and facility agriculture. Field agriculture needs to analyze the correct location to deploy the sensors/actuators. Facility agriculture collects environment-related data from the sensor, wireless devices, and actuators to activate the required device. The collected data send to the artificial intelligence model to make the right decision on time. In wireless communication technology, sensors/actuators use based on a short distance, central distance, and long-distance. Especially for the long-distance mode uses ZigBee, LoRa, and NB-IoT these techniques [3]. IoT is used in agriculture to monitor farms from anywhere in the world and reduces human resources. This method is achieved with the help of sensors and actuators. Farmers will know the details of temperature, fertilizer use, moisture level, land irrigation level, etc. The collected data is preprocessed in the edge computing layer before it is sent to the cloud server. The preprocessed phase works with two steps; the first phase is to monitor the sensors and filter the incomplete data and outliers. The second phase uses to compress the collected data before it is sent to the next level. The deep learning technique uses to inspect the stored information. The deep mind is the combined model of various deep reinforcement learning models, such as deep learning and reinforcement techniques. In the vast majority of instances, the deep learning algorithm learns specific contextual information for high-dimensional raw data from the environment. This learning approach is used to assess the best policies for optimal cultivation and minimal resource utilization [8].

10.2 ROLE OF AGRICULTURE IN THE NATIONAL ECONOMY

Nowadays, meeting the basic needs of the world's population, such as food, milk, meat, sugar, and so on, is a primary issue for world countries. The population and food production of a nation are growing in separate poles. Agricultural exports such as wheat, milk, paddy, sugarcane, and other agricultural raw goods play an essential role in the national economy (GDP). Some nations, such as Brazil (Sugar), India (Milk), China (Wheat), and others, have a substantial role in the international agricultural export market. In India, GDP increased by 19.9% in 2020–2021 due to agricultural exports and employment for rural people [9]. As a result, we must ensure high yields in all agricultural sectors. Low yielding is caused by unhealthy soil, the failure to select suitable crops for the specific soil, the failure to apply fertilizer on time, water shortage, and insect attacks. The aforementioned factors are critical in reducing agricultural yielding potential [10, 11]. As a result, we must track farming land on a regular basis to avoid these factors. It is possible to track the farm without having a person present for the entire day. It is essential to identify the use of technology to make above mentioned effort.

10.3 IMPORTANCE OF WIRELESS SENSOR NETWORK BASED ON IoT

This is the ideal time to incorporate cutting-edge technology into conventional agriculture in order to turn it into intelligent agriculture and achieve full yields. Some of the promised technologies of wireless networks, like sensor nodes, are used to monitor agrarian land. The required sensors are placed throughout the farmland [12]. The sensor nodes are static and identified using GPS. Various sensor nodes are used to sense different information (like temperature, water level, moisture level) in different agricultural regions at a predetermined time interval. In the smart agrarian sector, the Internet of Things (IoT) is used to provide versatile functionality and fast access to functions from anywhere [13]. IoT reduces human activity and effort on agricultural land by deploying automation devices. These devices enable farmers to access all of their activities, information, and real-time environmental details from anywhere in the world. An IoT-based smart agricultural system's essential task is collecting information in a series of measures from farming land to change crop growth based on real-time environmental data [14]. As a result, advanced technology can absolutely and flexibly reduce the farmer's burden.

The most recent technologies which are used in smart agricultural land are illustrated in Figure 10.1. It operates with various stages, such as data collection, data preprocessing, data transfer, and cloud service, as seen in the block diagram. Static sensor nodes are used to collect field data, and these nodes are placed in different locations in the farmland. Over a fixed time span, the sensor nodes collect field data in a sequence of measurements from land and water. Each sensor node collects specific parameters (temperature, moisture, oxygen level, water level, and NPK ratio) from different locations at a set time interval. Then the parameters are passed to the data collection section. Before the data is sent to the next stage, it has to be preprocessed. In this stage, the collected data is split into two portions, the first portion is complete data, and the second portion is incomplete data. By discarding incomplete data from the whole, the transferring bandwidth is reduced efficiently. In the next level, the transferred data is being analyzed by the various types of algorithm to make an effective decision without delay [8].

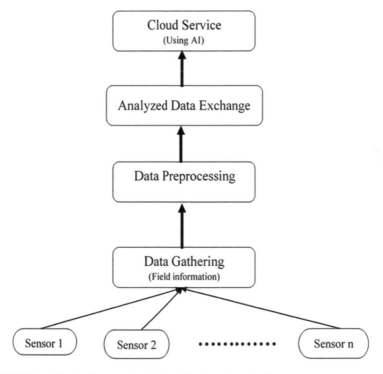

FIGURE 10.1 Block diagram for IoT-enabled smart agriculture.

The components shown in Figure 10.2 are used in smart agriculture. Multiple sensors are deployed in different locations to monitor the farmland. Each sensor senses unique information (Temperature, humidity, moisture, etc.), and sends that to the central gateway (Base Station). The central gateway gathered all of the data and sent it to the cloud services, where it was saved for later use. The data analyzed in a proper way to predict the possible solution for the maximum cultivation. The forecast is then sent to the farmer via the appropriate channel (i.e., mobile SMS alert).

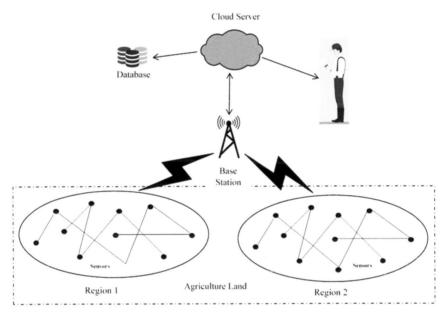

FIGURE 10.2   Architecture of IoT-based WSN.

10.4   ISSUES IN AGRICULTURAL SYSTEM IN RURAL AREAS

10.4.1   SOIL ANALYSIS

Soil analysis is a crucial action to be taken before we choose any crops for cultivation. Because good and fertile soils are mandatory for the production of healthy crops. Analyzing soil nutrient levels is an integral part of assessing whether soil fertility needs to be increased.

10.4.2   FARM MONITORING AND CONTROL THE USE OF FERTILIZER

Farmers need to monitor their cultivation of land routinely to ensure maximum production. IoT helps farmers to insight into their lands via technology. Consequently, they can effectively foresee and prevent problems before they arise. The soil's levels of Potassium, Phosphorus, and Nitrogen (NPK) must be tracked. The notable primary reason for producing low yielding from the cultivation is due to the improper use of fertilizer. Monitor the soil's nutrient concentrations so fertilizer can be added at the right time.

10.4.3   IRRIGATION MANAGEMENT

Water is a pivotal element in predicting the health of crops as well as maximum yielding. The use of cutting-edge technology is critical in ensuring that crops receive the proper amount of water at the appropriate time.

10.4.4   INSECTS MONITORING

This method is essential to safeguard crops from seasonal pest attacks and monitor the cropland to avoid unwanted pest attacks both day and night. The Pest monitoring system significantly decreases pesticide use in crops, ensures healthy products, and raises income.

10.5   TECHNOLOGIES FOR PRECISION AGRICULTURE AND FARMING

10.5.1   SENSORS USED IN IOT-BASED SMART AGRICULTURE/ PRECISION AGRICULTURE

Different sensing technologies are used in PA to give accurate real-time field information to the farmers to help them monitor and enhance the crop. In addition to responding to dynamic environmental factors, location sensors use GPS satellite signals to assess latitude, longitude, and altitude to about a few miles. To triangulate a location, at least three satellites are needed. PA relies heavily on precise positioning. Location sensors include GPS-integrated circuits such as the NJR NJG1157PCD-TE1.

Optical sensors use light to determine soil properties. The sensors measure varying wavelengths of light reflectance in the near-infrared, mid-infrared, and polarized light spectrums. Sensor nodes are used in various applications, including drones, vehicles, robots, and satellites. Optical sensors may be used to measure clay, organic matter, and soil moisture content. Just two examples of variables that can be aggregated and evaluated are optical sensor data on soil reflectance and plant color. There are plenty of photodetectors and photodiodes on the market, which are the basic components of optical sensors (Figure 10.3).

FIGURE 10.3   IC photo sensor.

In precision agriculture (PA), some of the crucial data provided by electrochemical sensors, such as pH and nutrient ratios in the soil, is useful for achieving maximum yielding. Sensor electrodes detect unique ions in the soil. Sensors mounted on specially built "sleds" are currently used to collect, process, and map soil chemical data.

Some mechanical sensors use to measure Soil compaction, or "mechanical resistance." The sensors record resistive forces using a probe that penetrates the soil and load cells or strain gauges. Ground-engaging machinery like tractors uses the same technologies to predict pulling requirements. Another useful sensor for irrigation is tensiometer (Honey-well FSG15N1A), which monitors the root forces to absorb the water. So that farmer gets accurate plant information for irrigation (Figure 10.4).

FIGURE 10.4   Honeywell force sensor.

Specific sensor nodes such as 'dielectric soil moisture sensors' are used to estimate the soil's moisture level. It measures the moisture level in farmland (a property of electricity that varies depending on the amount of moisture in the air).

Sensors called 'airflow sensors' has specially designed for monitoring the soil air humidity. This evaluation could be done in some fixed area or when in action, dynamically. Soil condition, composition, and moisture level are only a few of the soil properties that create differentiated distinguishing signatures.

Different information should be needed to help the cultivating process so that various agricultural weather monitoring towers have been located in multiple regions to collect the data. These agricultural weather monitoring towers are self-contained units that gather data on crop growth and weather patterns in a particular area. Some critical parameters such as temperature (soil, air), moisture level (land, crop, air), leaf wetness, Wind speed and direction, and atmospheric pressure are collected by weather stations in some fixed time spare. This stored data is composed in a specific arrangement and transferred to the central data center through WSN. Due to their portability and low cost, agricultural weather stations are ideal for any kind of farmland [15].

10.5.1.1 SYSTEM COMPONENTS IMPLEMENTED IN THE AGRICULTURE FIELD

The hardware devices used for implementation are described in Table 10.1, along with their functionality and the reason for which they were used [16].

TABLE 10.1   List of Hardware Devices

SI. No.	Hardware	Functionality
1.	Raspberry Pi	It is an operating system as well as a central processing Unit used to make the decision.
2.	Temperature sensor	The sensor will collect the water level from the soil, and the same will be conveyed to raspberry pi.
3.	Gas sensor	This sensor will intelligence any type of gas is available in the agriculture area.
4.	PIR sensor	This sensor will intelligence the signal primarily based upon the warmth of moving objects.
5.	URD sensor	This sensor will enhance intelligence as well as calculate the space of the traveling item.
6.	DHT sensor	This sensor will intelligence the moisture of the agriculture area.
7.	FAN	This actuator will start automatically if the moisture level crosses the edge value.
8.	Buzzer	This device is used to make noise where ever the gas is sensed in the agriculture area.
9.	Motor	It is a device linked with the sprayer to spray water if no water in the agriculture field
10.	Camera	It will take a photograph of the agriculture area if any object movement is sensed.

10.5.2 IOT-BASED WSN TECHNOLOGY USED FOR SOIL ANALYSIS

Soil analysis plays a vital role in smart agriculture/PA to ensure maximum yield using minimum resources. While selecting crops, a soil nutrient analysis is needed to achieve a high harvest. By using the traditional method of farming, maximum yielding is not possible. Smart agriculture/ PA is a concept used to represent new technologies used in agricultural practices to maximize yields [17]. With smart farming technologies, farmers should know valuable field instructions with their hand device

(SMS notification). Hence, they will take the requisite steps to develop their cultivation as soon as possible, based on real-time field instructions. As a result, by successfully using scarce resources such as water and fertilizer, the quality and quantity of crops can be effectively improved [18]. The majority of the farmers are now discussing a lot about using innovative agricultural technologies to take their farming to the next level because of the recent development in Wireless Sensor Networks (WSN) and the IoT. The modern technologies main goal is to implement a cost-effective, energy-efficient wireless system to monitor various farmland regions. There are a variety of well-proven Artificial Neural Network (ANN) algorithms for determining soil nutrient levels [19].

The maximum yielding has to be achieved through the intelligent soil estimating method. So, it is mandatory to design such a WSN model for the agricultural sector. Figure 10.5 represents that type of design. Multiple sensor nodes are deployed in various locations to sense the soil parameters (moisture, temperature, water level, etc.) [20]. The depicted sensor nodes communicate with the cloud server through the gateway using the internet. The main objective of the cloud service is the data stored in the cloud server can be easily accessed from any electronic device (e.g., mobile, tab, desktop, laptop, etc.) in an easy manner. Once the data is transferred to the cloud, artificial intelligence techniques (i.e., ANN) are used to test the soil's phosphorous level. This nutrient is a vital parameter in soil fertility, so the ANN monitors its level and reduces the time for traditional laboratory testing. As a result, the farmer will choose appropriate crops for their land based on the phosphorus level in the soil. Smart agriculture/PA can be used to reach the maximum yield target.

10.5.3 *MONITORING SOLUTIONS USING SMART AGRICULTURE*

Farmers will be able to raise their production rates by 70% by the year 2050, thanks to the IoT, so the future looks bright. In any case, IoT has a lot to say when it comes to relieving the pains that farmers experience on a daily basis.

Nowadays, farmers are able to face their daily challenges regarding cultivation with the help of modern technologies (AgriTech). Planting, irrigation, crop harvesting, and pest control are only a few of the activities that agriculture field monitoring gathers.

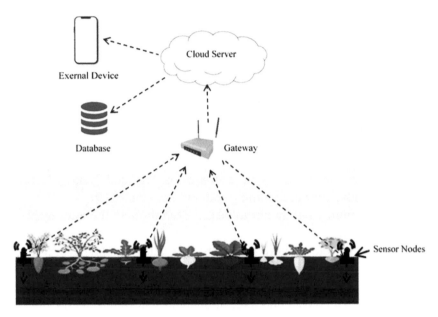

FIGURE 10.5   Innovative agricultural applications using advanced WSN.

10.5.3.1   *MONITORING THE CONDITION OF THE SOIL*

Soil quality is a vital predictor for farmers when deciding when to plant and harvest their crops. Farmers are immediately notified of soil moisture and salinity using IoT sensors that control soil conditions. Farmers would be able to plan their irrigation and insect operations in farmland based on specific essential parameters such as temperature (air and soil). A combination of hardware and software systems is needed to respond to real-time problems and to alert certain critical real-time field data.

10.5.3.2   *MONITORING ON WEATHER*

One of the most popular IoT application fields is weather monitoring in agriculture. Yields in crop farming are highly reliant on the climate, which is fundamentally unstable. The agricultural weather observation stations are regularly alert the farmers if any change happens in humidity, temperature, wind speed and direction, and solar radiation. As a result, the farmer is ready to react based on real-time information. Some of the real-time agricultural weather observation stations such as Smart element, Pycno, and allMETEO are examples of how these modern techniques help the farmers get timely data related to climate through their electronic devices (laptops and smartphones).

10.5.3.3 MONITORING ON CROPS

When a crop gets mature and ripens, many things have wrongly happened: Unpredictable weather conditions, insect attacks, and unnoticed diseases on crops could cause the crop to mature and ripen before the farmer notices it. As a result, the farmer will cause irreversible sadness and loss before they notice it's ripe. Hence, modern technologies such as smart sensing techniques are adopted to monitor crop growing, and collect actual facts in farmland (humidity, water level, air temperature, etc.). Semios and arable are real-world examples of detecting grain ripe in agriculture and informing farmers about harvesting.

10.5.3.4 SYSTEMS FOR KEEPING TRACK OF LIVESTOCK

Agriculture sensor systems are widely used in livestock and crop farming. SCR is the foremost company that contributes highly to a cattle tracking system. SCR uses a unique instrument attached to the cow's neck to observe the cattle's information (like cow movements, health, and diseases).

10.5.3.5 AUTOMATION DEVICES FOR GREENHOUSES

A delicate and responsive greenhouse environment necessitates constant monitoring and control. Growlink, Farmapp, and GreenIQ, smart agriculture applications for greenhouse automation, demonstrate the use of remote sensing in agriculture. They aid in the maintenance of ideal microclimate conditions by controlling lighting, humidity, CO_2, and temperature. Greenhouse farming is more productive thanks to instant alerts and improved management capabilities.

Advantages of monitoring solutions in precision agriculture:

- Productivity has been increased;
- Quality has improved;
- Pesticides are used less frequently;
- Control and predictability;
- Increased selling price; and
- Forecasting the future.

10.5.4 WSN FOR SMART IRRIGATION MANAGEMENT

It is difficult to maintain water management in agricultural land because it needs to consider various factors such as irrigation, watering the crop, and Drip irrigation. Another important considerable factor in water management depends upon the type of crops, soil (Alluvial Soil, Black Soil, Red Soil, and Mountain Soil), soil fertility, and land (arid and semiarid areas) [21]. Before selecting irrigation techniques, consider the soil's nutrients level, such as nitrogen, phosphorous, and potassium. Farmers in some regions use briny water for irrigation, depending on the land type. As a result of the high saline level in the water, the yielding level is decreased. Therefore, in order to encourage peasant practices and water monitoring, using the geological dissemination system of water to control irrigation in such areas is essential [22].

Farmers obtain irrigation water from ponds, lakes, rivers, and rain. As a result, irrigation methods differ based on water supplies and nutrient levels. Therefore, the common traditional way of irrigation techniques and practices does not find suitable for aiming maximum yielding. Thus, conventional irrigation techniques and technologies do not seem to be suitable for achieving maximum yields. It pushes farmers to the next step, encouraging them to migrate to smart irrigation strategies to avoid water wastages during irrigation. Smart irrigation's primary aim is to supply water for agricultural purposes to both dry and wet fields [23]. Converging from conventional irrigation to smart irrigation has been shown to increase yields in both quality and quantity. Farmers would be able to track their agriculture and supply water when required without the need for human interference using mechanized irrigation methods [24].

Farmers can now control the water level in their fields and monitor crop development from anywhere due to modern technologies. Static sensor nodes provide authentic and real-time field pieces of information related to water to farmers; thus, the farmers can make effective decisions on time to develop crops. WSNs can help in creating the IoT framework. It is made up of various network nodes (sensors) that are each powered by a solar-powered removable battery. A Group of sensor nodes and actuators is commonly referred to as a Cyber-Physical System (CPS) capable of processing low-level data, information storage, and networking. These are self-governing units and perform low-level processing without delay [25]. Based on the application's concerns, the network can be constructed using various topologies (ring, mesh, and bus). Message Queuing Telemetry Transport (MQTT) or Constrained Application Protocol (CoAP) are the transfer protocol used to share the information between the sensor nodes. Multiple sensor nodes/actuators are mounted in different farmland regions to sense accurate factors. The central gateway is in charge of collecting data from various nodes and transferring it to the cloud server over the internet. Artificial intelligence methods can be used to reach optimal yielding milestones. Different machine learning (ML) methods are used to inspect the data for effective decision-making. So that users can retrieve the data and take the necessary actions to improve yields based on real-world factors [26].

10.5.5 PEST MANAGEMENT IN PRECISION AGRICULTURE

Pesticide overuse is harmful not only to the environment, but also to people and the economy of the country. Insects and rodents are the primary cause of agricultural economic loss. As a result, farmers commonly use pesticides to combat weeds, insects, and plant diseases.

10.5.5.1 REGULATORS OF PEST GROWTH (RPG)

RHCS suppresses the growth of insects in farmland by using insecticides. Many regulators of insect growth (RPG) are combined with adult insecticides. By interfering with molting, RPG prevents an insect from reaching adulthood. Humans are less harmed by RPGs in general.

10.5.5.2   TOOLS FOR COMMUNICATION

Mobile technologies are widely used in pest management to find factual information about the location of insects in farmland and save it in a cloud server to access by the insect control expert and admin. This modern technology makes it possible to monitor the land from far away and allows the farmers to take necessary action against insects.

10.5.5.3   FLY BAITS

Fly bait stickers may be used in places where flies congregate, such as in food storage areas. When flies come into contact with the tiny tag, it is coated in insect food and an insecticide that can take them down in under a minute [27].

10.5.5.4   ULTRASONIC GENERATOR

Ultrasonic sound is described as audible sound with a frequency greater than 20,000 Hz. Ultrasonic can be generated using a variety of methods, including mechanical, piezoelectric, and magnetostriction. The ultrasonic waves are produced by a piezoelectric process.

A sound transducer is a device that transforms electrical current into sound waves. The fusion of iron and nickel is used to produce ultrasonic magnetostriction.

10.5.5.5   IMAGE PROCESSING

Extracting valid information from the captured picture is referred to as image processing. It captured the actual location of insects in farmland and compared it to the saved picture to identify the presence of the insect. The following measures are used in image processing:

- The image captures and transfers it to the microcontroller;
- Analysis of the transferred image in microcontroller to detect the data.

Analog and digital image processing are the two methods of image processing [28–30]. It allows for the capture of a visual record of a moving object.

KEYWORDS

- **digital image processing**
- **geographic information systems**
- **information and communications technology**
- **Internet of things**
- **precision agriculture**
- **wireless sensor network**

REFERENCES

1. Ahmed, N., De, D., & Hussain, I., (2018). Internet of things (IoT) for smart precision agriculture and farming in rural areas. *IEEE Internet of Things Journal, 5*(6), 4890–4899.
2. Navarro-Hellín, H., Martínez-del-Rincon, J., Domingo-Miguel, R., Soto-Valles, F., & Torres-Sánchez, R., (2016). A decision support system for managing irrigation in agriculture. *Computers and Electronics in Agriculture, 124*, 121–131.
3. Feng, X., Yan, F., & Liu, X., (2019). Study of wireless communication technologies on Internet of Things for precision agriculture. *Wireless Personal Communications, 108*(3), 1785–1802.
4. Ferrández-Pastor, F. J., García-Chamizo, J. M., Nieto-Hidalgo, M., & Mora-Martínez, J., (2018). Precision agriculture design method using a distributed computing architecture on internet of things context. *Sensors, 18*, 1731.
5. Ojha, T., Misra, S., & Raghuwanshi, N. S., (2015). Wireless sensor networks for agriculture: The state of the art in practice and future challenges. *Computers and Electronics in Agriculture, 118*, 66–84.
6. Tordera, E. M., et al., (2016). *What is a Fog Node? A Tutorial on Current Concepts Towards a Common Definition.* arXiv preprint arXiv:1611.09193 [Online]. Available: https://arxiv.org/abs/1611.09193 (accessed on 11 August 2022).
7. Armbrust, M., et al., (2010). A view of cloud computing. *Commun. ACM, 53*(4), 50–58.
8. Bu, F., & Wang, X., (2019). A smart agriculture IoT system based on deep reinforcement learning. *Future Generation Computer Systems, 99*, 500–507.
9. https://www.downtoearth.org.in/news/agriculture/agri-share-in-gdp-hit-20-after-17-years-economic-survey-75271 (accessed on 11 August 2022).

10. Tamoghna, O., Sudip, M., & Narendra, (2015). WSN for agriculture: state of the art in practice and future challenges. *J. Comput. Electron. Agric.*, 66–84.
11. Ben-Dor, E., & Banin, A., (1993). Near-infrared analysis as a rapid method to simultaneously evaluate several soil properties. *Soil Sci. Soc. Am. J.*, 364–372.
12. Lavanya, G., Rani, C., & Ganeshkumar, P., (2020). An automated low cost IoT based fertilizer intimation system for smart agriculture. *Sustainable Computing: Informatics and Systems, 28*, 100300.
13. Gubbi, J., Buyya, R., Marusic, S., & Palaniswami, M. (2013). Internet of Things (IoT): A vision, architectural elements, and future directions. *Future Generation Computer Systems, 29*(7), 1645–1660.
14. Harun, A. N., Kassim, M. R. M., Mat, I., & Ramli, S. S. (2015, May). Precision irrigation using wireless sensor network. In 2015 International Conference on Smart Sensors and Application (ICSSA) (pp. 71–75). IEEE.
15. https://www.mouser.in/applications/smart-agriculture-sensors (accessed on 11 August 2022).
16. Laxmi, S. S., & Hemavati, B. B., (2018). *Design and Implementation of IOT-Based Smart Security and Monitoring for Connected Smart Farming,* Elsevier.
17. McLoud, P. R., Gronwald, R., & Kuykendall, H., (2007). *Precision Agriculture: NRCS Support for Emerging Technologies.* Agronomy Technical Note (1).
18. Bongiovanni, R., & Lowenberg-DeBoer, J., (2004). Precision agriculture and sustainability. *Precision Agriculture, 5*(4), 359–387.
19. Jiang, H., & Cotton, W. R., (2004). Soil moisture estimation using an artificial neural network: a feasibility study. *Canadian Journal of Remote Sensing, 30*(5), 827–839.
20. Ferrández-Pastor, F. J., García-Chamizo, J. M., Nieto-Hidalgo, M., Mora-Pascual, J., & Mora-Martínez, J., (2016). Developing ubiquitous sensor network platform using internet of things: Application in precision agriculture. *Sensors, 16*(7), 1141.
21. Estrada-López, J. J., Castillo-Atoche, A. A., Vázquez-Castillo, J., & Sánchez-Sinencio, E., (2018). Smart soil parameters estimation system using an autonomous wireless sensor network with dynamic power management strategy. *IEEE Sensors Journal, 18*(21), 8913–8923.
22. https://easternpeak.com/blog/smart-agriculture-monitoring-solutions-to-optimize-farming-productivity (accessed on 11 August 2022).
23. Saad, A., & Gamatié, A., (2020). Water management in agriculture: A survey on current challenges and technological solutions. *IEEE Access, 8*, 38082–38097.
24. Bradaï, A., Douaoui, A., Bettahar, N., & Yahiaoui, I., (2016). Improving the prediction accuracy of groundwater salinity mapping using indicator kriging method. *Journal of Irrigation and Drainage Engineering, 142*(7), 04016023.
25. Chen, A., Orlov-Levin, V., & Meron, M., (2019). Applying high-resolution visible-channel aerial imaging of crop canopy to precision irrigation management. *Agricultural Water Management, 216*, 196–205.
26. Koduru, S., Padala, V. P. R., & Padala, P., (2019). Smart irrigation system using cloud and internet of things. In: *Proceedings of 2ⁿᵈ International Conference on Communication, Computing and Networking* (pp. 195–203) Springer, Singapore.
27. Akyildiz, I. F., Su, W., Sankarasubramaniam, Y., & Cayirci, E., (2002). Wireless sensor networks: a survey. *Computer Networks, 38*(4), 393–422.

28. Ojha, T., Misra, S., & Raghuwanshi, N. S., (2015). Wireless sensor networks for agriculture: The state-of-the-art in practice and future challenges. *Computers and Electronics in Agriculture, 118*, 66–84.

29. https://www.intechopen.com/online-first/modern-technologies-for-pest-control-a-review (accessed on 11 August 2022).

30. Saranya, K., (2019). *IoT Based Pest Controlling System for Smart Agriculture*. IEEE.

CHAPTER 11

Blockchain-Based Distributed Transactions for Industrial Applications

GARGI LOHIA[1] and K. SANTHI[2]

[1]Student, Computer Science and Engineering, VIT, Vellore, Tamil Nadu, India

[2]School of Information Technology and Engineering, VIT, Vellore, Tamil Nadu, India

ABSTRACT

This chapter discusses blockchain technology, how distributed ledger works, transactions function in blockchain, and how distributed transactions are operated. We then look at the consensus system of blockchain and digital signatures. Next, we look at the major industrial applications like cloud computing in blockchain, software engineering frameworks using blockchain, cryptocurrencies, smart contracts, energy trading using blockchain, supply chain management, healthcare, etc. We have proposed a model for manufacturing using blockchain-based distributed transactions, which aims to solve major industrial problems using techniques highlighted in the chapter.

11.1 INTRODUCTION

Blockchain is a technology that is gaining popularity not only in the industry but also among people outside it. Due to its nature and the number of people

Hybridization of Blockchain and Cloud Computing: Overcoming Security Issues in IoT.
M. Lawanya Shri, E. Gangadevi, K. Santhi, & Chiranji Lal Chowdhary (Eds.)

working on it, a wide range of applications of blockchain are discovered in the industry, that will not only revolutionize it and drive innovation, but also make existing processes way more efficient. Blockchain technology is an area of extensive research and investment. Its nature enables it to be secure while maintaining anonymity. This chapter takes into account generic papers written on the basis of research over individual applications over blockchain. One can observe that the applications follow a similar route. As a result, this chapter can aid in the development of further studies on industrial applications of blockchain-based distributed transactions. We have proposed a model for manufacturing using blockchain-based distributed transactions, which aims to solve major industrial problems using techniques highlighted in the chapter. It helps in the following ways:

i.   It aims to empower small-scale owners, farmers, and manufacturers;
ii. By employing blockchain and it promises to uniquely benefit startups and new businesses that make use of various processes and entities;
iii. It pushes for a decentralized model for business operation and eliminates the need for middlemen with the help of tokens and distributed transactions on blockchain.

The objective of this chapter is to be able to apply blockchain and distributed transactions for industrial purposes.

11.2   DISTRIBUTED LEDGERS

The underlying technology behind The underlying technology behind blockchain is distributed ledger technology (DLT), often called DLT. Blockchain is a kind of DLT and is the most popular application of the same.

As the name implies, a distributed ledger works like a ledger that maintains records, but the data that it holds isn't centralized. The ledger is maintained by multiple different servers that can be geographically separated, which share and maintain replicated versions of the data that is held by the ledger. This absence of central authority is the main feature of distributed technology [3].

The distributed servers, called nodes, maintain the peer-to-peer network that votes using consensus deciding the correct version of the transaction. The transaction is introduced by an update, and using special consensus algorithms (based on proof of stake or proof of work). The nodes determine which transaction is legitimate [14].

Permissioned ledgers only allow certain approved parties to participate in the transactions. This involves the existence of a central authority, since for anyone to be a part of the network, someone needs to give an approval.

Permissionless ledgers allow everyone to run nodes in the network and are open to all. These ledgers used proof of work (determined by the number of resources held by a node) to allow nodes to validate transactions. Since resources cannot be centralized, it allows for decentralization, while ensuring that only those with maximum computing power can legitimately mine blocks and add transactions. This can be executed through different methods. In Bitcoin, to discover a block, nodes have to find solutions to hash functions which take up a huge amount of computation power (72,000 GW).

11.2.1 DISTRIBUTED TRANSACTIONS

Distributed transactions in the context of blockchain are transactions on a distributed ledger, which aren't handled by a single entity. There exists an authority that can provide the resources, and a single entity that manages these transactions, but the database network spans two or more nodes [6].

These transactions have all ACID properties, ensuring the data remains valid even if errors occur. The 'A' stands for 'atomicity,' which means that a single transaction should be treated like a single unit, implying that either all of it is processed, or it completely fails, ensuring that either the database is completely updated, or is left unchanged (and not partially updated). 'C' stands for 'consistency,' which means that a transaction cannot leave the database in an invalid state, meaning that database constraints and other rules should be maintained after a transaction. This saves the database from being corrupted with invalid data, but does not guarantee the correctness of the transaction. 'I' refers to 'isolation,' which translates to the database reaching the same final state irrespective of whether the transactions occur sequentially or concurrently (concurrency control), implying that each transaction is isolated from the rest. Finally, 'D' stands for 'durability,' which ensures that transactions, once committed, aren't affected if the system fails.

Since these transactions happen with the help of multiple nodes/databases, synchronization is an important property they must satisfy.

The serializability of transactions refers to the outcome of a group of transactions remaining the same if they are executed serially compared to being executed concurrently, which separates these transactions in time and makes them serializable. To confirm global serializability, strict two-phase locking (SS2PL) is used, which allows a transaction to block data from being accessed by other transactions while that transaction is being executed. The two-phase commit protocol (2PC) is a popular algorithm that enables the processing of distributed transactions by coordinating between the different processes using 'commit' and 'abort' and logging the states [11].

One type of distributed transaction is long-lived transactions, which do not make use of 2PC as these might take a lot of time and, therefore, cannot block the data for long. These long-lived distributed transactions are then executed with the help of web services.

11.2.2   BLOCKCHAIN EXECUTES DISTRIBUTED TRANSACTIONS

Blockchain is a distributed ledger that consists of a series of blocks as data structures. The main ledger that contains all valid blocks that have been approved by the peer-to-peer network is called the blockchain [7, 13].

Blocks are added to the long-term chain through a process called mining. Miners are people who contribute to the blockchain by adding blocks to it. Blockchain verifies transactions through the elliptic curve distributed signature algorithm (ECDSA). The Equation of an elliptic curve is:

$$y = x' + ax + c$$

11.2.3   TRANSACTIONS VALIDATION

The people who discover the block (miners) can decide what transactions to include in the block. However, to validate a transaction, a block must be added to the long-term blockchain through consensus [30]. The miners keep adding their blocks to the chains they think are legitimate. The longest chain gets added to the long-term permanent chain that cannot be changed. Each block holds a number of transactions that need not be related to each other [8].

11.2.3.1 MINE THE BLOCKS

Miners include anyone who has the necessary resources to discover blocks. The resources include computational capacity (proof of work) or the stake in a particular blockchain (proof of stake). The proof of work system ensures that finding a block takes a significant amount of time, and protects against centralization and too many solutions at once. The miners get block rewards (BRs) after mining a block that gets added to the long-term consensus chain, which forms an incentive mechanism for miners to keep mining. In private blockchains, however, this peer-to-peer network-based validation doesn't need to happen since parties unrelated to the transactions shouldn't be informed about the same. Corda is an example of a private distributed ledger system.

11.3 THE BLOCKCHAIN CONSENSUS SYSTEM FOR DISTRIBUTED TRANSACTIONS

We have understood that the blockchain consists of blocks that contain a number of transactions. However, for resources to be exchanged between two or more parties, it has to be verified that the resources aren't illegally distributed, before they are added to the long-term chain. This is where digital signatures come in [5]. In Blockchain, a way through which objects are given identities is through tokens. Tokens represent objects/parts of objects and can be exchanged as they hold value.

11.3.1 DIGITAL SIGNATURES

A digital signature, much like a real-world signature, is a proof that a message or a transaction (which is signed) comes from the source it claims. The signature is a code that is impossible to counterfeit. The process of producing a digital signature involves asymmetric cryptography, which makes the use of two keys to secure messages and transactions. The keys also ensure that the message wasn't changed before it reaches the receiver. This is exceptionally important in industrial systems and supply chains where it is important to ensure that the materials aren't tampered with. Another property of these signatures is non-repudiation which means that after signing a transaction, the sender cannot claim that they haven't made the transaction.

11.3.2   HASH FUNCTIONS

Hash functions are used to create digital signatures and link blocks with each other. As mentioned, a key pair is randomly generated, after which the document containing the transaction and one of the keys (called the private key) is hashed (transformed into another key representing the data using a hash function). The person receiving the document makes use of the other key (public key – that is visible to everyone) to verify that the sender made the transaction. If the transaction is tampered with, the hash doesn't match the public key, and the transaction becomes invalid.

11.4   PROPOSED METHOD INDUSTRIAL COMPONENTS TOKENIZED IN TRANSACTIONS ON BLOCKCHAIN

Any industry has 4–5 main factors of production, like land, labor, capital, entrepreneurship, and marketing. These components function individually, but have to be managed at a macro level. These components have to be managed, and a lot of effort has to be put in to make sure they function together efficiently as well as in isolation.

For upcoming entrepreneurs, small scale productions, gathering each For upcoming entrepreneurs and small-scale productions, gathering each of these factors in isolation can be a huge task. The land is extremely expensive, and it is very difficult to buy pieces of land, especially in industrial regions due to high demand for the same [32]. Brokers and middlemen that help in acquiring land take up huge sums of money. Similarly, manufacturing machines are huge and few, while being expensive. They take up space and also need to be maintained. Most processes also do not require these machines continuously. Finding the right workforce is another huge issue. Skilled laborers are extremely hard to find at an optimal cost.

Another major problem is finding enough capital to fund the business and keep it going. Small-scale owners such as farmers and startup owners are extremely gullible and do not have the means to take huge loans. Middlemen thus take advantage of this fact and charge high rates of interest on the loans they provide. Owners of a business/organization thus have to end up paying for more than what they actually use.

As we have observed, blockchain enables giving identification to entities using tokenization and allows the trade of the same using distributed transactions. Landowners, laborers, and machine owners/traders can divide the land, machines, capital they use, and the labor force available in the market into entities, e.g., 1 square hectare of land can be used as a single token. Individual laborers and machines can similarly be given tokens. Transactions on the same can be performed on a single platform by small-scale owners and interested people. Use of multiple blockchains (or, a blockchain of blockchain) to divide ownership of individual components as tokens (much like ownership of stocks, but here all components of the industry can be involved) based on time agreements using smart contracts, small industries can afford to function. This helps them use certain entities temporarily without having to spend money to buy the same.

This helps in the following ways:

1. **Cost Saving:** It helps in reducing huge amounts of money as it does away with the need for middlemen and saves transaction time. Business might even profit from these transactions if they happen over blockchain-based cryptocurrencies.
2. **Accessibility:** By placing all requirements on a single blockchain that can be securely operated by everyone, it makes all these components accessible to everyone having the means to access the blockchain.
3. **Standardization:** Given that everything can be tokenized, these tokens can have a standard cost, which will help in reducing total costs for the industry.
4. **Accountability:** Even though transactions on a blockchain allow users to be anonymous, given how smart contracts work, users are accountable for their transactions.

The available tokens and the requirement of certain tokens can be published to the peer-to-peer network, and transactions can be agreed upon. After transactions have been made, they are validated through the consensus algorithm. The consensus algorithm for such a blockchain is very similar to the consensus algorithm for bitcoin.

11.4.1 CONSENSUS ALGORITHM

➢ **Step 1:** The transactions that have been agreed upon are sent to the peer-to-peer network.
➢ **Step 2:** Every node in the peer-to-peer network collects transactions into a block.

> ➤ **Step 3:** The block that is randomly chosen decides what transactions to add.
> ➤ **Step 4:** The block is validated if other nodes include its hash in the next block.

Smart contract-based land, labor, and machinery agreement–by providing identities to pieces of land and groups of labor (in terms of hours of work/efficiency) can enable industries to operate with land, labor, and machines without having the cost to buy/rent these factors for longer periods of time (even when they are not in use). Digital marketing agreements, capital (or ownership) can also be operated block-wise, with distributed transactions. These pay-per-use models can prove highly advantageous for technical organizations that have to make use of certain technology for developing a product for a short period of time. This enables quicker growth of the industry, as small-scale manufacturers and products do not have to rely upon dedicated investments and can drive their industry forward. Note that this approach is decentralized. A centralized approach can be adopted when an organization wants to operate on a blockchain while issuing a certain amenity. For example, a retail owner executing a gift card scheme through blockchain operates on a centralized blockchain, as they issue cards and make transactions based on their will.

11.5   INDUSTRIAL APPLICATION

Let us now understand how blockchain and its components can be used for distributed transactions for industrial applications.

11.5.1   *SMART CONTRACTS*

Smart contracts are transactions that are executed by themselves with the help of certain conditions/limits. This mode of transaction does away with the need for intermediate parties that have to be trusted, e.g., Banks. The transactions need not be monitored and are executed based on predetermined time limits, e.g., if Bill's grandmother has to pay him a certain amount every month, she can make a smart contract that will automatically transfer that amount from her bank account to Bill's account. A smart contract, once made, cannot be changed [15, 16].

11.5.2 CLOUD COMPUTING

Cloud technology is a dynamic network that enables transfer of data in real-time. Thus, blockchain can help in securing, locating data and tracking data [1]. Blockchain provides anonymity to the users by enabling users to verify transactions using digital signatures that cannot be traced to user identity. Coupled with cloud technology, this transaction system can become more convenient with greater security features (by using digitally powered wallets that store private keys in the cloud platform) [17].

Storage of data, replication of data, access to the database can be enabled using cloud technology. In the existing system, if the private key of a transaction is lost, the coins are lost forever. Industries require management of a number of transactions on a daily basis, and in the absence of efficient and secure storage platforms, these keys can be stolen/lost. Task, user, and data management can be achieved through cloud technology. This can prove useful in supply chains, healthcare management and in detecting the spread of diseases [18].

11.5.3 SOFTWARE ENGINEERING FRAMEWORKS WITH BLOCKCHAIN

A number of blockchain-based products, like storage with the help of blockchain and blockchain as a service (BaaS), are being adopted by major companies. There are three main factors industrialists check while employing blockchain frameworks: security, scalability, and performance [18]. Due to its guaranteed features like transparency, traceability, and immutability, blockchain is being adopted in the software engineering industry, where development of a product involves multiple organizations. It removes the necessity of trust and operates on technical expertise. Products and processes can be grouped into blocks which can be identified with developers/consumers. This helps in easy export of products and identification and control of errors, as product development can be traced all the way back to its source. Decentralized apps (dApps) are also being adopted by the industry, although its adoption is restricted by latency issues [19].

11.5.4 CRYPTOCURRENCIES

The most popular use of Blockchain is in cryptocurrencies, especially Bitcoin and Ethereum. They are operated with a proof-of-work blockchain that allows miners to come up with blocks every 10 minutes [20]. Even though a number of altcoins have come into the industry, Bitcoin remains popular due to three factors: rate of unit production, competition level in producers and mining algorithm difficulty [21]. Blockchain helps in direct payments without the involvement of banks/ any centralized authority. Through incentivization (BRs and transaction fees), people are forced to remain honest and not succumb to malpractice. There are various ways through which these bitcoins are stored, and decentralized identity management ensures that payments are verified without revealing the identities of the users. The cryptocurrency market is growing by the minute as research in the field is increasing market trust in the currency, thus attracting investors, which are shown in Figure 11.1.

FIGURE 11.1 Bitcoin logo.

11.5.5 ENERGY TRADING (USING INDUSTRIAL INTERNET OF THINGS)

Energy trading is the commercial trade of energy. Energy is a major requirement and is undeniably the most important industry. An example of blockchain-based energy trading is net metering [2]. It allows producers to trade with consumers without involving middlemen based on consumers' requirements. For instance, people producing electricity from renewable resources can provide the same to the consumers directly or themselves use this electricity whenever they want (after a period of time), rather than having to use it immediately after it is produced. It thus helps in cost saving, as consumers don't have to pay for slabs of electricity if they aren't using as much, and can transfer that amount of electricity to the next month. Distributed Transactions in Blockchain helps in keeping track of the blocks of energy that are available, and the consumers who purchase them. In the Industrial Internet of Things, energy trading exists in peer-to-peer networks (harvesting of energy, microgrids, etc.), and the use of blockchain enables overcoming security hurdles by securing these transactions and eliminating the need for a trusted third party between the producer and the consumer [22]. This also helps in reducing delays and allows for efficient energy usage and increases privacy to a huge extent [23].

11.5.6 SUPPLY CHAIN MANAGEMENT

In supply chains, it is important and very advantageous to be able to trace where materials come from. It can help in increasing profit margins by decreasing losses incurred due to damages and faults in the supply chain, and help in preventing losses due to gray markets. It helps in efficient management of supply chains, thereby increasing efficiency in production. Presently, organizations include third-party software/organizations to be able to integrate supply chain management. This increases integration costs and lowers diffusion [24].

Blockchain not only increases transparency of the whole supply chain process, but also reduces paperwork using smart contracts. It thus enables the stakeholders in the management industry to remain engaged in the process by allowing end-to-end tracking.

Physical entities that have to be traded have identities and are added to the distributed ledger, which is immutable. This improves consumer trust as it increases the visibility of the product in the chain while making the process secure [9]. There is also lesser need for other communication resources between entities through which materials have to pass, since the blockchain makes it visible for everyone. In supply chains currently, it is difficult to detect and locate problems since there remain gaps in communication. Also, organizations issue hundreds of transactions every day, thus making not only the process difficult to manage, but also the payments difficult to record.

Supply chains employ permissioned blockchains. Specific uses of blockchain in supply chain are summarized below:

1. **Food Supply:** Food products are susceptible to being damaged with time. Blockchain allows us to track the contamination and edibility of food by giving identities to products. Companies like Walmart and IBM are already on board for using blockchain to track their meat supplies.

2. **Mining:** Gems like diamond, etc., are extremely expensive and are prone to black markets and doping. Ever ledger partnered with IBM's tracking service to check ethical mining.

Blockchain helps in overcoming inter-organizational, intra-organizational, technical, and external barriers related to blockchain. Businesses are motivated to integrate blockchain due to its sustainable management of the supply chain [25, 26].

11.5.7 HEALTHCARE

Figure 11.2 shows an electronic health records of a patient are important for healthcare management. However, due to the unavailability of secure sharing platforms, information about patients is not secure, and is based on the trust patients have in the hospitals and organizations that are given this data directly. This, however, results in data leak, as hackers and other third parties can easily steal patient data. Another problem from a patient's perspective [10] is filling and sharing data over and over again, which results in time being spent in sharing the same data again. Another issue in the healthcare industry is managing pharmaceuticals and supply of verified medications [27].

Blockchain provides solutions to these problems due to its attack-resistant chain, which can hold patient details under unique patient IDs. Patients can sign the blocks using private keys and share this information to the required organizations. This information stays permanent, and anyone who wants to alter it has to alter all of the blockchain. This data is also stored over a lot of nodes without being completely visible, making blockchain an ideal platform for healthcare data [28].

FIGURE 11.2   Healthcare implementation using smart contracts in blockchain.

Using IoT, data can also be remotely monitored with the help of mobile applications. Researchers have conducted tests for a few tests, where data is shared in real-time using cloud technology, and is stored in blockchain which makes it secure and tamper proof. Healthcare organizations like hospitals that require this data can then provide necessary help to the patient in no time. In China, blockchain is being used to track health insurance and speed up the process of providing the same.

11.5.8   OTHER APPLICATIONS

The IoT [12] and sharing economy both include peer-to-peer networks and thus are set to benefit from the rise of distributed transactions in blockchain. Voting made online, and online library systems are a few other applications that can be made possible with the help of distributed transactions. Any manufacturing process that can be divided into subparts can be achieved with the help of distributed transactions. The materials can then be traced with the help of the same distributed transactions and can be located easily [3, 4].

11.6   CONCLUSION

Blockchain-based distributed transactions prove to be highly advantageous for industrial use, as they fill up loopholes in the industrial process and make a number of tasks more efficient. As investments and research in the field gain more popularity, blockchain coupled with other advancing technologies like industrial IoT, deep learning, and artificial intelligence can drive innovations in the industry. This chapter has given an insight into the major applications of blockchain as it functions today in various fields and can be used for further research on the same.

KEYWORDS

- **blockchain as a service**
- **blockchain technology**
- **cloud technology**
- **hash functions**
- **peer to peer network**
- **permissioned and permissionless ledgers**
- **proof of work**

REFERENCES

1. Sarmah, S. S., (2019). Application of blockchain in cloud computing. *International Journal of Innovative Technology and Exploring Engineering, 8*(12), 2278–3075. 10.35940/ijitee.L3585.1081219.
2. Creative Commons, (2020). Net metering. Wikipedia. https://en.wikipedia.org/wiki/Net_metering#Virtual_net_metering (accessed on 11 August 2022).
3. Javed, M. U., Rehman, M., Javaid, N., Aldegheishem, A., Alrajeh, N., & Tahir, M. (2020). Blockchain-based secure data storage for distributed vehicular networks. *Applied Sciences, 10*(6), 2011.
4. Fan, W., Sang, Y. C., Shawn, E., & Xiaobo, Z., (2020). Blockchain-based distributed banking for permissioned and accountable financial transaction processing. *IEEE 29th International Conference on Computer.* 10.1109/ICCCN49398.2020.9209687.
5. Zhao, D., & Tonglin, L., (2020). *Distributed Cross-Blockchain Transactions.* In Databases. https://doi.org/10.14778/xxxxxxx.xxxxxxx.
6. *The Difference Between Blockchain and Distributed Ledger Technology,* (2018). N.P.: Tradeix. https://tradeix.com/distributed-ledger-technology/ (accessed on 11 August 2022).
7. Ray, S., (2016). *Blockchains: The Technology of Transactions.* Towards data science. https://towardsdatascience.com/blockchains-the-technology-of-transactions-9d40e8e41216 (accessed on 11 August 2022).
8. Gupta, S., Jelle, H., & Mohammad, S., (2021). *Fault-Tolerant Distributed Transactions on Blockchain Synthesis Lectures on Data Management.* N.P.: Morgan and Claypool Publishers. https://doi.org/10.2200/S01068ED1V01Y202012DTM065.

9. Li, X., Peng, J., Ting, C., Xiapu, L., & Qiaoyan, W., (2020). A survey on the security of blockchain systems. *Future Generation Computer Systems, 107*, 841–853. https://doi.org/10.1016/j.future.2017.08.020.

10. Chen, H. S., et al., (2019). Blockchain in healthcare: A patient-centered model. *Biomedical Journal of Scientific & Technical Research, 20*(3), 15017-15022.

11. Beck, R., Stenum, C. J., Lollike, N., & Malone, S., (2016). *Blockchain–the Gateway to Trust-Free Cryptographic Transactions*. Research Papers. 153. https://aisel.aisnet.org/ecis2016_rp/153 (accessed on 11 August 2022).

12. Kravitz, D. W., & Cooper, J., (2017). Securing user identity and transactions symbiotically: IoT meets blockchain. In: *2017 Global Internet of Things Summit (GIoTS)* (pp. 1–6). Geneva, Switzerland. 10.1109/GIOTS.2017.8016280.

13. Kiayias, A., & Panagiotakos, G., (2019). On trees, chains and fast transactions in the blockchain. In: Lange, T., & Dunkelman, O., (eds.), *Progress in Cryptology – LATINCRYPT 2017; LATINCRYPT 2017: Lecture Notes in Computer Science* (Vol. 11368). Springer, Cham. https://doi.org/10.1007/978-3-030-25283-0_18.

14. Tiwari, H., (2017). Merkle-damgård construction method and alternatives: A review. *Journal of Information and Organizational Science, 41*, 283–304. 10.31341/jios.41.2.9.

15. Christidis, K., & Devetsikiotis, M., (2016). Blockchains and smart contracts for the internet of things. In: *IEEE Access* (Vol. 4, pp. 2292–2303). doi: 10.1109/ACCESS.2016.2566339.

16. Lin, W. C., & Zhiguo, H., (2019). Blockchain disruption and smart contracts. *The Review of Financial Studies, 32*(5), 1754–1797. https://doi.org/10.1093/rfs/hhz007.

17. Park, J. H., & Park, J. H., (2017). Blockchain security in cloud computing: Use cases, challenges, and solutions. *Symmetry, 9*(8), 164. https://doi.org/10.3390/sym9080164

18. Gaetani, E., Aniello, L., Baldoni, R., Lombardi, F., Margheri, A., & Sassone, V., (2017). Blockchain-based database to ensure data integrity in cloud computing environments. *Italian Conference on Cybersecurity* (p. 10). Italy. https://eprints.soton.ac.uk/411996/ (accessed on 11 August 2022).

19. Julien, P., Jérémy, R., & Yves, L. T., (2020*).* Permissioned blockchain frameworks in the industry: A comparison. *ICT Express*. ISSN 2405-9595. https://doi.org/10.1016/j.icte.2020.09.002.

20. Beck, R., Müller-Bloch, C., & King, J. L., (2018). Governance in the blockchain economy: A framework and research agenda. *Journal of the Association for Information Systems, 19*(10), Article 1.

21. DeVries, P. D., (2016). An analysis of cryptocurrency, bitcoin, and the future. *International Journal of Business Management and Commerce, 1*(2), 1–9.

22. Adam, S. H., (2017). Cryptocurrency value formation: An empirical study leading to a cost of production model for valuing bitcoin. *Telematics and Informatics, 34*(7), 1308–1321, ISSN 0736-5853, https://doi.org/10.1016/j.tele.2016.05.005.

23. Li, Z., Kang, J., Yu, R., Ye, D., Deng, Q., & Zhang, Y., (2018). Consortium blockchain for secure energy trading in industrial internet of things. In: *IEEE Transactions on Industrial Informatics, 14*(8), 3690–3700. doi: 10.1109/TII.2017.2786307.

24. Gai, K., Wu, Y., Zhu, L., Qiu, M., & Shen, M., (2019). Privacy-preserving energy trading using consortium blockchain in smart grid. In: *IEEE Transactions on Industrial Informatics* (Vol. 15, No. 6, pp. 3548–3558). doi: 10.1109/TII.2019.2893433.

25. Kari, K., Hallikas, J., & Dahlberg, T., (2017). Digital supply chain transformation toward blockchain integration. *The Digital Supply Chain of the Future: Technologies, Applications and Business Models Minitrack*, 1–10. 10.24251/HICSS.2017.506.
26. Sara, S., Mahtab, K., Joseph, S., & Lejia, S., (2019). Blockchain technology and its relationships to sustainable supply chain management *International Journal of Production Research, 57*(7), 2117–2135. doi: 10.1080/00207543.2018.1533261.
27. Casado-Vara, R., Javier, P., Fernando De La, P., & Juan, M. C., (2018). How blockchain improves the supply chain: case study alimentary supply chain. *Procedia Computer Science, 134*, 393–398, ISSN 1877-0509, https://doi.org/10.1016/j.procs. 2018.07.193.
28. Agbo, C. C., Mahmoud, Q. H., & Eklund, J. M., (2019). Blockchain technology in healthcare: A systematic review. *Healthcare, 7*(2), 56. https://doi.org/10.3390/healthcare7020056.
29. Mettler, M., (2016). Blockchain technology in healthcare: The revolution starts here. In: *2016 IEEE 18th International Conference on e-Health Networking, Applications and Services (Healthcom)* (pp. 1–3). Munich, Germany. doi: 10.1109/HealthCom.2016.7749510.
30. Tasatanattakool, P., & Techapanupreeda, C., (2018). Blockchain: Challenges and applications. In: *2018 International Conference on Information Networking (ICOIN)* (pp. 473–475). Chiang Mai, Thailand. doi: 10.1109/ICOIN.2018.8343163.
31. Sankar, L. S., Sindhu, M., & Sethumadhavan, M., (2017). Survey of consensus protocols on blockchain applications. In: *2017 4th International Conference on Advanced Computing and Communication Systems (ICACCS)* (pp. 1–5). Coimbatore, India. doi: 10.1109/ICACCS.2017.8014672.
32. Bennett, R., Miller, T., Pickering, M., & Kara, A. K., (2021). Hybrid approaches for smart contracts in land administration: Lessons from three blockchain proofs-of-concept. *Land, 10*, 220. https://doi.org/ 10.3390/land10020220.
33. Desiree, D., & Ifejika, S. C., (2020). The role of blockchain in documenting land users' rights: The canonical case of farmers in the vernacular land market. *Frontiers in Blockchain 3*, 19. 10.3389/fbloc.2020.00019.

CHAPTER 12

Consensus Mechanism of Blockchain for Industrial Internet of Things (IIoT)

CHARIT GUPTA PALURI[1] and K. SANTHI[2]

[1]*Student, Computer Science and Engineering, VIT, Vellore, Tamil Nadu, India*

[2]*School of Information Technology and Engineering, VIT, Vellore, Tamil Nadu, India*

ABSTRACT

The Industrial Internet of Things is also known as IIoT. It mainly refers to an industrial structure where many electronic devices are interconnected under a wireless network. IIoT plays a huge role in Industry 4.0 (a fourth industrial revolution of traditional manufacturing and industrial practices, using the newest technologies). One of the main aims of Industry 4.0 is to incorporate IIoT across various industries. But however, the current IIoT is liable to failures such as malicious attacks, network hacks, and other digitalized attacks, which cannot supply stable and reliable services to fulfill the needs of IIoT in an industry. Combining blockchain and the Internet of Things (IoT) can help to overcome these failures because implementing blockchain can increase the security and resilience of an IIoT system. In this chapter, we will explore diverse types of consensus mechanisms and choose suitable mechanisms for IIoT devices and networks. But however, IIoT networks require vast computational resources, also limited communication capabilities. In this chapter, we can understand how the implementation of blockchain can hugely impact IIoT networks. On the

Hybridization of Blockchain and Cloud Computing: Overcoming Security Issues in IoT.
M. Lawanya Shri, E. Gangadevi, K. Santhi, & Chiranji Lal Chowdhary (Eds.)

other hand, we can look at current consensus techniques which have been implemented and improve these techniques to prevent network failures.

12.1 INTRODUCTION

The Industrial Internet of Things (IIoT) is an integration of to automate and digitalize the industry, so the efficiency of manufacturing or producing goods increases. At the same time, reducing the cost of manufacturing and labor, and cutting down on errors. Overall, the implementation of IIoT can only give out a positive outcome to the industry [1].

However, a global IoT can face various challenges, such as security attacks or failures. This one negative aspect can overcome all the positive aspects of IIoT. IIoT network is subjected to various cyber-attacks on industrial control systems (ICS). Some specific cyber-attacks are device hijacking, man-in-the-middle attacks, distributed denial of service (DDoS), and permanent denial of service (PDoS). These attacks are single-point failures since the data in these IIoT is centralized [2].

One of the best ways to deal with these cyber-attacks is to implement a blockchain along with IIoT. Blockchain has the potential to solve IIoT security issues. Since blockchain's core is distributed digital ledger which means transactions between users, systems, and clients are transparent and cannot be amended or removed from the log. Incorporating blockchain in the IIoT network can alleviate the security issues in the network in numerous ways [3]:

i.   IIoT network becomes tamper-proof, due to blockchain ledgers and eliminates the trust among devices, and no single party has control over the data generated by IIoT devices.
ii. It provides transparency, allowing authorized members to track the history of transactions or current transactions. Also, this factor can help identify data leaks in the network using previous transactions.
iii. Adding blockchain to the IIoT network can increase the security of the network by adding a robust level of encryption, which makes it hard for hackers to bypass the security and overwrite the stored data.

These are just a few ways in which blockchain can enhance the security of IIoT. Blockchain also provides coordinators between n-number of devices, making it viable to support many transactions in the network. We can also leverage the consensus mechanism of blockchain in IIoT to overcome cyber failure. Even though the incorporation of blockchain can increase the security of IoT, but there are few challenges we must consider:

1. **The Trade-Off Between Security and Efficiency of the IoT Network:** Blockchain's consensus mechanism can definitively help improve security for IIoT devices, but these mechanisms force the nodes to work on high complexity hash algorithms for verification of transactions. These consensus mechanisms require high space and power thus making it overloading for IoT devices. For example, Proof of Work (PoW) is the most common type of consensus mechanism used for blockchain. If we eliminate PoW the efficiency of transactions can boost up, but we will be comprising on the security of the network. As a result, the best option is to identify a way that provides efficiency and security for IoT devices [4].

2. **IIoT Network Should be Transparent and Private at the Same Time:** One of the main characteristics of the blockchain is transparency, in which anyone can join the network, and all the information will be visible to that person. But on the other hand, the IIoT system requires privacy because these systems collect some sensitive data that should only be accessed by authorized personnel. As a result, the IIoT network should be transparent yet private at the same time [4].

3. **A Conflict Between Low-Throughput and High-Concurrency:** IoT devices report knowledge incessantly in IIoT systems, resulting in a high concurrency. But however, complicated blockchain security mechanisms mostly limit the throughput of blockchain. Besides, the synchronous agreement model in chain-structured blockchains cannot modify the use of information measures in IIoT systems. Therefore, the way to improve the turnout of blockchain to satisfy the requirement of frequent transactions in IIoT systems becomes the third challenge [4].

Our contributions to this chapter are:

i. Identifying a few of the main challenges in integrating IIoT with Blockchain technology and providing a viable solution to these challenges;

ii. Providing an IIoT network that is intergraded with blockchain consensus mechanisms which provide a secured and scalable system;

iii. Creating a consensus mechanism that has all the characteristics.

12.2 RELATED WORK

Blockchain is a decentralized and distributed ledger and tamper-free database that can share and access all the members of the blockchain. But what is blockchain? It consists of three main components: block, nodes, and miners. Block is a 32-bit number which is also known as Nonce, and contains data. Every time a block is created, it takes up 32-bit, then generation of block header hash is followed by. A hash is 256-number bit which is linked with 32-bit. Nodes are essential to blockchain technology since blockchain is decentralized nodes that help to maintain copies of the blockchain and provide a fully functional network [7]. Lastly, miners help create a new block for the blockchain. Mining is the process of creating a block, but however, mining a block isn't easy. Block has a unique 32-bit number and hash, and each block uses the previous block's hash as a reference [8].

There are two types of blockchain technologies that are currently implemented in today's world: private blockchain and public blockchain.

A public blockchain is an open network, and information is available in the public domain. Since public blockchain doesn't require any permission, anybody can view, read, or add data to the blockchain, and most importantly anyone can access the data on the blockchain. Public domain blockchain is decentralized and immutable. The advantages of public blockchain are immutable, open-source, and distributed ledger. An example of public blockchain would cryptocurrency such as Bitcoin, Ethereum, or Litecoin. The data on these cryptocurrencies can be accessed user if the user is present on the blockchain [7, 9].

Private blockchain works on permission operations unlike public blockchain and works on closed networks. This type of blockchain is applicable for organizations which selected members are a user of a blockchain network. The organization controls the level of security, authorization, permissions, and accessibility of blockchain, unlike public blockchain. Advantages of private blockchains are low cost, their efficiency, and controlled process, and it's safe. Examples of private blockchain are multichain and hyperledger. For example, Maersk, an international shipping company use blockchain to track container during shipping. Another example is IBM Watson, which has the ability to create a small and private blockchain that allows data transactions between client and company [9, 10].

In today's world, some applications with a combination of blockchain and IoT have the brilliant potential for companies to create services between devices and also give an opportunity to create value from collected data [11]. Using the basic idea of the blockchain-IoT application, we can implement these ideas with insignificant changes in Industrial IoT. A few examples of blockchain-IoT applications [3] are Chain of Things (CoT), International Office of Technical Assistance (IOTA), and Modum.io.

Industrial IoT is a subcategory of the internet of things (IoT), the basic idea of industrial IoT is that connected devices are sensors-embedded machines and infrastructures which send data using the internet as a medium [13]. IIoT devices can be implemented for a small environment in a complex industry. Industrial IoT can be applied to various fields such as production, supply chain, healthcare [14], etc.:

1. **Production:** IIoT technology can be implemented for predicting problems and monitoring a machine's performance. It can increase the efficiency of overall production.
2. **Supply Chain:** IIoT can help restock the necessary resources, which help the workers to focus upon the production of goods rather than worrying about resources.
3. **Healthcare:** Implantation IIoT can help notify healthcare workers if a patient's condition becomes serious, making healthcare to be precise and responsive. This also increases the chances of saving a patient's life in a critical situation.

IIoT devices can be supported with the Hyperledger, which was developed by IBM, which provides distributed ledger system for resources with a consensus mechanism, thus speeding up the application [15, 16]. This was only one example of blockchain integration with IIoT; there are more, such as Multichain, Lisk, etc. These blockchain platforms help to achieve safety, maintaining a record of transactions, prevention of data leakage and cyber-attack. Along with these advantages, these platforms can have computational requirements such as Central Processing Unit (CPU) and memory utilization, the energy consumption of IIoT network [12].

The application of IIoT and blockchain is supercomputing system. In this application, when machines in an industry produce data, each piece of data is timestamped, showing the user when and what happened exactly. Using these timestamped data can be used to resolve accidents and boost up production [16].

Since blockchain technology works on distributed ledger technology (DLT), to maintain agreement on data among the user of the blockchain, we introduce consensus mechanism. It's a fault-tolerant mechanism, that is used blockchain technology [5, 17]. Also, consensus mechanism enhances the security for industrial IoT networks. This makes the network safe and prevents technical glitches caused by outside sources. The mechanism works on a few basic objectives which define consensus mechanism [18, 19]:

1. **Unified Agreement:** The primary goal of consensus mechanisms is to achieve collective understanding between user of the blockchain.

2. **Fair and Equitable:** This objective makes blockchain technology open source and decentralized, which allows anyone to participate in the network.

3. **Prevent Double Spending:** The consensus mechanism work on certain algorithms, that allows the ledger to contain legitimate transactions. These certain algorithms prevent double spending issue. For example, if a node needs to use a resource based upon previous transactions, these algorithms ensure that same recourse isn't being spent twice.

4. **Align Economic Incentive:** Blockchain consensus mechanisms supply economic incentives that are governed itself, by constructing a trustless structure. These incentives also reward the user depending upon their behavior in blockchain.

5. **Fault Tolerant:** This mechanism ensures blockchain is immune to attacks and faults. Also, it enhances consistency and secures the blockchain. In case of cyber-attacks or technical failures, the system will work without any issues.

These are the main goal of the consensus mechanism, which enhances blockchain technology. But however, the main challenge lies in choosing the appropriate mechanism for the blockchain, or it will lead to poor results. The output of choosing poor consensus mechanisms is a lack of performance, consensus failures, and blockchain forks.

So far, we have discussed the aims of consensus mechanisms and briefly touched on the outcome of choosing a poor consensus mechanism. Now, lets us talk about the characteristics of the consensus mechanism.

The characteristics of consensus mechanisms of blockchain are [19, 20]:

i.   **Egalitarian:** Every node in the blockchain has a vote that is given equal value and weight.
ii. **Safety:** All the nodes in the blockchain are eligible to produce true results depending upon the rules of the consensus mechanism which is used in the system.
iii. **Inclusive:** This characteristic ensures that the network nodes in the blockchain are active during the voting process.
iv. **Participatory:** This ensures that all the nodes are constantly contributing for updating of the blockchain and involved in networks.

If a consensus mechanism has all these characteristics, then it is a strong mechanism which endure any technical failures or cyber-attacks.

There are several types of consensus mechanism which can be applied to a blockchain technology, which are [21]:

- Proof-of-work;
- Proof-of-stake;
- Delegated proof-of-stake;
- Leased proof-of-stake;
- Proof of elapsed time;
- Practical byzantine fault tolerance;
- Simplified byzantine fault tolerance;
- Delegated byzantine fault tolerance;
- Directed acyclic graphs;
- Proof-of-activity;
- Proof-of-importance;
- Proof-of-capacity;
- Proof-of-burn;
- Proof-of-weight.

These are 13 different consensus mechanisms [6] these help archive agreement among the users in the blockchain. But let's look at a few common consensus mechanisms such as proof-of-work (PoW), proof-of-stake (PoS), and delegated proof-of-stake (DPoS):

1.   **Proof-of-Work (PoW):** A consensus mechanism that prevents double-spending. This mechanism is applied in Bitcoin and Litecoin. In this mechanism, the nodes are needed to prove work is done, and submit their work. This qualifies the nodes for adding new transactions to the blockchain [21]. This consensus mechanism

requires high computational energy and processing time. PoW was implemented in Bitcoin as a basic consensus mechanism, where the main idea was to create a public blockchain. In this mechanism, miners compete against each other to add new blocks to the blockchain. A miner's success rate is proportional to a miner's computational capabilities. These miners get various puzzles to solve, such as client or computational puzzles or functions related to CPU, as in CPU cost function or CPU pricing function. But these puzzles are hard yet they are possible depending on the miner's computational abilities [22].

2. **Proof-of-Stake (PoS):** It is an alternative for PoW, which uses less computational power and has less processing time to complete its processes. In this mechanism, the nodes of blockchains are chosen by an algorithm to record the transactions. The chosen nodes depend on how much cryptocurrency a node owner owns. The algorithm is designed in a way to access the details of how much cryptocurrency is owned by each node owner. In this consensus mechanism, if a node holds a high stake in cryptocurrency, it can be chosen to record a transaction. In this approach, it's attainable to dramatically decrease the complexness of cryptography, resulting in large outturn gains for the total network. As every node should stake its own currency to participate, it will be expensive if the network undergoes cyberattacks [21].

3. **Delegated Proof-of-Stake (DPoS):** It is related to PoS, its transaction representation in the network. The main idea of DPoS was to integrate democracy among the nodes. This means each node can get a vote during the election to protect the blockchain and keeping it decentralized from cyber-attack or technical failures. DPoS is a combination of Pow, and PoS, DPoS is energy efficient and it enhances the security of the blockchain. DPoS is more scalable and secured compared and this mechanism can process more transactions in the blockchain compared to Pow and Pos. DPoS was established in 2014 in cryptocurrencies, for example, Lisk, BitShare, and Ark [21, 23].

As we only discussed few main and fundamental consensus mechanisms are used in today's world. In other words, DPoS is a better version of PoS and PoW combed. PoS is effective and use less computation power compared to PoW. These mechanics focus on achieving decentralized governance for blockchain [23].

The consensus mechanism's main aim is to bring an agreement between all the blockchain users. This allows the blockchain to be secured and more reliable. When we incorporate one of these mechanisms into industrial IoT, it enhances the security of the network and decreases the chance of malicious attacks or technical failures. All these consensus mechanisms are effective and secure the network, but Proof of Work (POW) can easily implement in the IIoT.

12.3 PROPOSED WORK

POW is one of the most secure ways to ensure that the transactions being entered into the blockchain, and thence, the data transfer between the nodes in the network is happening correctly. In an IIoT network, only the devices belonging to the network to ensure no new device with malicious intent enters the network. This can be achieved by having a node that verifies each device that enters the network. Since we are dealing with industry-level data, our main aim is to keep the data and the machines that produce the data safe. But only one node cannot be used for verifying all the devices constantly so we propose this system verification in the blockchain [26].

In POW, we have a node confirm (also known as validator) the new nodes entering the network. Using a validator, we can reduce the chances of a cyber-attack, also prevent nodes with malicious intentions to enter the IIoT network. In this system, a node is nothing but a machine that produces valuable data and is connected to an industrial IoT network. A validator only confirms a device joining the network. The validator node uses a private key and a public key which the validator uses for authenticating the new device joining the network or the existing device in the network. The signature of the validator is stored in the device's memory. The nodes in use this signature to verify if the incoming message is from a valid node or if it an attack [21]. Let's keep in mind that the main job of the validator is to assign his signature to the nodes of the IIoT network, but doesn't verify if data transaction is valid between existing nodes [4].

The verifying of transactions will be done by a set of nodes we call checkers or miners. The miners in the Industrial IoT network would be a set of devices, which sole purpose is to check if transactions are recorded properly in the blockchain database. Also, to ensure that the data is transferred correctly without any data leakage or miscommunication between the nodes. Firstly, the miners must gain the node's trust by sending their proof of work [4, 24]. A work that clearly says that the miners have entered a correct transaction by creating a new ledger into the blockchain. Thus, later this blockchain is distributed among all the nodes of the IIoT network.

In this POW mechanism, miners are assigned a certain calculation to be computed. Whichever miner completes the calculation first will be entering the transaction into the blockchain and the other miners will copy this blockchain and overwrite it. For the IIoT network, we propose a simple calculation puzzle, which calculates a random number generated by the miner itself [22]. All the miners in the network must try to solve this puzzle, miners will have a random number generator that will be continuously calculating numbers until the target is achieved or another miner has calculated the target first [22, 25]. However, the target number or value changes over the difficulty. But whichever miner number calculates the target number first will be entering the transaction into the blockchain.

This consensus mechanism is a practical possibility for IIoT compared to other mechanisms because POW is simpler to implement compared to other mechanisms. PoW acts like a portal for devices to verify if data transactions between nodes are valuable. Also, it ensures that data is not being manipulated from third-party sources, and data is genuine [26]. This consensus mechanism increased the security of IIoT networks.

12.4 CONCLUSION

Industrial IoT is the implementation of IoT network in the industry to increase the productivity and efficiency of machines. Integration of blockchain with IIoT increases the security of the network by overcoming cyber-attacks and malicious intruders entering the network. This can be achieved by introducing consensus mechanisms, in IIoT networks. The most suitable mechanism would be Proof of Work because it's secure and can be integrated well with the network. This enhances the network, by preventing malicious attacks. This mechanism prevents data loss between the nodes and keeps the data genuine with any manipulation from malicious nodes. To summarize, the given proposal of adding PoW to industrial IoT can outperform the negatives and improve the network.

KEYWORDS

- **delegated proof-of-stake**
- **distributed denial of service**
- **industrial control system**
- **Internet of things**
- **permanent denial of service**
- **proof of work**

REFERENCES

1. *IIoT-the Industrial Internet of Things (IIoT) Explained,* (2020). Retrieved from: https://www.i-scoop.eu/internet-of-things-guide/industrial-internet-things-iiot-saving-costs-innovation/industrial-internet-things-iiot/ (accessed on 11 August 2022).
2. Ahmad-Reza, S., Christian, W., & Michael, W., (2015). Security and privacy challenges in industrial internet of things. In: *2015 52nd ACM/EDAC/IEEE Design Automation Conference (DAC)*. IEEE.
3. Somayaji, S. R. K., Alazab, M., Manoj, M. K., Bucchiarone, A., Chowdhary, C. L., & Gadekallu, T. R. (2020, December). A framework for prediction and storage of battery life in IoT devices using dnn and blockchain. In *2020 IEEE Globecom Workshops (GC Wkshps* (pp. 1–6). IEEE.
4. Huang, J., et al., (2019). Towards secure industrial IoT: Blockchain system with credit-based consensus mechanism. *IEEE Transactions on Industrial Informatics, 15*(6), 3680–3689.
5. Wang, W., et al., (2019). A survey on consensus mechanisms and mining strategy management in blockchain networks. *IEEE Access, 7*, 22328–22370.
6. Salimitari, M., & Mainak, C., (2018). *A Survey on Consensus Protocols in Blockchain for IoT Networks*. arXiv preprint arXiv:1809.05613.
7. Wüst, K., & Gervais, A., (2018). Do you need a blockchain? In: *2018 Crypto Valley Conference on Blockchain Technology (CVCBT)* (pp. 45–54). Zug, Switzerland. doi: 10.1109/CVCBT.2018.00011.
8. Singhal, B., Dhameja, G., & Panda, P. S. (2018). How blockchain works. In *Beginning blockchain* (Vol. 1, pp. 31–148). Apress, Berkeley, CA.
9. Joshi, N., (2020). *Public vs Private Blockchain: Who Wins?* Public blockchain. Retrieved from: https://www.allerin.com/blog/public-vs-private-blockchain-who-wins (accessed on 11 August 2022).
10. Chowdhary, C. L. (2020). Growth of financial transaction toward bitcoin and blockchain technology. In *Bitcoin and blockchain* (Vol. 1, pp. 79–97). CRC Press.

11. Prodan, R., (2021). *Blockchain for Social Media - Blockchain as a Service (BaaS)*. Retrieved from: https://articonf.eu/blockchain-for-social-media/ (accessed on 11 August 2022).

12. Wang, Q., et al., (2020). Blockchain for the IoT and industrial IoT: A review. *Internet of Things, 10*, 100081.

13. Raposo, D., et al., (2018). Industrial IoT monitoring: Technologies and architecture proposal. *Sensors, 18*(10), 3568.

14. Gilchrist, A., (2016). *Industry 4.0: The Industrial Internet of Things*. Apress.

15. Attia, O., et al., (2019). An IoT-blockchain architecture based on Hyperledger framework for health care monitoring application. *NTMS 2019-10ᵗʰ IFIP International Conference on New Technologies, Mobility and Security*. IEEE Computer Society.

16. Wang, Q., et al., (2020). Blockchain for the IoT and industrial IoT: A review. *Internet of Things, 10*, 100081.

17. Seibold, S., & George, S., (2016). *Consensus: Immutable Agreement for the Internet of Value*. KPMG. https://assets.kpmg/content/dam/kpmg/pdf/2016/06/kpmg-blockchain-consensus-mechanism.pdf (accessed on 11 August 2022).

18. Bhardwaj, C., (2020). *What do I Need to Know About Blockchain Consensus Algorithms?* Retrieved from: https://appinventiv.com/blog/blockchain-consensus-algorithms-guide/ (accessed on 11 August 2022).

19. Cachin, C., & Marko, V., (2017). *Blockchain Consensus Protocols in the Wild*. arXiv preprint arXiv:1707.01873.

20. Vuong, A., (2020). *Consensus Algorithms: The Root of the Blockchain Technology*. Retrieved from: https://101blockchains.com/consensus-algorithms-blockchain/ (accessed on 11 August 2022).

21. Zhang, S., & Jong-Hyouk, L., (2020). Analysis of the main consensus protocols of blockchain. *ICT Express, 6*(2), 93–97.

22. Kiayias, A., & Dionysis, Z., (2019). Proof-of-work sidechains. *International Conference on Financial Cryptography and Data Security*. Springer, Cham.

23. Miah, S., (2019). *Comparison of PoW, PoS and DPoS Governance Models*. Retrieved from: https://medium.com/@salmanmiah/comparison-of-pow-pos-and-dpos-governance-models-dcea481140f8 (accessed on 11 August 2022).

24. Wu, Y., et al., (2020). Consensus mechanism of IoT based on blockchain technology. *Shock and Vibration, 2020*.

25. King, S., (2013). *Primecoin: Cryptocurrency with Prime Number Proof-of-Work, 1*, 1–6.

26. Zhao, S., Shancang, L., & Yufeng, Y., (2019). Blockchain enabled industrial internet of things technology. *IEEE Transactions on Computational Social Systems, 6*(6), 1442–1453.

CHAPTER 13

Security and Privacy Trade-Off in Cryptocurrencies: An Implementation of Blockchain Technology

S. SANJAY[1], V. ANANYA[1], S. KAMAL PRASAT[1], P. KISHORE[1], and K. SANTHI[2]

[1]Student, Computer Science and Engineering, VIT, Vellore, Tamil Nadu, India

[2]School of Information Technology and Engineering, VIT, Vellore, Tamil Nadu, India

ABSTRACT

The chapter examines the evolution of various security threats related to the most common and popular digital currency, a cryptocurrency that employs booming blockchain technology. A cryptocurrency is a form of exchange, such as the Indian rupee; however, it is virtual and uses encryption strategies to manipulate the advent of financial units and confirm the switch of funds. However, security issues and privacy challenges mostly expose downfalls in cryptocurrency, such as cyber-attacks, that must be taken seriously and addressed to function safely. This chapter sheds light on various security threats and highlights the concept of various attacks with a focus on cryptojacking, one of the severe unsafe threats in cryptocurrency history. It also discusses the privacy concerns involving cryptocurrencies, stating various novel approaches to the challenges that force security and privacy trade-offs and the influential role of blockchain technology.

Hybridization of Blockchain and Cloud Computing: Overcoming Security Issues in IoT.
M. Lawanya Shri, E. Gangadevi, K. Santhi, & Chiranji Lal Chowdhary (Eds.)
© 2024 Apple Academic Press, Inc. Co-published with CRC Press (Taylor & Francis)

13.1 INTRODUCTION

Blockchain technologies have been steering up the boom in the field of the financial world with the birth of various cryptocurrencies, especially bitcoins. The general features of fiat currency, along with easy electronic transactions, provide us with the concept of cryptocurrency. For a few years, the general public has been informed about this emerging cryptocurrency through media and various sources and its rising prices. At the same time, it is also possible to transfer this into fiat currency. It is often a bit confusing to understand the working of cryptocurrencies, the security behind cryptocurrencies, and how they work. It doesn't require a trusted third party for its transaction to take place securely. The basic framework for this cryptocurrency is its book-keeping ledger that records and keeps a check on who has what, and it is a full-fledged control system in regard to the money and its owner. Hence, it is one of the safe ways regarding finances and its transaction. But there are certain drawbacks in the security of these cryptocurrencies which have been solved using various solutions and some are still left unsolved. Cryptocurrency has emerged as the monetary resource of desire by a cybercriminal. Its unique characteristics of decentralization and pseudo-anonymity also are appealing to criminals in general. The excessive quantity of cryptocurrency used for crime is due to the price rise. Even though the cryptocurrency marketplace price has reduced for the first sector of 2018, the price is higher compared to the remaining year. The preference to have those cryptocurrencies has caused using unlawful ventures. The occurrence of cryptocurrency has kept on developing during the last decade, and this has attracted the interest of cybercriminals. Thus, the security behind these cryptocurrencies is highly crucial and important to the effective and efficient use of cryptocurrencies implementing blockchain technology [11–14].

- With practicality, the chapter has contributed to the existing literature on security and privacy in digital currencies.
- The holistic security and privacy analysis with the underlying technology in the digital currencies are critically examined, emphasizing the most advanced and complex technicalities as well as issues with the state-of-the-art ways of securing the cryptocurrencies.
- A wide range of security challenges faced by the countries across the globe is completely taken into the analysis process and their respective solutions are provided.

- This chapter has contributed to the existing theory of security attacks by analyzing a wide range of cyber-attacks and their impact with state-of-the-art solutions to secure against them.
- Blockchain's basic technology and the function of cryptography in the security of digital currencies is evaluated with critical analysis, hence contributing to the existing theory of Blockchain Technology coupled with cryptography in the security of digital currencies.
- Over 10 plus, the recent state-of-the-art research literature has been critically analyzed with proposed novel solutions.
- In addition to the state-of-the-art security analysis, this chapter also provides a deep analysis of privacy in digital currencies, emphasizing it with the facelessness of the end holder of the digital currency, and in turn, contributing to the existing literature on privacy in digital currencies.

13.2 RELATED WORKS

The dependency on the organization's data over the internet has become common nowadays because everything operating online needs improved security [1]. Bitcoin is considered a functional data nowadays, requiring increased security. In this chapter, there is a discussion related to the rising blockchain technology, which is responsible for preventing bitcoins from malicious attacks, and how it has taken over traditional transactions. Current cryptosystems employ cryptography for the purpose of data privacy, but the information outbreak causes is not tolerable, which makes the user themselves doubtful upon their data. This chapter covers the countermeasures for the existing worldwide cryptology and security requirements that are currently used with bitcoin [2].

In today's scenario, digital currencies are surging up in which bitcoin has a special mention [3]. Although it has its advantages, it is mixed with some serious risks related to security and privacy. This chapter explores digital currency from a conventional asset pricing view and slowly discusses the various fluctuations in terms of pricing of bitcoin. Another important aspect discussed in this chapter is regarding the systemic risks faced in the price of bitcoin.

With the current focus on bitcoin and another cryptocurrency that uses encryption techniques for transactions, blockchain technology has reached its peak with enormous potential in regard to industrial applications. On the other hand, it faces various security issues that must be listed. In this chapter, the plight of cryptocurrencies with respect to its security and the issues related to it are discussed detailed in Ref. [4].

Ref. [5] begins with the rise of decentralized blockchain systems and cryptocurrencies. Later it moves to the part where other countries view the cryptocurrencies with respect to its security mode and why it has been abolished in a few countries. It also compares the security mode utilized in cryptocurrency and other traditional payments. Lastly, it provides solutions to overcome the security concerns related to it and also provides an overview of the future of cryptocurrencies.

The prosperity of bitcoins at the early stages of cryptocurrencies is a point to be highlighted. With lots of advantages that it possesses, it has gained more importance in the peer-to-peer payment network. One of its main points to be noted is its anonymity through the means of delivering the data transactions blatantly network. However, the existence of adversarial attacks makes bitcoin vulnerable to loss of anonymity and privacy. This chapter aims to provide improvements regarding the anonymity and privacy of bitcoins and also explains various malicious attacks that bitcoins are prone to [6].

In Ref. [7], zero coins are the ones that tackle a few privacy issues like the existence of transactions in public ledger that are faced by bitcoins. This chapter primarily focuses on the development of zero cash and highlights the decentralized anonymous payment schemes (DAP schemes) that enable the users to pay among themselves privately. The famous emerging blockchain technology has become the reason for the favorable outcome in terms of bitcoin in various fields like the healthcare industry, e-voting, and duplication in IoT applications. With all such benefits, bitcoins face serious security threats, which this chapter has highlighted with a detailed analysis of double-spending attacks. This is followed by the countermeasures required for the issue faced by them. Finally, a glimpse of Bitcoin peer-to-peer network security risks and Bitcoin storage security has been provided in Ref. [8].

With the exponential rise in the financial value of digital currencies, the usage of digital currencies also increased significantly. In this chapter, the author discusses the various core functional expressions for the enactment of virtual cryptocurrencies., along with their security requirements, and primarily focuses on two possible security attacks, a 51% attack and an Android Java RNG attack [9].

As cryptocurrency mining reaps huge benefits [10], miners have tried to find various alternative methods of utilizing computational resources instead of the traditional mining methods. One such method of exploiting the computational resources of a client with their consent or often without their knowledge by running extra workload scripts behind the scenes of a website is known as cryptojacking. It detects the attacks using CMTracker and analyzes the roots, impact, and effectiveness of cryptojacking. The chapter takes the initial direction towards a systematic, detailed study of this attack.

In Ref. [15], the authors explain that cryptojacking has been extensively abused over the internet affecting over 10 million users worldwide. The worst part of the attack is that it's scripts often hide under the plain sight of normal websites like in-browser mining. The author discusses the different types of mining, threats involved and especially the algorithms to detect such threats. The chapter mainly focuses on aggressively detecting crypto jacking with deep neural networks by using the CoinPolice technique. In Ref. [16], as discussed in earlier papers [10, 11], cryptojacking has become a major threat to be solved and hence various countermeasures against it are being invented. In this chapter, the author takes a look at web extensions that combats against in-browser mining and does a detailed study of its methodology, testing, and results on a web extension called CMBlock, which is devised to detect and prevent in-browser crytojacking using blacklist and behavior methods.

13.3 SECURITY IN CRYPTOCURRENCY

13.3.1 SYSTEMATIC RISKS

The leading cryptocurrency is bitcoin, which represents 93% of cryptocurrency market capitalization. Price variation may be risky for naïve investors. However, an experienced investor will try to spread out his investment portfolio in a divergent manner to reduce the risks involved. They invest in assets with minimal market variation. Systematic risk asset follows the fluctuation in the market while a non-systematic risk asset does not. Mature investors will be willing to invest in bitcoin if it is a non-systematic risk asset. There is a huge price fluctuation in bitcoin and it may fudge the risk. In other words, the risk in the investment portfolio will be diversified if bitcoin lacks systematic risk. Bitcoin doesn't face systemic risk as confirmed by various models; Fama-French's three factors model, capital asset pricing model, etc. The place where the investment is located determines the diversification of the risk portfolio. The results of various tests on the success as well as robust characteristics suggest that bitcoin does not have systematic risk as well as the optimal proportion of bitcoin in a portfolio for investment is almost identical to the main results.

13.3.2   SECURITY CHALLENGES ACROSS THE GLOBE

Arvind Narayanan, a computer scientist at Princeton University, states that digital money is a combination of both cryptography and cash. He has also said that the use of cryptography for developing cryptocurrency acts as a safety component due to its encoding principles and the framework in which it is viewed.

Five nations have declared owning or executing cryptographic forms of money unlawful by receiving an enactment as of March 2018. Before that, it was first enabled in Kyrgyzstan in 2014, when the Kyrgyz government banned the inhabitants from the usage of virtual cryptocurrency. Also, Ecuador has declared it illegal to use cryptocurrency in the financial market and so banned its flow within the country. The same has been devised in the country of Bolivia by its government and in extreme cases also capturing the natives for the usage of cryptocurrency that includes both Bitcoins and Altcoins. In 2017, Bangladesh banned bitcoin and other virtual monetary forms within the country, and the exchanges utilizing Bitcoin or other virtual monetary forms are considered to be unlawful, and people not abiding by the law are liable to a sentence of as long as 12 years in jail. Nigeria also has faced similar kinds of situations like the above-mentioned countries regarding the use of cryptocurrency. Starting in mid-2017, the Central Bank of Nigeria limited virtual monetary standards, expressing that there were many attacks and threats due to the usage of cryptocurrency, which is mostly left untraceable and making them vulnerable to further issues also. This happened particularly in illegal tax avoidance and financing of psychological warfare.

13.3.3 SECURITY ISSUES

Currently, there are many hackings related to cryptocurrency happening in today's world with the introduction of newcomers to the market. The main loss for the people indulged in this is the loss of their cryptocurrency or being hacked but not during its exchange. All of this begins with the password which will ask for combinations of different characters in order to create a secret phrase that cannot be decoded by malicious actors. Developers generally use dictionary calculation which is much similar to Blockchain hub that takes split seconds to convert into a word which is secret. Else, they will simply differentiate it from a word called secret phrase which is connected with the particular individual. Usually, passwords around 18 digits in size are advisable with a blend of irregular letters. Irregular capital letters in the middle of words will get converted into some exclamation marks or question marks, which seem simple but mostly forgotten. As a backup password and for the second measure of security, two-factor authentication is used. After logging into the necessary platform using the appropriate username and password, two-factor authentication is activated, which generates a numerical code for the specific platform one is using which is time-dependent. The time-dependent feature means the code lasts for several seconds to a minute and gets refreshed once the time is up and a new one is generated subsequently. This is possible with the help of mobile applications on both Apple and Android, such as the Google Authenticator app, the Orpheum, etc. It is a must for every cryptocurrency platform to provide the option of two-factor security. After downloading the app, the QR code is scanned for the respective platform which generates an ongoing numerical password for all individual login. This acts as a crux in cryptocurrency to where it is easy for somebody to get access to the users' passwords and usernames. But this is prevented due to the use of the two-factor which stops them by keeping track of the activity while using it on the phone or any other device which hinders the act of breach. When a user is holding cryptocurrency in a wallet, an automatically generated private key is to know whether the user's wallet is being compromised or not, which is the most essential piece of information that one has to secure as a secret at all costs. If it is not taken care of properly, then it may land us in a disadvantageous situation.

Cryptocurrencies are similar to e-money, which means they also face similar problems as that of the classic electronic payment systems. In addition to that, the operating principles specific to cryptocurrencies are more disturbing and there are a certain number of risks that are particularly related to cryptocurrencies. They are:

1. **Spoofing Payment-Related Information and Phishing:** While transferring money to a friend, copying the other party's wallet address correctly may be done, but the malware tends to replace the copied address with another one. Most of them usually don't check the address after copying it, especially as the address is a long set of random characters. The main victims of these cyber thieves are the ones who use a traditional bank system. But the advantage of a traditional system is that it is possible to cancel the transfer.

2. **Hacking a Payment Gateway:** Loss of money can take place even during the usage of a genuine looking payment gateway. For example, in June 2017, the most trusted online wallet for the Ethereum Classic cryptocurrency all of a sudden started stealing money from users' wallets unknowingly where the hackers managed to convince the users that they were the original domain owners which turned out to be a social-engineering method of convincing. After gaining access, they started getting information regarding cash flows. For example, in Brazil this year, hackers have taken down the whole bank of Brazil and were hijacked once by hackers.

3. **User Address Error:** In cryptocurrency, the risk of losing the money due to a mistake in the beneficiary address to which the cryptocurrency is transferred is very common. The seriousness is huge since even a change in one digit can result in the loss of money and sometimes the transferred money that is under threat gets multiplied by a large number, say 256.

4. **Loss of a Wallet File:** Cryptocurrency wallet files are usually stored by the users on their computers. Hence, there is a high chance of getting lost when the hard disk gets impaired or being stolen with the help of malware. So, making a hard copy of the secret key and the purchase of a USB hardware wallet are followed by the high-end skilled users who are generally in a small ratio. Usage of centralized e-money is preferred currently. It is a rare Internet bank that does not need two-factor authentication and

transactions getting confirmed with the help of OTP through SMS. It is necessary to use USB tokens in case of large amounts.

5. **Insecure ICOs:** One type of fundraising is Initial Coin Offering (ICO) which is popular among cryptocurrency holders. Above 1.7 billion dollars has been generated in the year 2017 through ICOs.

13.3.4 SECURITY REQUIREMENTS

The necessary security needs required for the cryptocurrency area are but not limited to:

i. **Security and Verification of the Crypto Coins:** It must be taken care of during their creation without leading to any failure. Proving the amount of work invested must be expended.

ii. **Proof of Work:** It has to be taken care of that no coin must be re-spent and must be owned by a single person. The records of all transactions are maintained by a central authority that keeps all the entities using the network. Transactions must happen securely between two parties even without a central authority which ensures greater security.

13.3.5 ROLE OF CRYPTOGRAPHY

Bitcoin has been categorized as crypto-currency because of its usage of public-key cryptography for safety and security. User-made payments are sent by broadcasting digitally signed messages which transfer ownership of Bitcoins that are considered to represent the unit currency. Verification and timestamping of all transactions are done through a decentralized network of specialized computers using a proof-of-work system. Bitcoins being open-sourced, every single line of codes used in Bitcoin transactions are visible. There isn't a single owner of BTC and its ownership is divided amongst open-source developers in the BTC Foundation. A state-of-the-art encryption method employed for military and government applications is widely used for the verification of every cryptocurrency transaction. The Bitcoin user is anonymously represented during a particular transaction within the system due to which they can be identified only using public keys. Everything will become a failure once the cryptosystem is broken and usually the cryptographic code is practically infeasible to crack due to which the hackers are tempted to attempt brute force methods for shutting down exchanges and subsequently getting hold of the cryptocurrencies. Distributed-denial-of-service attack overloads the servers by sending recurring instances of automated data visitors by bots. When a cryptocurrency exchange gets attacked, the value of Bitcoins depreciates which benefits the hackers who see a profit from those. The value of these virtual forms of money is restored when the exchange is restored. Hackers intentionally also crash the service. The DDoS attack could be prevented, as long as the main cryptography frame is protected. Bitcoin uses no complex cryptography; its sophisticated design reflects a surprising amount of ingenuity.

13.3.6   ROLE OF BLOCKCHAIN TECHNOLOGY

Digital transaction's safety for Bitcoin has emerged in a quick leap due to blockchain technology and requires no concern related to its destruction, which mainly resembles a group of hackers. The data relating to the transactions are kept safe by implementing blockchain technology, and there is no such possibility in interfering with that information. Before the existence of Bitcoin, there were other digital currencies in use. But their major disadvantage was the inability to solve the double-spending attack which has been successfully solved by Bitcoins. This was why there was a fall in other digital currencies. It is possible for the digital currency to be used twice for transactions in dissimilar scenarios and adds to the chance of getting replicated since it doesn't involve any physical cash. Also, the double-spending attack can occur during bitcoin transactions because a particular person cannot authenticate the possibility of being duped Bitcoins as in the case of physical cash, which a physical entity can verify. So, both in the case of coins and bits, it is possible for the occurrence of two different transactions. Hence Bitcoins also have a larger possibility of the attack of the double-spending problem. The owner may himself initiate such an attack and meddle with the network by performing fraud transactions. For other currencies, the double-spending problem can't be solved. But in the case of Bitcoin, even though the problem of double-spending occurs, it can be solved due to the maintenance of all the transactions in a ledger called a Universal ledger which is the same as that of Blockchain. All the transactions are stored in the ledger, which foresees the inclusion of a new block, after every 10 minutes, and the node contains the replica of the ledger that gets resumed for every new transaction that resembles the one in the global ledger. When the sender uses the same bitcoin to complete a transaction with a merchant, it gets added into the pool of unconfirmed transactions, which the miners check for its legality. While these miners check, only they get approved and get included in the next block for the further process while the second one is dropped down by proving and considering it as an invalid one. When both fraudulent and honest transactions simultaneously go for verification, the one with a larger number of confirmations is approved while the other one is disregarded.

13.4   CYBER SECURITY ATTACKS

13.4.1   TYPICAL ATTACKS

1. **Attacks on Wallet Software:** Stealing and destroying the key present are the two ideas of attack during the wallet software attack. By doing so, the money of the user is lost which can't be tracked. This type of attack is stopped by using a more efficient and secure user wallet.

2. **Greater Than 50% Attack:** The attacker gains command over the whole mining pool if the mining power is more than 50% of the hash-rate required for mining a network. Following this, DoS attacks can also take place because the attacker has full access to the network. Fortunately, this attack doesn't bring much loss to the users and miners. Further, a scheme called two-phase proof-of-work is implemented for its prevention.

3. **Selfish Mining:** This attack is also called a block withholding attack where the other miners are denied access to a validated block in a particular mining pool by the attacker. Successively, the attacker will be able to proceed with the mining of the next block. Another approach implemented by the attacker is by holding the private branch and the solution until the length of the private branch exceeds the public branch which finally showcases the proof-of-work of the attacker having a higher probability than the other miners in the given pool.

4. **Eclipse Attack:** For the Eclipse attack to be implemented, gathering 50% malicious attacks by the attacker is a criterion that must possess a 41% mining strength. The attacker controls the node by directing all the connections to his ID in place of the P2P network. The miners generally note down the pool members considering whether they are honest or attacker nodes. In this way, this attack can be prevented. Another solution is the use of an overlay network.

5. **Distributed Denial of Service (DDoS) Attack:** This tries to bring down the operations that are performed in a pool which makes the honest miners remove themselves from the pool due to the rage caused during the process. Solutions for this attack are Traffic Monitoring and botnet detection.

13.4.2   ANDROID JAVA RNG ATTACK

This section explains the flaw that makes the Java Pseudo Random Number Generator attack an option due to the poorly generated pseudo-random numbers and how the bitcoins were stolen. A bug within the Android implementation of the Java SecureRandom class prevented the generation of secure random numbers. The SecureRandom class is obtained as an entropy seed, which is considered essentially as pseudo-random data generated by the operating system, from a file situated at /dev/random. But accessing the file was not possible as in the occurrence of a bug implying a random seed was not produced to generate the random number. These poorly generated random numbers were then used to create the ECDSA signature.

13.4.3   DOUBLE SPENDING ATTACK AND ITS FORMS

A bitcoin used more than once for different transactions for any fraudulent activity performed by attackers to disrupt the network is called a double-spending attack. By creating the duplicate of the already used original, the attacker initiates this attack. It is tough for the decentralized system to identify whether it is a duplicate copy of the original one. It is impossible to find out whether all the inputs given are honest because they can also be fraudulent by being used or spent earlier. For such an act, verification is done by the miners who legalize and validate the BTC used. The inputs are validated by cross-checking with already stored information in the blockchain to prevent the input of the next transaction to be a fraudulent one. After this whole process of getting approved, the block gets added to the chain. The whole mining process is made the costlier and resource-intensive operation to prevent the attacker from introducing any malicious block into the chain. Legitimate proof of work is required to mine and establish a block of transactions in the blockchain.

Various forms of double-spending attacks are race attack, Finney attack, Vector76 attack, 51% attack, and many more:

1. **Race Attack:** In this type of attack, the merchant without waiting for confirmation, provides the products and services to the payer. Hence, the transaction stands in a position where it is not confirmed yet. To manipulate the merchant, the attacker comes up with two kinds of transactions: (i) a transaction that pays the merchant an amount of BTC in return for a product/service and (ii) a fraudulent transaction that pays the same amount to the wallet of the attacker. Same, malicious BTC is spent in both kinds of transaction which the attacker releases simultaneously into the Bitcoin network making the miner think about the validity of both the transaction until one of them gets added to the Blockchain a.k.a. the confirmed transaction whose input can't be used for any other future transaction. This leads to the possibility of a malicious transaction being verified first instead of the merchant-paying transaction which will be considered as the invalid one and will be dropped off from the mining pool system. The prevention method is to wait for the confirmation and see to it that the honest block gets added to the blockchain before the merchant finishes off his deal with the payer. For this, a suggested waiting period would be at least six confirmations of the honest block being successfully added to the Blockchain, which prevents the attacker from reversing the transaction.

2. **Finney Attack:** This attack was introduced through the Bitcoin forum. The acceptance of this attack is possible only when the merchant abides with the unconfirmed transactions and also involves initiation and successively the process of mining of the blocks containing two transactions that look similar to each other just like that in the race attack. If the first block gets mined successfully, the attacker proceeds with the next one as fast as he can to finish off the deal with the merchant and also to prevent the merchant from confirming the transaction. As soon as the block

gets mined, it is automatically added to the chain and the transaction initiated by the merchant becomes null. Unfortunately, the attacker is rewarded with a mining reward for successfully making his block entry into the Blockchain.

3. **Vector76 Attack:** Unlike the above-mentioned Race and Finney attacks, the merchant can't proceed with mining the next block, unless the already mined block has been validated and appended to the chain in the case of the Vector76 attack. A fork is generated in the Blockchain to retreat the transaction. This whole attack consists of two parts of the network. One part is where the forking of the Blockchain takes place along with the visible transaction by the attacker. While on the other, we cannot see this initiated transaction. Also, we can determine whether the double-spending has taken place or not by determining whether the fraudulent transaction started by the attacker is longer than the honest one created by the merchant.

4. **51% Attack:** Most dangerous attack amongst all is this 51% attack in the BTC system where the attacker controls greater than 50% computational power of the system due to which is also called majority attack. During this attack, the integrity is completely lost due to the loss of opportunity of other miners to take part in the transaction. The success of this attack entirely depends on the resources produced as the outcome is measured in terms of financial and computational power which is shown in Figure 13.1.

13.4.4 CRYPTOJACKING: A CASE STUDY

Cryptojacking is the unauthorized use of computational resources to mine cryptocurrency without the consent of the goal device's owner. Cryptojacking is malware that hides on non-public computing machines, tablets, or cell devices and employs the machine's asset to mine virtual currencies referred to as cryptocurrencies. In easier words, the unauthorized usage of another individual's machine to acquire cryptocurrencies is referred to as cryptojacking. Similar to different protection attacks, the goal of cryptojacking is money. This attack is typically finished without the expertise of the individual whose machine has been compromised. It is likewise referred to as malicious crypto-mining.

RACE ATTACK
Sending coins to different
vendors with the help of
two distinct machines.

FINNEY ATTACK
Here, the attacker plays the role of
miner where he sends coins to
himself without broadcasting.

VECTOR67 ATTACK
Here, the attacker will create two nodes where
one is linked to the exchange node and the
other linked to the peer-to-peer network.

51% ATTACK
Here, the attacker possesses the ability to block the new
transactions from to be taking place/from being confirmed
in the blockchain network.

FIGURE 13.1 Comparison of the types of double spending attacks based on the role of attacker.

The damage inflicted on cryptojacking sufferers relies upon the hardware used in the assault, and the context. For computer systems and plugged-in laptops/cellular devices, the damage is composed particularly of an accelerated electric powered bill, decreased performance, and heat. This assault is extra dangerous to customers with cellular devices strolling on battery power because it shortens the battery existence span and finally causes the tool to close down. Cryptojacking scripts which the malicious adversaries use does it with the intention of profits. But how much extra power do they expend in order to gain such profits is an inquisitive question to ask. The profits gained by the malicious adversaries and the additional energy they expend is illustrated mathematically:

$$\text{Profit} = \Sigma[(v \times d \times hs \times r)/dif]$$

$$\text{Energy} = \Sigma(v \times d \times p)$$

where; 'v' stands for visitors; 'd' stands for duration; 'hs' stands for Hash-Speed; 'r' stands for reward; 'dif' stands for difficulty; 'p' stands for power.

Let's assume the values of each given variable to be of a certain number in its own unit from the data collected, which is ideal for gaining profit and the ideal energy consumed. Those values are:

Variable	Value
Visitors	211.5
Duration	326s
HashSpeed	50 hash/sec B
Reward	$1,095
Difficulty	56.2G hash
Power	32.5

According to Hong et al. [10], in-browser cryptojacking is wherein malicious adversaries have been making use of an internet person's CPU sources to mine cryptocurrency with the aid of injecting malicious payloads into the compromised websites. This new shape of cryptojacking can without difficulty skip antivirus with the aid of hiding within the browser's process, which makes it undetectable.

13.4.4.1   COINPOLICE TECHNIQUE

CoinPolice is a system for hidden cryptojacking detection that has been considered as one of the main solutions for this cryptojacking. We have diagnosed capabilities that may be used to hit upon malicious cryptocurrency mining on webpages. Also, a brand-new lively probing method that locates hidden miners that are seeking to keep away from detection through decreasing their CPU utilization has been advanced under this methodology. Based on the diagnosed capabilities and a deep neural community classifier we've advanced a system called CoinPolice with high performance rates. An overall performance evaluation towards the cutting-edge kingdom of the artwork has proven that CoinPolice outperforms it in detecting surprisingly throttled miners with a decreased quantity of fake alarms. Evaluation of CoinPolice on present miners and have completed a massive scale research and feature observed 6,700 mining websites, 447 of which are in Alexa's Top 1 million list. It has additionally been checked mining web sites observed through sample matching within the Public WWW base. The results display that the handiest 43% of those web sites are efficiently mining cryptocurrency.

13.4.4.2 CMBLOCK APPROACH

The current countermeasure method, that is the blacklist technique on web extension has a few troubles concerning it. An attacker may want to effortlessly avoid the net extension that simplest makes use of the blacklist technique. This blacklisting technique isn't always a powerful method for the countermeasure to in-browser cryptojacking due to an adaptive attacker can usually keep away from detection via way of means of recreating a new URL that isn't always determined in the public list of blacklisted URLs that been utilized in net extension. So, to counter cryptojacking, we introduce an extra method combining with the current countermeasure method, which is making use of conventional method blacklisting and detection for capability mining behavior in the loaded cryptojacking script. This extra method will discover capability mining behavior inside the loaded script on the website. The detection technique will even intercept the crypto mining inline script wherein the attacker embedded the script internal HTML (referred to as Hypertext Markup Language for growing net pages and net application) to run the in-browser crypto mining for the implementation of this methodology, a device has been advanced known as CMBlock.

The CMBlock software is created using react, consisting of a consumer interface primarily based totally on the google chrome platform as a special platform requiring a special software programming interface (API). The consumer interface will display if the crypto mining script is blocked on every occasion the consumer visits the website. This segment is also in which this system is examined. The software is examined to make certain that the consumer interface applied paintings and software features running at the meant platform. Next is a show for the reputation to reveal to the consumer that block miner reputation is blocked if the website includes cryptojacking miner script. Below the region of the display, there will be two buttons.

13.4.5 ATTACK PROFITABILITY

The reasons behind most security breaches and attacks are either for monetary benefits or for defamation, denial with personal propaganda against the victim. Cryptocurrencies having high exchange rates are exploited for financial gains. Also, the above-mentioned attacks involve a significant amount of cost to be spent and hence it won't be logical and sustainable if the returns are not higher than the amount utilized to carry these attacks.

13.4.5.1 ILLUSTRATION

Consider an attacker Alice and a vendor Bob having transactions of goods worth × bitcoins. As a general practice, Bob waits for a certain number of confirmations before releasing the goods to Alice. Once Alice receives the goods, she decides to carry out a double-spend attack by initiating another fresh transaction that sends the same bitcoins to her own address. This would be deemed invalid by the other honest nodes; hence Alice has to mine one more block (n blocks) than the number of confirmations to include her transaction in the longest chain by over-riding the existing one with the first spend. The probability with which Alice can overturn this is the success probability Ps. While doing so, Alice bears a mining cost that includes money spent on electricity E(t) and the mining gear that depreciates D(t) but also receives the mining reward that includes block reward (BR) and transaction fees (TF) for every block mined.

Revenue = Worth of good purchased + Success probability × (BTC spent + Mining reward)

$$= X + Ps \times (X + n \times (BR + TF))$$

$$Cost = BTC \ spent + Mining \ cost$$

$$= X + (nE(t) + d(t))$$

From the above equations, we can interpret that if the number n increases, cost increases and decreases the feasibility of a double spending attack exponentially. Hence a global norm is to wait till 6 confirmations, where the probability of successfully conducting a double spend attack becomes very low and feasibly impossible.

13.5   PRIVACY AND PRACTICALITY IN CRYPTOCURRENCY

13.5.1   *FACELESSNESS IN CRYPTOCURRENCY*

Generally, a bank is considered to be the third party during a transaction that possesses accurate details regarding their customer's financial activity. They keep all the information so safe and can be wholly trusted. On the other hand, Bitcoin's transactions are kept distinct and apparent with the transaction being open but the public keys meant only for the person involved in the transactions. User's names are generally pseudo names hidden, meanwhile people in a particular transaction network can keep track of the path and the status of the money of a person's transaction. The peculiar feature of the usage of pseudonyms creates anonymity in bitcoins. These pseudo names also help in representing the address of the BTC transaction and monitor it regularly. It is mandatory for revealing the identity of the payments regarding the goods and services at the time of the Bitcoin interchange happening between the trader and the user. The way the user handles bitcoin and his behavior towards bitcoin validates the extent of privacy the user has. A new key pair is generated during every transaction and using it has been devised as a counteragent which helps in determining the value of the bitcoin possessed by the holder. Different wallets can be used for varied transactions. The user must be sure that he doesn't disclose the address for achieving a safe transaction. The service hosts are aware of the user's address which is present in the server of the wallet service containing information related to the data and its transaction.

13.5.2   *ZEROCOIN: AN EPITOME OF PRIVACY*

For safeguarding the spending habits of the public, data related to that, and the account balances by various groups of people, an automatic guarantee is required for the protection of their privacy. One of the ways for this guarantee is the Anonymous transactions which make the market value of the coin independent of its history thereby the owner's coin remains fungible. For this purpose, the concept of Zerocoin was devised, which provides strong anonymity guarantees for Bitcoin. Prevention of transaction graph analysis is achieved by Zerocoin by employing zero-knowledge proofs which resonate with the e-cash protocol. But the difference of this Zerocoin from e-cash protocols is that validation of the coin doesn't require a digital signature, and also it does not need any centralized authority to avoid double-spending. But for all this, it uses zero-knowledge for the authentication and the proof that they are a part of the public list of valid coins. To bring the fact into the highlight, Zero Coins are not fully anonymous but considered as a decentralized mix, where the bitcoins are treated via this Zerocoin protocol regularly. Although Zerocoin satisfies the basic e-cash scheme, it doesn't come in accord with some important requirements regarding full-fledged anonymous payments. Firstly, Zerocoin employs the concept of a solid and stable denomination where there will be no changes made after a particular transaction. Secondly, Zerocoin doesn't follow a particular convention where one user has to pay another directly. And thirdly, it has no purpose in hiding the amount or the metadata regarding the transactions that happen in a given network.

Decentralized Anonymous Payment Scheme is developed and constructed in order to have state-of-the-art privacy which works on top of any ledger-based CryptoCurrency. In addition to privacy, this construction, in addition, provides complete transparency of the ledger at any moment of time. The working and the construction of this scheme is detailly explained in a mathematical way in the following six steps with the base coin as bitcoin:

> **Step 1: Making Users Anonymous with the Help of Constant-Valued Coins:** Let COMMIT be the variable denoting a commitment scheme which is non-interactive as well as hiding more probabilistically. If random text is denoted as RAN and the message as MES, the commitment shall be denoted with $c: = COMMIT_{RAN}(MES)$ and hence, c can be revealed with the knowledge of RAN and MES, and it can be verified that $COMMIT_{RAN}(MES)$ is the same as c. For spending c, by initiating a spend transaction ST that has the coin's serial number(s) and a NP statement stating *"I know RAN such that $COMMIT_{RAN}(s)$ appears in the list of coin commitments."* User anonymity is accomplished due to the fact the evidence π is zero-knowledge: at the same time as s is revealed, no records approximately RAN is, and locating which of the several commitments in the list corresponds to a selected spend transaction ST is equal to inverting $f(x): = COMMx(s)$, that's assumed to be infeasible. Thus, the foundation of the charge is anonymous.

➤ **Step 2: Decreasing the List of Coin Commitments:** In this process, the time and space complexity are converted from linear to logarithmic. Also, the NP statement is modified as *"I know RAN such that COMM$_{RAN}$(s) appears as a leaf in a CRH-based Merkle tree whose root is R."*

➤ **Step 3: Extension of Coins for Anonymous Payments:** Using the processes mentioned above creates problems while transferring c to another user. So, we create three pseudorandom functions for the seed y represented as PF_y^{adr}, PF_y^s, PF_y^{pk}. In this model, we assume that PF_x^s is collision-resistant. Next is the generation of address key pair for each and every user in action denoted as (ad_{pk}, ad_{sk}) where ad_{pk}: $= PF^{adr}_{adsk}$ (0). Another important thing in this step is the spending coins by pour operation where the por transaction is represented as PT. If the new coins created during this process are denoted as nc_1 and nc_2, PT: $= (R, s_{old}, nc_1, nc_2, \pi_{POUR})$.

➤ **Step 4: Sending Coins:** If a_{pk}^{new} is the address public key of user u_1, a new coin nc_1^{new} is created which must somehow send the secret values to u_1 for it to spend the coin. For this purpose, the address key-pair is modified. Each user now has a key pair (adr_{pk}, adr_{sk}), where $adr_{pk} = (ad_{pk}, pk_{ec})$ and $adr_{sk} = (ad_{sk}, sk_{ec})$. In addition, (pk_{ec}, sk_{ec}) is a key pair for a key-private encryption scheme.

➤ **Step 5: Receiving Public Outputs:** Till now, the processes mentioned above allow the user to mint, merge, and split coins but not convert it back to its base coin form (Bitcoin). For the latter part to be feasible, we include public outputs in pour transaction. Hence, v_{pb} is publicly declared and is targeted by the string info which together is now included in the pour transaction PT.

➤ **Step 6: Non-Malleability Property:** To protect the pour transaction PT from malleable attacks, further modification is done in the NP statement using digital signatures. This includes:

- One-time signature scheme by introducing the key-pair (pk_{sg}, sk_{sg});
- Computation of h_{sg}: $= CRH(pk_{sg})$;
- Computation of h_1 and h_2 which serves as MACs to h_{sig};
- Introduction of h, h_1, h_2 in the pour transaction PT and proving that h_1, h_2 are computed without any mistake.

13.5.3   *NOVEL APPROACH TO CHALLENGES*

Cryptocurrencies also face challenges in the real world. For these problems faced by it, there are various solutions for it to make it an efficient and secure system. This clarifies all the concerns related to it. Some problem approach is listed down below:

1. **Technical Knowledge and Resource Creation:** Cryptocurrencies and Blockchain technologies are considered to be a growing field in the finance sector, and the government needs to take it into account as a future trend and satisfy all the obligations related to it. Hence, it is the responsibility of the government to impart the knowledge to the government in regards to the knowledge creation and all the technical expert recruitment in a particular company. A trustworthy Certification Authority (CA) is required for this purpose to keep in accounts related to the performance in this area also an international council of countries can be set for helping the users and trade-off.

2. **Scalability:** It is an issue that is common to both cryptocurrency and Blockchain technology where small transactions are not possible due to the size of the blocks being smaller which also causes a time lag during the transaction. This issue can be solved by employing a more efficient and orderly transaction. One more way to prevent this is by creating a Mini-Blockchain that is connected with the network directly, which leads to the establishment of small proofs to prevent the non-empty addresses and the coin identity from being lost and in turn, enhances the security. By doing so, the network synchronization is considerably increased which is made capable of faster transactions and increased anonymity.

3. **Key Management or User Anonymity:** Another shared problem of cryptocurrency and Blockchain is the Private Key Management which has been a worrying security threat regarding identity authentication and information encryption. For this issue, many complicated algorithms and enhanced computer trends have been employed for the user's anonymity and data security. They are:

   • Preimage attacks on the mining header target such as Proof of Work can be prevented by employing a small number of transactions so that the attacker cannot start an attack using the coin-based transaction.

- New address types can be brought into use which employs an even stronger hashing and new signature schemes than the previous one.
- In the Main Hash, the use of nested hashes must be prevented and the use of old primitives must be avoided.

13.5.4　GUIDE FOR CRYPTO-OWNERS AND CRYPTO-INVESTORS

Verification of the web wallet's address, and not following the links to an internet bank or web wallet must be properly followed. Double-checking the recipient's address, the amount being sent, and the size of the associated fee must be done thoroughly before the transaction.

i.　Writing down the mnemonic phrase will help us to recover a crypto wallet in case a person has lost it or forgotten the password;

ii.　Be calm and careful while crypto-investing especially while making decisions related to that;

iii.　Use separate hardware (such as a USB device) to keep the cryptocurrency safe;

iv.　Always keep the crypto wallet devices and all the exchanges related to its anti-virus protected.

13.6　CONCLUSION

From this chapter, one can wonder whether such security and privacy issues prevail in cryptocurrencies which are ironically famous for its encryption with strong cryptography and with the implementation of blockchain technology. However, any system has some vulnerability, and cryptocurrencies are no exception. But even such challenges have novel solutions with which one can overcome the security threats have been elaborated on this chapter. The key point stressed over here is that they are not secured by people or by trust, but by the algorithmic math of cryptography. So, it is the responsibility of the crypto-investors to be familiar with the loopholes of vulnerability and meticulously follow the protocols and guidelines provided in this chapter with caution to prevent cyber-attacks. Also, the cryptocurrency market is a volatile, unstable dynamic environment that requires proper management, stability, and scalability. Hence, this work is a sole attempt to highlight the security and privacy issues in cryptocurrency and also with the hope that future researchers also find novel solutions to tackle the prevailing challenges.

KEYWORDS

- **blockchain**
- **block reward**
- **certification authority**
- **cryptocurrency**
- **cryptojacking**
- **decentralized anonymous payment**
- **hypertext markup language**
- **transaction fees**

REFERENCES

1. Nalavade, A., (2018). Blockchain technology: Most secure database I. Introduction II. database threats. In: *2018 Second Int. Conf. Intell. Comput. Control Syst.*, no. ICICCS (pp. 1356–1362).
2. Reza, T. S., (2018). A study on digital currency: The safety of future money. *Transparansi J. Ilm. Ilmu Adm., 1*(1), 134–139. doi: 10.31334/trans.v1i1.145.
3. Gilbert, S., & Loi, H., (2018). Digital currency risk. *Int. J. Econ. Finance, 10*(2), 108. doi: 10.5539/ijef.v10n2p108.
4. Goel, N., Ku Ojha, N., Kumar, P., Mishra, S., & Kumari, V., (2018). *Security Issues in Blockchain and Crypto Currency Security Issues in Blockchain and Crypto Currency* (pp. 1–12)
5. Pandya, S., Mittapalli, M., Gulla, V. T. S., & Landau, O., (2019). Cryptocurrency: Adoption efforts and security challenges in different countries. *HOLISTICA – J. Bus. Public Adm., 10*(2), 167–186. doi: 10.2478/hjbpa-2019-0024.
6. Soni, D. K., Sharma, H., Bhushan, B., Sharma, N., & Kaushik, I., (2020). Security issues & seclusion in bitcoin system. In: *2020 IEEE 9th Int. Conf. Commun. Syst. Netw. Technol.* (pp. 223–229). doi: 10.1109/CSNT48778.2020.9115744.
7. Ben-Sasson, E., et al., (2014). Zerocash: Decentralized anonymous payments from bitcoin. *Proc. –IEEE Symp. Secur. Priv.*, 459–474. doi: 10.1109/SP.2014.36.
8. Zaghloul, E., Li, T., Mutka, M. W., & Ren, J. (2020). Bitcoin and blockchain: Security and privacy. *IEEE Internet of Things Journal, 7*(10), 10288–10313.

9. Lee, Y., Son, B., Park, S., Lee, J., & Jang, H. (2021). A Survey on Security and Privacy in Blockchain-based Central Bank Digital Currencies. *J. Internet Serv. Inf. Secur.*, *11*(3), 16–29.

10. Hong, G., et al., (2018). How you get shot in the back: A systematical study about cryptojacking in the real world. *Proc. ACM Conf. Comput. Commun. Secur.*, 1701–1713. doi: 10.1145/3243734.3243840.

11. Petrov, I., Invernizzi, L., & Bursztein, E., (2020). *CoinPolice: Detecting Hidden Cryptojacking Attacks with Neural Networks.* [Online]. Available: http://arxiv.org/abs/2006.10861(accessed on 11 August 2022).

12. Razali, M. A., & Mohd, S. S., (2019). CMblock: In-browser detection and prevention cryptojacking tool using blacklist and behavior-based detection method. *Lect. Notes Comput. Sci. (including Subser. Lect. Notes Artif. Intell. Lect. Notes Bioinformatics)*, *11870 LNCS*, 404–414. doi: 10.1007/978-3-030-34032-2_36.

CHAPTER 14

A Study of Data Storage, Data Retrieval, and Streaming Architectures Across Various Platforms

J. GEETHA, RITU PRAVAKAR, PALLAVI D. NAIK, and S. SIRISHA REDDY

Department of Computer Science and Engineering,
Ramaiah Institute of Technology, Bangalore, Karnataka, India

ABSTRACT

The growth of smart gadgets and devices in the field of the Internet of Things (IoT) has been exponential. This prompts a requirement for developing effective information storage systems. In any case, in the following years, it is normal that we will be unable to deal with the tremendous measure data produced by the IoT gadgets using cloud computing effectively because of transmission capacity constraints. Edge and fog data processing is getting pervasive in the field of information examination and analysis. The assessment is dependent upon the steady nature of the data being taken care of in the cloud and its availability around at that point. In this chapter, we present a comprehensive study of different techniques for capacity across fog gadgets and edge frameworks. While two or three works outlined the benefits of these foundations specifically for IoT applications, basic Cloud benefits that can exploit the geo-dispersion of assets have not been proposed at this point. In a future IoT-commanded condition, most of the information will be delivered at the edge, which might be moved to the system center. We also present the usage of filters for data retrieval from the storage

Hybridization of Blockchain and Cloud Computing: Overcoming Security Issues in IoT.
M. Lawanya Shri, E. Gangadevi, K. Santhi, & Chiranji Lal Chowdhary (Eds.)
© 2024 Apple Academic Press, Inc. Co-published with CRC Press (Taylor & Francis)

device and present a comparison of Bloom and Cuckoo filters. Finally, we present a study of the various kinds of protocols of the P2P system for the architectural arrangement of the devices.

14.1   INTRODUCTION

In a future IoT-dominated environment, most of the information will be delivered at the edge, which might be moved to the system center. Neighborhood stockpiling administrations can be utilized to cushion IoT and client-produced information at the edge, before information cloud synchronization. Nearby capacity and handling at the edge of the system gives a rich arrangement, as indicated by which information is incidentally put away [7]. Sensors can be integrated with multiple edge devices like Raspberry Pi. They are used consistently on private and wide-zoned frameworks for data generation, assessing the neighborhood and transmission to the cloud. This venture concocts a productive method to store and oversee information with the assistance of substance-based revelation and furthermore ensure straightforward access. It offers further development registering for additional investigation or total and furthermore forward information to the cloud. Edge-local federated Store (Elf Store) [1] is an edge-neighborhood combined store for surges of information squares. Various fog devices are arranged in a super-peer overlay network. They are used to screen the edge assets, offer united metadata ordering utilizing the Bloom filters, find information inside 2-jumps, and keep up surmised worldwide insights about the quality and capacity limit of edges. Information produced on the edge and fog is just momentarily accessible on them, as they are in the end moved to the cloud for steadiness. This is the key explanation behind edge devices being normally less solid. This makes the applications using this kind of data to run primarily on cloud or left with the option of sending them back to the edge devices. However, the purpose of concern is that cloud alone can be relied on for information constancy. Assistance ought to be created which can oversee information on fog and edge gadgets somewhat just on the cloud. In the event of hub disappointments, likewise, the administration ought not stop. Advancement of such administrations on the edge and fog layers likewise offers straightforward information revelation and simpler access to information for different applications. The most popular content

(MPC) caching strategy is an extremely good methodology for caching. Fog nodes are liable for checking demands for content which is absent in the store. The popularity table stores the count. When the popularity threshold is reached, the content is termed as popular and after that it is cached. When Fog node's buffer is full, it removes the content which is least popular to make space for the new content. Subsequently after this, the customer will get the information truly from the noteworthy Fog node. Hence the customer need not fetch it from the Content delivery network (CDN) server or the primary unavailable cloud server, with the exception of if the cached data item has been replaced. The issue of time while downloading the content and also to search for content availability is proposed to be solved by CDNs. It suggests to deliver content through edge cache servers which can be deployed at different locations globally [2]. Systems are developed to distribute the data parts to various processing systems. These systems form the nodes of the system. Since the amount of energy consumed, a large focus is on reducing the amount of energy consumed [10]. Response time for the various requests made to a processing system which is computing the given task in a distributed manner is an important factor to determine the efficiency. Various approaches are studied to improve this, some of them being combining simulated annealing and genetic algorithms [11]. The gap between dispersed information stockpiling administration on layers fog drives the requirement for reserving. Cloud assets are utilized to a great extent for information storage [19–23]. In any case, the purpose of concern is that the cloud alone can be relied on for information perseverance. A help ought to be created which can oversee information on edge gadgets fairly just on the cloud. If there should be an occurrence of hub disappointments additionally the administration ought not stop. Advancement of such administrations on the edge layers additionally offers straightforward information disclosure and simpler access to information for different applications [1].

This chapter is organized as follows: Section 14.2 explains about "Fog Computing and Caching." An overview of how it is spread across various classes of users is presented here. Section 14.3 introduces "Edge Computing Systems and Mobile Data Storage Services." Section 14.4 presents various "P2P Systems." In Section 14.5, we describe "Use of Filters for Data Extraction." In further sections, we describe various streaming architectures (Figure 14.1).

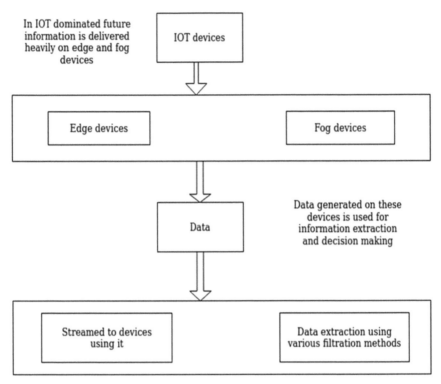

FIGURE 14.1 Flow of information generated on IoT devices.

14.2 FOG COMPUTING AND CACHING

14.2.1 MOBILE USERS

The other name for Fog computing is "cloud close to ground." The compute facility of the Fog servers is light-weight and is at a close proximity to various mobile users. Some of the major applications of Fog computing are live video streaming and dissemination of ads. A Fog computing framework is of a three level Mobile-Fog-Cloud structure. The versatile clients get administrations required from the Fog servers with the assistance of local wireless connections. The contents of the Fog servers can be refreshed by utilizing wired or cell systems. The major disadvantage is the higher cost while updating the content in cases where the bandwidth between cloud and fog servers is expensive [6] fog computing gives incredible cloud benefits in the physical closeness of clients. Fogs can be considered for offering computational power and breaking point cutoff focuses, with low inaction and high information move limit. This means to improve organizational transmission capacity and protection.

14.2.2 DISTRIBUTED GRAPH

The significant inquiry which needs tending to in fog computing is the determination of gadgets for storing the data, its circulation, and the procedure of recovery. A scoring framework can be used for referencing the issue of choice of the gadget. In this proposed framework, the higher centrality user gadgets are viewed as best up-and-comers. This depends on their ability to give the necessary content.

The system network over the gadgets can be represented as a chart. The centrality idea from the system can be utilized for ID of significant nodes. This will permit higher centrality devices to union or leave an appropriated system of fog devices by working together with the close by device. A centrality measure is the total amount of the most concise ways to the extent the number of jumps from all customers to all content [3].

14.2.3 LARGE DATA ANALYSIS AND INCREASED COVERAGE OF COMPUTATION

The nature of Fog Computing is because of remarkable virtualization. Each Fog hub involves at any rate one gadget. These contraptions can be switches or arrangements of neighborhood servers. Edge gadgets can be related with the Fog Computing layer, which in this manner can be related with the united cloud computing layer [4]. The potential issues of computing infrastructure and the moderate reaction time of distributed computing can be relieved. This should be possible by a multi-level fog processing model that has huge scope information investigation administration. A versatile framework level test system assesses the fog-based analytics service and the QoS schemes. Regarding the likelihood of employment blocking and the utility of analytics service, fogs can be utilized to improve the presentation of examination over keen urban areas in contrast with cloud just models. With the effective help of different dispersed figuring motors, the enormous scope investigation administration can be run over the frameworks of multi-level fog calculation [5].

14.3 EDGE COMPUTING SYSTEMS AND MOBILE DATA STORAGE SERVICES

In a future IoT-overwhelmed condition, most of the information will be delivered at the edge, which might be moved to the system center. Information management methodology directs how an eyeball organization facilitates the administration of edge information put away at a store. For example, Wi-Fi access points can be used at the edge of the system. Such local storage administrations can be utilized to cushion IoT and client produced information at the edge, before information cloud synchronization. The comparison of various data management strategies are listed in Table 14.1 [7].

TABLE 14.1 Comparison of Data Management Strategies

Proactive	Reactive	Data-Specific
Data transfer is done proactively	Transfer is done only when it's necessary.	Data attributes are used.
The local repositories move the approaching information proactively to the expected goal like cloud storage	Registration of name of data item to name resolution system is done to enable access and notification is sent to the destination of the data.	Data attributes are used to decide on the action for each data item. Data attributes can be scope and shelf life.

Recovering information which is put away at far off areas causes blockage in the network also requires high latencies. This prompted the need for frameworks that are focused at versatile clients and use little scope, decentralized capacity hubs at the outrageous edge of the system. vStore is a system that is fit for context aware micro-storage. The choice where to store information is caused by decisions that can either be pushed all around to the system or made independently by clients [8].

14.4 P2P SYSTEMS

14.4.1 CHORD

The location of nodes having the data item is the fundamental issue with peer-to-peer applications. Certain distributed lookup protocols like Chord address this problem. The only operation supported by Chord is mapping a key to its node. On top of Chord, data location can be implemented by mapping the key to the data item. After mapping, the key/data pair can be stored at the node onto which it has been mapped. Chord can adjust proficiently as various nodes leave and join the framework. It is equipped for noting questions regardless of whether the framework is ceaselessly evolving [9].

14.4.2 IPFS

Another peer-to-peer distributed file system is interplanetary file system (IPFS). This connects various devices involved in the computation with the same file system. It could be viewed as a solitary BitTorrent swarm, trading objects inside one Git archive. A summed-up DAG is framed by IPFS. IPFS doesn't have a solitary purpose of disappointment. Consequently, hubs need not have trust on one another. This counts as its major advantage. IPFS nodes are in constant communication with other nodes in the network, majorly across the internet [15].

14.4.3 SUPER-PEER NETWORK

A super-peer node can work as both for example a server to specific customers and as an equivalent in a system of other super-peers. The viability of super-peer systems is because of their effectiveness in consolidating the client-server model with load adjusting and vigorous dispersed search. Also, they utilize the heterogeneity of capabilities across other peers. This means that peers in a peer-to-peer system need not be similar to each other. Peers have heterogeneous properties. Super-peers are more efficient than the individual client since they act like centralized servers to clients. A properly designed super-peer network is expected to provide huge performance improvement in the P2P system [14].

14.4.4 DECENTRALIZED SYSTEMS

Since decentralized systems are gaining importance, it's necessary to check how dependable they are. The "dependability" here means the extent to which information can be extracted. It is usually defined using any type of information exchanged, the capabilities of the nodes involved and the data distribution amongst nodes. To overcome the unreliability of nodes comprising the system, these hierarchically grouped systems self-organize [13].

14.5 USE OF FILTERS FOR DATA EXTRACTION

A bloom filter is a productive portrayal of a set which on queried decides the participation of the data item on which it is queried upon. Bloom filters can also be used to decide if content is present in the cache. When the client demands a data item or information, the bloom filter algorithm will decide whether the information now exists in the store or needs to be fetched from the server itself. Bloom filter allows false positives and this is its biggest disadvantage. A bloom filter can only suggest that the data may be present. It never guarantees. However, it guarantees if the data is not present. Suppose if the data is not found, then there is an overhead. This is the major disadvantage of bloom filters [12]. Significant disadvantages of bloom filters incorporate their failure to allow the cancellation of data items from the set. Cuckoo filters support and emptying things effectively while achieving better than Bloom channels. For applications that store various things cuckoo filters have lower space overhead than space-smoothed out bloom filters [16]. Cuckoo filters are simpler to execute and furthermore uses less space than Bloom directs in various feasible applications. Cuckoo hashing and fractional key cuckoo hashing make cuckoo channels on a very basic level, capable of allowing development reliant on simply the set aside remarkable imprint [16]. A comparison of filters from data drawn from Ref. [16] is given in Table 14.2.

TABLE 14.2 Comparison of Filters

Comparison Metric	Bloom Filter	Cuckoo Filter
Addition and deletion of items	Items cannot be deleted from the set	Can add or remove items dynamically
Performance	Lower performance in comparison to cuckoo filters	Higher performance
Space overhead	Higher space overhead	Lower space overhead
Lookup performance	Lower lookup performance	Higher lookup performance
Efficiency	Less efficient	More efficient

14.6 STREAMING ARCHITECTURES

Architectures like lambda use Apache Storm to implement a speed layer. This allows data interaction from different sources. For processing it as batch and storage, MongoDB is very useful [17]. Platforms for real-time streaming can gather geospatial knowledge from open-source. Inputs for these originate from IoT and social media platforms. These don't address the integration of spatiotemporal data from IoT devices [18]. Architectures for scalable cloud-based real-time data processors work on integrated sensor data. A publish-subscribe which is topic-based can be used for associating the gadgets to cloud in message-broker. A stream processing engine is used for stream processing. This processing engine is distributed. Robotics applications use these kinds of architectures extensively [24]. Streaming platforms are also based on Apache Storm. These platforms use Apache Kafka to put information in the Storm cluster. Apache Kafka is a commit log service. The created information, which can start, for example, the Web or different sources, is put away in the Kafka group, with the end goal that Storm can get to it in this way. Databases like MongoDB are used by some frameworks for writing results obtained from streaming. This will help the clients of these frameworks to query the result of concern in real-time [25].

14.7 CONCLUSION

The importance of data generated on devices such as edge/fog increases with increased data generation on IoT platforms—nonattendance of the data results in a huge loss of data enthusiasm. Most of the implementations catering to the processing of these data open the data generated on these devices and move them to the cloud for persistence. Hence, these devices are less trustworthy. Caching will address problems in the appropriated information stockpiling administration on the edge/fog layer and abstain from relying entirely upon the cloud for information perseverance. It will likewise construct a solid help to store and oversee information on fog and edge layers even within sight of disappointments. Fog and Edge Computing foundations have been proposed to address the idleness issue of the present Cloud Computing stages.

14.8 FUTURE WORK

Future work can be carried out by studying cuckoo filters. The disadvantage of bloom filters is it does not allow the items to be removed from a particular set. Then again cuckoo channel permits us to include and erase the things productively from the set and is considerably more impressive than bloom filters. Bloom filter only predicts if data is present or not, but never explicitly guarantees. This may cause performance degradation, if data is not present. Also, genetic algorithms can be studied in depth since edge servers cannot meet requirements in mobile computing environments due to the shortage of resources. Genetic algorithms have shown magnificent results in terms of effectiveness in improving the efficiency of computing.

KEYWORDS

- **content delivery network**
- **edge-local federated**
- **genetic algorithms**
- **Internet of things**
- **interplanetary file system**
- **most popular content**

REFERENCES

1. Monga, S. K., Ramachandra, S. K., & Simmhan, Y., (2019). ElfStore: A resilient data storage service for federated edge and fog resources. In: *2019 IEEE International Conference on Web Services (ICWS)* (pp. 336–345) IEEE.
2. Alghamdi, F., Mahfoudh, S., & Barnawi, A., (2019). A novel fog computing-based architecture to improve the performance in content delivery networks. *Wireless Communications and Mobile Computing, 2019.*
3. Khan, J. A., Westphal, C., & Ghamri-Doudane, Y., (2019). Information-centric fog network for incentivized collaborative caching in the internet of everything. *IEEE Communications Magazine, 57*(7), 27–33.

4. Moysiadis, V., Sarigiannidis, P., & Moscholios, I., (2018). Towards distributed data management in fog computing. *Wireless Communications and Mobile Computing, 2018.*

5. He, J., Wei, J., Chen, K., Tang, Z., Zhou, Y., & Zhang, Y., (2017). Multitier fog computing with large-scale IoT data analytics for smart cities. *IEEE Internet of Things Journal, 5*(2), 677–686.

6. Mayer, R., Gupta, H., Saurez, E., & Ramachandran, U., (2017). Fogstore: Toward a distributed data store for fog computing. In: *2017 IEEE Fog World Congress (FWC)* (pp. 1–6). IEEE.

7. Psaras, I., Ascigil, O., Rene, S., Pavlou, G., Afanasyev, A., & Zhang, L., (2018). Mobile data repositories at the edge. In: *{USENIX} Workshop on Hot Topics in Edge Computing (HotEdge 18).*

8. Gedeon, J., Himmelmann, N., Felka, P., Herrlich, F., Stein, M., & Mühlhäuser, M., (2018). vStore: A context-aware framework for mobile micro-storage at the edge. In: *International Conference on Mobile Computing, Applications, and Services* (pp. 165–182) Springer, Cham.

9. Stoica, I., Morris, R., Liben-Nowell, D., Karger, D. R., Kaashoek, M. F., Dabek, F., & Balakrishnan, H., (2003). Chord: a scalable peer-to-peer lookup protocol for internet applications. *IEEE/ACM Transactions on Networking, 11*(1), 17–32.

10. Chen, C. A., Won, M., Stoleru, R., & Xie, G. G., (2014). Energy-efficient fault-tolerant data storage and processing in mobile cloud. *IEEE Transactions on Cloud Computing, 3*(1), 28–41.

11. Wu, H., Deng, S., Li, W., Fu, M., Yin, J., & Zomaya, A. Y., (2018). Service selection for composition in mobile edge computing systems. In: *2018 IEEE International Conference on Web Services (ICWS)* (pp. 355–358) IEEE.

12. Broder, A., & Mitzenmacher, M., (2004). Network applications of bloom filters: A survey. *Internet Mathematics, 1*(4), 485–509.

13. Ledlie, J., Taylor, J. M., Serban, L., & Seltzer, M., (2002). Self-organization in peer-to-peer systems. In: *Proceedings of the 10th Workshop on ACM SIGOPS European Workshop* (pp. 125–132)

14. Yang, B. B., & Garcia-Molina, H., (2003). Designing a super-peer network. In: *Proceedings 19th International Conference on Data Engineering (Cat. No. 03CH37405)* (pp. 49–60). IEEE.

15. Benet, J., (2014). *Ipfs-Content Addressed, Versioned, p2p File System.* arXiv preprint arXiv:1407.3561.

16. Fan, B., Andersen, D. G., Kaminsky, M., & Mitzenmacher, M. D., (2014). Cuckoo filter: Practically better than bloom. In: *Proceedings of the 10th ACM International Conference on Emerging Networking Experiments and Technologies* (pp. 75–88).

17. Villari, M., Celesti, A., Fazio, M., & Puliafito, A., (2014). AllJoyn lambda: An architecture for the management of smart environments in IoT. In: *2014 International Conference on Smart Computing Workshops* (pp. 9–14). IEEE.

18. Thakur, G. S., Bhaduri, B. L., Piburn, J. O., Sims, K. M., Stewart, R. N., & Urban, M. L., (2015). PlanetSense: a real-time streaming and Spatio-temporal analytics platform for gathering geospatial intelligence from open source data. In: *Proceedings of the 23rd SIGSPATIAL International Conference on Advances in Geographic Information Systems* (pp. 1–4).

19. Chowdhary, C. L., Patel, P. V., Kathrotia, K. J., Attique, M., Perumal, K., & Ijaz, M. F., (2020). Analytical study of hybrid techniques for image encryption and decryption. *Sensors, 20*(18), 5162.

20. Tripathy, A. K., Das, T. K., & Chowdhary, C. L., (2020). Monitoring quality of tap water in cities using IoT. In: *Emerging Technologies for Agriculture and Environment* (pp. 107–113) Springer, Singapore.

21. Chowdhary, C. L., & Mouli, P. C., (2012). Design and implementation of secure, platform-free, and network-based remote controlling and monitoring system. In: *International Conference on Pattern Recognition, Informatics and Medical Engineering (PRIME-2012)* (pp. 195–198) IEEE.

22. Chowdhary, C. L., Ranjan, A., & Jat, D. S., (2016). Categorical database information-theoretic approach of outlier detection model. *Annals. Computer Science Series, 14*(2).

23. Chowdhary, C. L., Darwish, A., & Hassanien, A. E., (2021). Cognitive deep learning: Future direction in intelligent retrieval. In: *Research Anthology on Artificial Intelligence Applications in Security* (pp. 2152–2163). IGI Global.

24. Kamburugamuve, S., Christiansen, L., & Fox, G., (2015). A framework for real time processing of sensor data in the cloud. *Journal of Sensors, 2015*.

25. Zhou, L., Chen, N., & Chen, Z., (2017). Efficient streaming mass Spatio-temporal vehicle data access in urban sensor networks based on Apache storm. *Sensors, 17*(4), 815.

Index